Teaching Science

Reflective Teaching and Learning: A guide to professional issues for beginning secondary teachers

Edited by Sue Dymoke and Jennifer Harrison

Reflective practice is at the heart of effective teaching. This core text is an introduction for beginning secondary teachers on developing the art of critical reflective teaching throughout their professional work. Designed as a flexible resource, the book combines theoretical background with practical reflective activities.

Developing as a Reflective Secondary Teacher Series

These subject-specific core texts are for beginning secondary teachers following PGCE, GTP or undergraduate routes into teaching. Each book provides a comprehensive guide to beginning subject teachers, offering practical guidance to support students through their training and beyond. Most importantly, the books are designed to help students develop a more reflective and critical approach to their own practice. Key features of the series are:

- observed lessons, providing both worked examples of good practice and commentaries by the teachers themselves and other observers
- an introduction to national subject frameworks including a critical examination of the role and status of each subject
- support for beginning teachers on all aspects of subject teaching, including planning, assessment, classroom management, differentiation and teaching strategies
- a trainee-focused approach to critical and analytical reflection on practice
- a research-based section demonstrating M-level work
- a comprehensive companion website linking all subjects, featuring video clips of sample lessons, a range of support material and weblinks.

Teaching Mathematics
Paul Chambers

Teaching History
Ian Phillips

Teaching ICT
Carl Simmons and Claire Hawkins

Teaching English
Carol Evans, Alyson Midgley, Phil Rigby, Lynne Warham and Peter Woolnough

Teaching Science
Tony Liversidge, Matt Cochrane, Bernie Kerfoot and Judith Thomas

Teaching Science

Developing as a Reflective Secondary Teacher

Tony Liversidge, Matt Cochrane,
Bernie Kerfoot and Judith Thomas

Los Angeles | London | New Delhi
Singapore | Washington DC

First published 2009

SAGE Publications Ltd
1 Oliver's Yard
55 City Road
London EC1Y 1SP

SAGE Publications Inc.
2455 Teller Road
Thousand Oaks, California 91320

SAGE Publications India Pvt Ltd
B 1/I 1 Mohan Cooperative Industrial Area
Mathura Road
New Delhi 110 044

SAGE Publications Asia-Pacific Pte Ltd
33 Pekin Street #02-01
Far East Square
Singapore 048763

Library of Congress Control Number: 2006927540

British Library Cataloguing in Publication data

A catalogue record for this book is available from the British Library

ISBN-978-1-84787-361-3
ISBN-978-1-84787-362-0 (pbk)

Typeset by C&M Digitals (P) Ltd, Chennai, India
Printed in Great Britain by TJ International Ltd, Padstow, Cornwall
Printed on paper from sustainable resources

Mixed Sources
Product group from well-managed
forests and other controlled sources
www.fsc.org Cert no. SGS-COC-2482
© 1996 Forest Stewardship Council
FSC

CONTENTS

ABOUT THE AUTHORS

Matt Cochrane
Head of Science and PE
Currently Head of the Science and Physical Education Department in the Faculty of Education at Edge Hill, Matt has worked in teacher training for the last fifteen years, both as a mentor in school, and as a tutor in University.

As Head of Science at a comprehensive school in the North West of England, he was responsible for the induction of Newly Qualified Teachers, and for the mentoring of trainee teachers from HE institutions in the area, working on the course development committee at Liverpool Hope University for a time. He is carrying out doctoral research into the processes which influence pupils in Year 9 when they start to make their choices for GCSE study and beyond.

Bernie Kerfoot
PGCE Science Course Leader
Bernie, a chemistry specialist, has taught for 14 years in a number of secondary schools, holding a variety of posts of responsibility. Before coming to Edge Hill, his previous post involved responsibility for ICT in a partner school. He has recently successfully completed a Master's Degree in Education and has acted as a tutor for the Open University Initial Teacher Training team. He has recently presented to the National Conference of the Association for Science Education on the innovative use of ICT in the science classroom.

Tony Liversidge
Research Development Co-ordinator
Tony worked as a biology and science teacher and as a school–industry liaison co-ordinator in secondary schools before moving into teacher education. He has extensive experience of working with trainee teachers on both undergraduate and post-graduate programmes, having been a course leader for both BSc and PGCE Secondary Science Routes and Programme Leader for the BSc Secondary Undergraduate route at Edge Hill. He is currently the Research Development Co-ordinator in the Faculty of Education. He is the series co-ordinator and co-author of a set of three interactive starter and plenary CD-Roms produced by Hodder Murray for their Hodder Science course. He has considerable experience as a GCSE biology and science examiner and has worked as an external examiner for both undergraduate and post-graduate science teacher training courses. He is a regular contributor to ASE annual and regional conferences, including his popular

'Grossology' workshops. His doctoral studies involved looking at mentoring in science initial teacher training and his current research interests centre on creativity and innovation in science teaching.

Judith Thomas
Key Stage 2/3 Programme Leader
Judith taught science in local schools before being appointed Widening Access co-ordinator at Edge Hill in 2000. Within this capacity, Judith has enabled hundreds of secondary school children to participate in science-based activities on campus. Judith teaches specialist sessions on PGCE Science and is a tutor for the Open University. She now co-ordinates courses in Key Stage 2/3 Initial Teacher Training across a range of subjects.

ACKNOWLEDGEMENTS

We would like to thank Kevin Maddocks along with the staff and pupils of North Liverpool Academy for their help in preparing the video lessons which accompany this book.

Also thanks go to David Farley, Assistant Head Teacher at The Deanery C of E High School and 6th Form College, Wigan and Gill Dobson, Science AST at Fred Longworth School, Wigan for their contributions.

The following trainees contributed to the materials supplied online: Sukhbinder Mahay, Melanie Murray, Martine Weijland, Maegen Whitton, Alison Brady, Daniel Finnegan, Darren Chandler and Andrew Law.

Stephen Wyatt provided artwork.

HOW TO USE THIS BOOK

As you start your training to become a teacher, you will be faced with a bewildering array of information and requests for your personal details. A lot of the information will come from your training provider, and will give details about the course that you are starting. Your personal details will be required in order to compile a curriculum vitae (CV) that can be sent out to your placement schools; they will also be needed so that you can receive clearance from the Criminal Records Bureau (CRB) to work with children. Very early on, you will learn that your success on the training course depends on your ability to demonstrate competence in the Professional Standards for Qualified Teacher Status (QTS) that are laid down by the Training and Development Agency for Schools (TDA).

This book is designed to help you make a success of your training course. It shows you how to plan lessons, how to make good use of resources and how to assess pupils' progress effectively. But its main aim is to help you learn how to improve your classroom performance. In order to improve, you need to have skills of analysis and self-evaluation, and you need to know what you are trying to achieve and why. You also need examples of how experienced teachers deliver successful lessons, and how even the best teachers continually strive to become even better.

The book has a practical focus. It will help you to feel more comfortable about what is expected from you on teaching practice, through demonstrating good practice into a whole-school and a national context. You will, for example, find suggestions about how science lessons can contribute to whole-school initiatives such as developing pupils' thinking skills.

A key feature of this book is the accompanying website (www.sagepub. co.uk/secondary). The icon shown in the margin will appear throughout the text where additional material is available. The website contains simple links to sites that provide useful support for your science teaching. The book (in particular Chapter 4) makes extensive references to two science lessons. On the website you will find documents that give you a breakdown of the teaching and learning sequences for each lesson. Commentary in the text will refer to an incident or detail by the time; for example, you might be asked to view a teaching sequence which runs from 2:10/8:20, i.e. from 2 mins 10 secs to 8 mins 20 secs. The filmed lessons demonstrate key aspects of planning, teaching and student learning but the commentary will also draw your attention to particular aspects of a teacher–student dialogue or perhaps to the techniques being used to put the topics across to the pupils. The video clips are in Windows media video file format (.wmv), and give the best quality visuals if viewed with Windows Media Player. (Players that support this file type are Windows Media Player 7, Windows Media Player for

Windows XP, Windows Media Player 9 series, Windows Media Player 10 and Windows Media Player 11.)

Although the focus throughout is on improving your professional skills, there is no attempt to provide a 'tick list' of how to achieve each of the individual Professional Standards for QTS. We believe that a more holistic approach is better suited to this type of publication. The book addresses professional attributes, professional knowledge and understanding, and professional skills in a more holistic way than the way they are presented in the Standards. You will, however, find frequent reference to the Standards, and it is hoped that through using the book reflectively, you will acquire the general skills required to gather and present your evidence against each of the Standards statements. A rough guide to where the book addresses individual Standards is given in the following chart.

Table H.1 Professional Standards for Qualified Teacher Status

	Standard	Opportunities to learn more (chapter)
Professional attributes. Those recommended for the award of QTS should: Relationships with children and young people		
Q1	Have high expectations of children and young people including a commitment to ensuring that they can achieve their full educational potential and to establishing fair, respectful, trusting, supportive and constructive relationships with them	3. Planning to teach a science lesson 5. Managing learning in science 6. Managing learning; measuring learning
Q2	Demonstrate the positive values, attitudes and behaviour they expect from children and young people	3. Planning to teach a science lesson 5. Managing learning in science 6. Managing learning; measuring learning
Frameworks		
Q3a	Be aware of the professional duties of teachers and the statutory framework within which they work	2. What are you expected to teach in a science lesson? 7. Teaching different abilities; teaching different pupils
Q3b	Be aware of the policies and practices of the workplace and share in collective responsibility for their implementation	12. Refelctive practice and professional development 1. What is science teaching? Who are science teachers? curriculum: a public perspective' 2. What are you expected to teach in a science lesson?
Communicating and working with others		
Q4	Communicate effectively with children, young people, colleagues, parents and carers	2. What are you expected to teach in a science lesson? 4. Elements of a science lesson

Q5	Recognize and respect the contribution that colleagues, parents and carers can make to the development and well-being of children and young people and to raising their levels of attainment	3. Planning to teach a science lesson 6. Managing learning; measuring learning 11. Science outside the classroom 12. Reflective practice and professional development
Q6	Have a commitment to collaboration and co-operative working	3. Planning to teach a science lesson 5. Managing learning in science 6. Managing learning; measuring learning 11. Science outside the classroom 12. Reflective practice and professional development
Personal professional development		
Q7a	Reflect on and improve their practice, and take responsibility for identifying and meeting their developing professional needs	1. What is science teaching? Who are science teachers? 6. Managing learning; measuring learning 12. Reflective practice and professional development
Q7b	Identify priorities for their early professional development in the context of induction	
Q8	Have a creative and constructively critical approach towards innovation, being prepared to adapt their practice where benefits and improvements are identified	3. Planning to teach a science lesson 10. Creativity and innovation in science teaching and learning
Q9	Act upon advice and feedback and be open to coaching and mentoring	1. What is science teaching? Who are science teachers? 12. Reflective practice and professional development
Professional knowledge and understanding. Those recommended for the award of QTS should:		
Teaching and learning		
Q10	Have a knowledge and understanding of a range of teaching, learning and behaviour management strategies and know how to use and adapt them, including how to personalize learning and provide opportunities for all learners to achieve their potential	2. What are you expected to teach in a science lesson? 3. Planning to teach a science lesson 4. Elements of a science lesson 5. Managing learning in science 6. Managing learning; measuring learning
Assessment and monitoring		
Q11	Know the assessment requirements and arrangements for the subjects/curriculum areas in the age ranges they are trained to	2. What are you expected to teach in a science lesson? 3. Planning to teach a science lesson

	teach, including those relating to public examinations and qualifications	4. Elements of a science lesson 6. Managing learning; measuring learning
Q12	Know a range of approaches to assessment, including the importance of formative assessment	2. What are you expected to teach in a science lesson? 3. Planning to teach a science lesson 4. Elements of a science lesson 6. Managing learning; measuring learning
Q13	Know how to use local and national statistical information to evaluate the effectiveness of their teaching, to monitor the progress of those they teach and to raise levels of attainment	6. Managing learning; measuring learning 12. Reflective practice and professional development
Subjects and curriculum		
Q14	Have a secure knowledge and understanding of their subjects/ curriculum areas and related pedagogy to enable them to teach effectively across the age and ability range for which they are trained	1. What is science teaching? Who are science teachers? 2. What are you expected to teach in a science lesson? 3. Planning to teach a science lesson 4. Elements of a science lesson
Q15	Know and understand the relevant statutory and non-statutory curricula, frameworks, including those provided through the National Strategies, for their subjects/curriculum areas, and other relevant initiatives applicable to the age and ability range for which they are trained	1. What is science teaching? Who are science teachers? 5. Managing learning in science 7. Teaching different abilities; teaching different pupils 8. Teaching different ages: Key Stage 3 to post-16
Literacy, numeracy and ICT		
Q16	Have passed the professional skills tests in numeracy, literacy and information and communication technology (ICT)	
Q17	Know how to use skills in literacy, numeracy and ICT to support their teaching and wider professional activities	3. Planning to teach a science lesson 6. Managing learning; measuring learning 10. Creativity and innovation in science teaching and learning
Achievement and diversity		
Q18	Understand how children and young people develop and that the progress and well-being of learners are affected by a range of developmental, social, religious, ethnic, cultural and linguistic influences	6. Managing learning; measuring learning 7. Teaching different abilities; teaching different pupils 8. Teaching different ages: Key Stage 3 to post-16

Q19	Know how to make effective personalized provision for those they teach, including those for whom English is an additional language or who have special educational needs or disabilities, and how to take practical account of diversity and promote equality and inclusion in their teaching	6. Managing learning; measuring learning 7. Teaching different abilities; teaching different pupils 8. Teaching different ages: Key Stage 3 to post-16
Q20	Know and understand the roles of colleagues with specific responsibilities, including those with responsibility for learners with special educational needs and disabilities and other individual learning needs	5. Managing learning in science lesson 7. Teaching different abilities; teaching different pupils
Health and well-being		
Q21a	Be aware of current legal requirements, national policies and guidance on the safeguarding and promotion of the well-being of children and young people	2. What are you expected to teach in a science lesson? 5. Managing learning in science lesson 7. Teaching different abilities; teaching different pupils 8. Teaching different ages: Key Stage 3 to post-16
Q21b	Know how to identify and support children and young people whose, progress development or well-being is affected by changes or difficulties in their personal circumstances, and when to refer them to colleagues for specialist support	
Professional skills. Those recommended for the award of QTS should:		
Planning		
Q22	Plan for progression across the age and ability range for which they are trained, designing effective learning sequences within lessons and across series of lessons and demonstrating secure subject/curriculum knowledge	2. What are you expected to teach in a science lesson? 3. Planning to teach a science lesson 4. Elements of a science lesson 7. Teaching different abilities; teaching different pupils 8. Teaching different ages: Key Stage 3 to post-16
Q23	Design opportunities for learners to develop their literacy, numeracy and ICT skills	2. What are you expected to teach in a science lesson? 3. Planning to teach a science lesson 4. Elements of a science lesson
Q24	Plan homework or other out-of-class work to sustain learners' progress and to extend and consolidate their learning	10. Creativity and innovation in science teaching and learning 11. Science outside the classroom

Teaching	
Teach lessons and sequences of lessons across the age and ability range for which they are trained in which they:	
Q25a	use a range of teaching strategies and resources, including e-learning, taking practical account of diversity and promoting equality and inclusion;	3. Planning to teach a science lesson 4. Elements of a science lesson 5. Managing learning in science 10. Creativity and innovation in science teaching and learning
Q25b	build on prior knowledge, develop concepts and processes, enable learners to apply new knowledge, understanding and skills and meet learning objectives;	3. Planning to teach a science lesson 4. Elements of a science lesson 5. Managing learning in science 10. Creativity and innovation in science teaching and learning
Q25c	adapt their language to suit the learners they teach, introducing new ideas and concepts clearly, and using explanations, questions, discussions and plenaries effectively;	2. What are you expected to teach in a science lesson? 3. Planning to teach a science lesson 4. Elements of a science lesson 7. Teaching different abilities; teaching different pupils 8. Teaching different ages: Key Stage 3 to post-16 10. Creativity and innovation in science teaching and learning
Q25d	manage the learning of individuals, groups and whole classes, modifying their teaching to suit the stage of the lesson	
Assessing, monitoring and giving feedback	
Q26a	Make effective use of a range of assessment, monitoring and recording strategies	4. Elements of a science lesson 6. Managing learning; measuring learning
Q26b	Assess the learning needs of those they teach in order to set challenging learning objectives	6. Managing learning; measuring learning 7. Teaching different abilities; teaching different pupils 8. Teaching different ages: Key Stage 3 to post-16
Q27	Provide timely, accurate and constructive feedback on learners' attainment, progress and areas for development	6. Managing learning; measuring learning
Q28	Support and guide learners to reflect on their learning, identify the progress they have made and identify their emerging learning needs	6. Managing learning; measuring learning
Reviewing teaching and learning	
Q29	Evaluate the impact of their teaching on the progress of all learners, and modify their planning and classroom practice where necessary	12. Reflective practice and professional development

Learning environment		
Q30	Establish a purposeful and safe learning environment conducive to learning and identify opportunities for learners to learn in out-of-school contexts	2. What are you expected to teach in a science lesson? 3. Planning to teach a science lesson 4. Elements of a science lesson 5. Managing learning in science 11. Science outside the classroom
Q31	Establish a clear framework for classroom discipline to manage learners' behaviour constructively and promote their self-control and independence	4. Elements of a science lesson 5. Managing learning in science
Team-working and collaboration		
Q32	Work as a team member and identify opportunities for working with colleagues, sharing the development of effective practice with them	7. Teaching different abilities; teaching different pupils 8. Teaching different ages: Key Stage 3 to post-16 10. Reflective practice and professional development
Q33	Ensure that colleagues working with them are appropriately involved in supporting learning and understand the roles they are expected to fulfil	7. Teaching different abilities; teaching different pupils 8. Teaching different ages: Key Stage 3 to post-16

As the title of the series suggests, this book aims to help you to develop into a reflective practitioner. Each chapter contains several points for reflection. These encourage you to break off from your reading and consider the issue being discussed. Sometimes you are asked to compare the information in the text with your own experience; sometimes you are asked to complete a small task. It is hoped that you will not be in a hurry to read through the whole book; take your time, reflect on the issues presented and, if possible discuss the issues with other trainees.

The main focus of the book is on practical advice, but there is another area of your course where we hope that you will find the book useful. If you are undertaking an award-bearing course (for example, leading to a PGCE or a degree with QTS), then you will have to do some assignments, and this book will help you with that too.

1 WHAT IS SCIENCE TEACHING? WHO ARE SCIENCE TEACHERS?

Bernie Kerfoot

This chapter:

- considers the nature of science and the implications to science teaching
- attempts to justify science as a core subject in the National Curriculum
- examines the changing roles of science education and science teachers in England and explores the drivers for this change
- examines the typical motivations of science trainee teachers at the start of their career and describes some the challenges to science teachers
- discusses the strategies that novice teachers use to acquire subject knowledge competence in a multidisciplinary subject
- reflects on what is perceived as good practice in science teaching.

WHAT IS SCIENCE AND HOW DOES SCIENCE WORK?

I think it is fair to say that up until the introduction of the National Curriculum for England and Wales (1989) many practising 11–16 teachers of science did not feel the necessity to reflect too long over the nature of science, that is, 'what science is' and 'how scientists work'. Some school teachers would have worked in the wider scientific community in previous careers and would have had a subjective awareness of a scientist's role. This absence of reflection changed in 1989 with the introduction of the statutory National Curriculum (1989) when in the 17 sections labelled 'Attainment Targets' (ATs) was enshrined a commitment to allow children to 'explore science'. They were to use the vehicle of scientific investigations to develop their knowledge and understanding of the 'ways in which scientific ideas change over time' and the 'social, moral spiritual and cultural contexts in which they are developed'. The science teacher was now responsible for addressing issues other than the straightforward teaching of the body of knowledge that has been classed as science.

Even when the National Curriculum was revised in 1991 and again in 1996 most 11–16 science teachers tended to be too busy teaching the key scientific facts and key concepts to spend long hours exploring the link between the 'real' science that has been happening, I would argue, since the appearance of humankind, and the activities that teachers were asking pupils to do in the classroom.

The National Curriculum for Science (DfES, 2004b) placed greater emphasis on the way scientists work and how the body of knowledge that can loosely be labelled as 'science' moves forward, and by 2007 in the revised National Curriculum for Key Stage 3 (QCA 2007b) you can see that attainment target 1 on p214 is titled 'How Science Works'. This has targets for pupils that include, amongst others, the development of the key concept of the fair test, Also the QCA suggest that pupils need to develop the skills and attributes of a scientist. These include observational and measuring skills, also the abilities to select and use resources, analyse data, spot patterns if they exist and then communicate their findings to others effectively.

Described on p208 are the Key Concepts that straddle science and are linked to How Science Works. For example, in the scientific community theories are generated to explain phenomena. There is also the idea that the scientific community 'shares developments and common understanding across disciplines and boundaries'. In short it is as if the knowledge and understanding broadly described on pages 210 and 211 are the vehicle to deliver the skills of the scientist and an insight into how the scientific community works.

At Key Stages 1, 2 and 3 in the 2004 National Curriculum Science document we see the latest 'scientific enquiry' strand forming what has been commonly known to science teachers since the implementation of a National Curriculum for science as 'Sc1'. It consists of two interrelated sections that are found in all Sc1 sections in all key stages.

In one section there are descriptions of the practical and investigational skills that you are generally led to believe are intrinsic to scientists and as science teachers we need to develop. At Key Stage 4 these are the ability to

- plan a testable idea
- observe and collect data
- work safely autonomously or with others
- evaluate methodology.

Some science educationalists, for example, Millar, 1989) point out that, first, these skills are not unique to science and, secondly, that they are extremely difficult to learn. Like all skills they have to be practised to get any better and are in fact linked to what is now being called higher-level thinking skills. How many times do you think science teachers go into lessons with their primary objectives skill based? Consider 'today children I am going to give you the opportunity to develop your planning skills'. As an outcome of this 'you will be slightly better at planning testable ideas'.

If we consider the first section we see the instruction that 'teachers should ensure that the knowledge, skills and understanding of how science works are integrated into the teaching'. So pupils should be taught (and I paraphrase):

- how scientific data can be collected and analysed
- how data can be creatively interpreted and how it can provide the evidence to test ideas and develop theories
- how scientific ideas and models can explain phenomena
- that there are some questions that science cannot currently answer and some that science cannot address.

Later on we see that pupils should also be taught about the applications and implications of science (and I am careful not to paraphrase here!).

a. About the use of contemporary scientific and technological developments and their benefits, drawbacks and risks.
b. To consider how and why decisions about science and technology are made including those that raise ethical issues, and about the social, economic and environmental effects of such decisions.
c. How uncertainties in scientific knowledge and scientific ideas change over time and about the role of the scientific community in validating these changes. (DfES, 2004b: 37)

The science content in the latest version of the National Curriculum (2007) shows wholesale revisions to the Key Stage 3 programme of study and attainment targets (QCA, 2007a). We see that Mick Waters's curriculum development team (Mick's role at the Qualifications and Curriculum Authority is Director of Curriculum) have cut content substantially. Their aim is 'to develop a modern, world-class curriculum that will inspire and challenge all learners and prepare them for the future' and in doing so they have reduced the content from 94 statements of learning to 14 (http://www. qca.org.uk/qca8665aspx). The themes are constant but the specificity is gone. The team see this content as being relevant and the driver underpinning the key concepts that all pupils have to understand. These key concepts are:

1. Scientific thinking (developing models to test phenomena and theories).
2. Applications and implications of science (link between science and technology).
3. Cultural understanding (science is rooted in all societies and draws on a variety of approaches).
4. Collaboration (developments are shared across the scientific community).

Gone are the old divisions that labelled the knowledge as chemistry, biology and physics. Now we see the breadth of subject that teachers should draw on as very loosely defined. Just one example 'energy, electricity and forces' has three broad statements of what might be taught. The first states 'energy can be transferred usefully, stored or dissipated but cannot be created or destroyed'. The second statement leads us to teach about 'forces are interactions between objects and can affect their shape or motion'. Finally, we see that 'electric current in circuits can produce a variety of effects'.

Also at Key Stage 3 the pupils have to develop the 'skills and processes in science that pupils need to make progress'. Section 2 (2.1, 2.2, 2.3) is a reworking of the 2004 National Curriculum, and indeed previous incarnations, as it recognizes the skills intrinsic to the scientists but throws an increasing emphasis on risk assessment, group working and using secondary sources, and asks pupils to communicate by way of presentations and discussions, again mirroring how scientists work. In Chapter 2 we see the Every Child Matters (ECM) agenda hard at work. Pupils should be allowed to develop skills of discussion, research, creativity, enterprise and communication, as well as a recognition that science occurs in the work place.

In short the National Curriculum for Key Stage 3 for implementation in 2008 seeks to use a science education to develop a well-informed, globally aware, confident, critical audience. They need good communication skills to express this awareness and criticality. They also need an appreciation of how scientists work and the limitations of what science can do. There is an implicit belief that the development of the higher-level skills that science can hopefully develop in children can be used in the wider work place. That is the challenge to you as new science teachers in the coming decade and beyond.

So this 'how science works' strand in the National Curriculum describes a way of working that is indicative of the way that scientists work and it invites pupils to become scientists in school science and mirror the way that real scientists work. As a consequence they might gain an insight into the scientific way of working and the consensual way the scientific community collectively operates.

Perhaps at this point it is worthwhile very briefly reflecting on the observations of two twentieth-century scientists who are acknowledged as insightful and analytical observers of the way scientists and the scientific community works.

Karl Popper was an Austrian who later became a British national. He was born at the turn of the century and died in 1994. Popper argued that the theories and explanations of observable phenomena undergo over time a sort of evolutionary process similar to natural selection. A 'best fit' model exists at any one time (Popper, 1959).

Are there implications for you as a science teacher teaching Year 8 set six 'the things plants need to grow' or at post-16 'the functions of the Golgi apparatus' of Popper's ideas about science? Certainly if you are doing a class practical with Year 7 or Year 10 and eight of your groups find that their resistors fit Ohms law but two groups find that their data does not fit in with the rest, then is this not an ideal opportunity to explore a 'best fit' approach – the consensus? Might you then explore how the scientific community works? How do they deal with this type of data? Might you ask 'Shall we do it again and see if we get same, similar or different results?' Can you see that Popper's 'take' on how science collects theories and models, is found in the 'applications and implications of science, section C'?

Thomas Kuhn was a physicist who became Professor of the History of Science in 1961 at the University of California. He later went on to work in the Massachusetts Institute of Technology. In 1962 he published *The Structure of Scientific Revolutions* (Kuhn, 1970). Kuhn proposed that most scientists work within an accepted 'paradigm'. A paradigm is a generally accepted set of shared 'beliefs' about a particular model that can be used to explain phenomena. Most scientists busy themselves with simply enlarging the data bank that supports this accepted model. Kuhn points out that eventually anomalies will begin to show then slowly accrue – they will build over time. What is vital to Kuhn's analysis is that with *every* model, theory or explanation this inevitably happens. As the anomalies begin to stack up, the scientific community will reach a crisis and accept a new set of beliefs – a new paradigm emerges. This may seem pretty obvious but again it is built into 'how science works' and you have to teach it in some shape or form.

If you consider the current case of carbon dioxide-led global temperature rise, we are looking at a classic case of a legion of environmental scientists beavering away inside a commonly held model that attempts to explain an apparent climate change. Yes, I would agree that there is data linking rising carbon dioxide levels with a rise in global temperature but is it conclusive? Have we assessed the phenomena over a timeframe that allows a degree of certainty? If a scientist provides data that suggests an alternative model (for example, solar cycles, changing cloud distribution and pH changes in oceans) that disagrees with the broad consensus of scientists that blames carbon dioxide, then the community tends to dismiss such evidence as unreliable – almost heretical. What happens if other data also seems to suggest a new model? Might we eventually have a paradigm shift? I have to say that personally I have always been aghast at the First World's massive reliance on fossil fuels to provide energy – after all, fossil fuels will eventually run out and are far too precious to burn to make electricity when we have other ways to generate it. Can you also see that as *we* begin to move away from reliance on fossil fuels then the Third World will begin to crank up the fossil fuel engine even more? It is becoming obvious that China and India want what we have had in terms of material benefits, and oil, coal and gas are a big part of the package. Is there a political driver fuelling research into climate change? Might you explore aspects of funding issues here? Is there a political agenda in how scientific research is funded? These are all issues that you can explore in the classroom with pupils, and they are all highly relevant.

Now although you would probably agree with me that Key Stages 3 and 4 pupils do not require an in-depth consideration of Popper's and Kuhn's philosophies of science, it would seem that the National Curriculum demands some insight by pupils. You might also agree that only a small proportion of the population really need an in-depth bank of scientific knowledge and understanding for their future work. You would certainly agree with the sentiment that every adult should be able to look critically and analytically at scientific claims in the media, for example, 'scientists have evidence in recent years suggesting that there is a link between a factory pushing out a heavy metal into a river and mutations in fish'. Locally in the north-west of England we find issues such as 'Is there a link between the Sellafield site and leukaemia?'. Similarly claims that 'cell phones can cause brain damage' or 'there are only 200 Bengal tigers left in the world' cause immediate issues that require reflection and criticality. The public domain is awash with such scientific claims but very few people ever read the original paper that forms the basis of the claim. Even when they do their conclusions are often inconclusive. Let me describe an activity I did with a large group of trainee teachers.

Some years ago the scientific community got extremely excited about the discovery and subsequent analysis of a meteorite that was found in ice at the North Pole. Scientists Everett Gibson and David McKay, from NASA, were convinced with a high degree of certainty that meteorite ALH 8001 came from Mars and that it appeared to have nodules in the rock that appeared to be fossilized bacteria. The scientific paper on the rock was presented in the media as certain evidence that bacterial life had existed on Mars and that Earth had been seeded by such contamination from outer space. Scientists and religious clerics all passed comments on the claims. What were we to believe? We are not alone, or at least at some point were not alone? I gave the original paper to 100 trainee teachers and they spent an hour contemplating the evidence in the paper. About 10 thought it was clear evidence of life on Mars at some stage, 10 thought it proved nothing and 80 sat on the fence stating 'not enough evidence to make a decision'. If you read the paper, it presented a series of points about the rock that suggested the nodules could have been made by the fossilization of microbes but each point in isolation was not enough. It was rather like a court case where the evidence builds bit by bit and you have to give a verdict on the sum of the bits. Science is like that and it is important that young people realize this. You can go back to Karl Popper on this one. Science works by eliminating hypotheses that are seen to be false. It is impossible to prove anything absolutely in science – scientists do not deal in 'truths'. Part of the problem is that scientific journalists and writers hover around the scientific community and pick up on papers. They then talk to the publishers and derive their own slant on things, and it is published.

Now this may be difficult for children to come to terms with but the earlier you start the more chance they have of understanding how science works. If you look at the single page of learning objectives in the National Curriculum (DfES, 2004b) that relates to Key Stage 4 you will see that some objectives readily lend themselves to an exploration of 'how science works'.

- Human health is affected by a range of environmental and inherited factors.
- New materials are made from natural resources by chemical reaction.
- Radiations in the form of waves can be used to transfer energy and be used for communications.

This final section that allows teachers to explore the environment, the Earth and the universe is potentially a goldmine for exploring issues about the way scientists work, the nature of the scientific community and how ideas and evidence evolve. Recently published commercial schemes of work with their incredible range of resources such as 21st Century Science and suggested activities, have moved into the market to assist teachers in delivering the less content-orientated and more process-driven learning on offer (http://www.21stcenturyscience.org).

Similarly science is a valid vehicle for delivering health and safety awareness in pupils. Some years ago the Consortium for Local Education Authority for the Provision of Science Services (CLEAPSS) published a pack of risk assessment forms for pupils to consider and fill in prior to doing investigations with hazards involved – seemingly a great idea to involve Year 10 and above being actively involved in the health and safety aspects prior to doing it. I have never seen them in use! I would like to think that a scientific education would develop in pupils the skills to assess risk and know where to go for hazard information. After all, it is an important life skill.

If the main aim of the ideas and evidence section is to force science teachers into being frank about the very nature of science and the ways in which science works and feeds into society through technology, then surely it is a good thing. It should allow children to develop a better understanding of how individuals enquire. Everyone makes observations, everyone thinks about why that is the way it is, everyone questions, everyone tests out his or her explanation and everyone comes to some sort of conclusion which is often very personal. This is the way scientists work and it is also indicative of the human condition. In the meantime it will hopefully also allow science teachers to address issues which have recently been primetime news such as 'should the Japanese kill humpback whales for scientific reasons?' Hopefully it will make human the face of the scientists. It also gives science teachers an opportunity to make science teaching more interesting.

PUPILS' PERCEPTIONS OF SCIENTISTS

Lots of research has been done into pupil's images of science (for example, Driver et al., 1996). Many children think scientists are people that know loads of facts, can explain everything and are mostly men and grey people in white coats, all 'Mr Spock'-type logical thinkers with the capacity to explain all events. A research scientist once said to me 'all my imagination and creativity has been binned by 20 years of doing science research'. Surely this is a depressing view, and it is backed by the pupils in school who are choosing to go into marketing, banking, media and sports rather than science. Pupils should realize that all scientific explanations are models and models are the product of the mind. In some science laboratories you are surrounded by physical models made by hand. This should be made clear. Science teachers are 'pedlars' of creative models and imagination, and creatively are part and parcel of the nature of science and how science works. Does it help or hinder the image of scientists when, on the basis of Professor Roy Meadows's evidence in court, a number of women were jailed because of 'scientific evidence'? They were subsequently released because of flaws in the scientific evidence. In one way it is good in that it proves that working scientists are fallible and that even respected experienced scientists can get it 'wrong' and see correlations in data when none exist. In other ways it puts a human face on the scientist. As science teachers we can use these cases to inform observers and pupils that science is not about 'truth' but, rather, about the collection of data and the statistical interpretation of it.

Nevertheless, the scientist working inside the academic scientific community offers the 'best' answers we have to many questions. The community seeks to regulate itself by peer appraisal through publishing and discussion. Data that is non-reproducible, not valid or is unreliable goes down a cul-de-sac in the same way that the sabre-toothed tiger did. Yes there are questions, phenomena we do not understand, dark matter, and now dark energy is a good example, and we sometimes feel that we are 'making it up as we go along' but the science community offers the best, most reliable way we have of making any sense of the incredibly complex universe we live in.

Point for reflection

Think about your own views on science. What do you think is most important for children to learn: the facts and bits of knowledge that science offers, or an appreciation of how science works. Think about the influence of your view of science on how you might teach science. Develop a teaching resource that might be useful in the classroom to illustrate to children how scientists work.

SHOULD EVERY LEARNER STUDY SOME SCIENCE?

One thing you should be able to do is argue in any staffroom a watertight case for the inclusion of science as a core subject. Certainly every mathematics and English teacher would find it obvious and not have too much difficulty in building a case for their own subject. Since the implementation of the National Curriculum in 1989, science has been core alongside English and mathematics. The teachers who sit nervously in the classroom include linguists, technologists and many of the humanities department. Science teachers are 'safe' in the role since the committee that put together the original National Curriculum made us indispensable by arguing the case for science in the core curriculum.

Certainly one of the answers that scientists offer when asked 'Why is science important?' is that 'science gives you answers to things that go on all about you'. They expand on this with statements like 'You know how the trees make food or even how a car works!' This is fine and shows an appreciation of one aspect of science education. It shows at least that the person is inquisitive, curious and seems to have thought about the wide-ranging question.

In fact, in 1989 when the prescriptive National Curriculum was introduced, there were 10 subjects. It has of course been modified four times since then and has undergone further modification in 2007 and for implementation within Key Stage 3 in 2008.

Science was and is a core subject right through from ages 5 to 16 – everybody has science lessons. Why is this? Originally the arguments for its inclusion were:

- A need for scientists (economic argument).
- A scientifically literate population in a scientific and technical society (utilitarian argument).
- Pupils should learn about how science and scientists work.
- Science is part of a global culture and needs preserving and passing on.
- Science is an important vehicle for driving a young person's intellectual (cognitive) development in a wide range of aspects.

These reasons cannot be dismissed easily by politicians and curriculum developers but I do think we are now in a position nearly 20 years down the line to explore them again with a fresh perspective. If a pupil says to you 'I don't like science. I never asked to do it. I was forced into it but I don't see the point in it. I want to do plumbing like my Dad and earn £1,000 per week', what do you say to him or her?

Your answer has got to be rooted in the wider sense of what the pupil may learn and develop. It is not just about the acquisition of scientific knowledge and understanding – although it is obviously important in order to make sense of the real world and use scientific models to explain what is going on around them. I am sure you realize that it is also important to pass formal examinations as well!

First, let us explore the aspects of learning not strictly to do with knowledge and understanding. Patrick O'Brien (2003) offers an insight into how higher-level 'thinking skills' can be developed in children through problem-based learning that is rooted in scientific enquiry. The book gives many examples of tasks to do with 'gifted pupils' at Key Stage 3 but, of course, the ability to 'think' beyond the simple absorption of facts is something that all pupils need to develop. Children can, through a science education, develop all the 'thinking' that will equip them to function as autonomous learners for the rest of their lives. So, for example, pupils need practice to develop creative thinking to synthesize facts in a new or original way. They also need to be able to use thinking that is reflective and centres on how well the synthesis fits the purpose. Although O'Brien points out that these skills are hard to define, surely as a science teacher you can develop in pupils creative thinking – how might the information be redesigned for another use?.

You might also develop in pupils the skills of analysis. These might contain grouping and classifying, spotting patterns and modelling. Also the ability to evaluate might be developed where issues such as validity reliability, and an appraisal of the strengths and the weaknesses of a performance might develop higher-level thinking. These are all aspects of learning that the good science teacher can develop and, moreover, feels the duty to develop. Now I agree that it is not that easy to explain this to the potential plumber but as a science teacher it is important to recognize this and for your reluctant learner to appreciate it. Science can help him or her take a 'thinking skills tool kit' out to his or her adult job.

Similarly on page 8 of the National Curriculum (DfES, 2004b) we see defined the role science has in developing key skills. They are linked to the notion of thinking skills and we see seven listed in black and white:

- Communication: Scientific writing and presentations perhaps?
- Application of number: Collecting and analysing data?
- IT: spreadsheets, databases, word processing, on line research etc.
- Working with others: Is group work in Science done because we don't have enough kit?

- Improving own learning and performance: Thinking about what they have just done and highlighting the strengths and weaknesses of the data and the procedure
- Problem solving: finding ways to answer the questions with creative solutions. So that pond is covered with algae but the other isn't. Why is this? Have I any ideas? How will I test them? What do I think I will find?

Alongside these key skills being developed you are also going to tell the student that he or she will gain an awareness of how science works and so develop a critical eye to scientific claims. He or she will also pick up an awareness of health and safety and risk assessment through practical work. The student might also develop his or her motor skills as a result. I once heard a Year 8 pupil muttering mutinously about why he did not see the need for science and, more specifically, practical work. I asked him to put 30 cm^3 of water into a nearby measuring 100 cm^3 cylinder. He opened the tap and in rushed 60 cm^3. He then tried to empty 30 cm^3 out and ended up down to 20 cm^3. He then went back to the tap and put some water in again – back up to 70 cm^3! I think he could have spent all day measuring out water. He had a huge grin on his face and laughed all the way out the door but I guess there was some recognition that fiddling around in the laboratory might develop in him some useful science techniques and perhaps even develop his 'touch' about the house and work place.

Although I think it is fair to say that many children will never see another bunsen burner after they leave school, there are some scientific techniques they can acquire and if they have lots of practice fiddling about with the kit in the preparation room they may well get better at such skills as observation – noticing changes that may be fine and subtle. Again this is an aspect of learning that is going to be valuable after formal schooling is over. Give them lots of observational tasks. For example:

- What happens to copper sulphate as you heat it and then add water?
- What can you see under your microscope?
- What's growing on the school's field?

The list available to you as a science teacher is endless and can be generated by the pupil. As science teachers we are developing all these aspects of learning and it is crucial the good science teacher conveys these learning aspects to the children. This is why you are doing science. It is not just to pass an examination or even get them to recognize that an insect has six legs, wings and three body segments. I can hear you now: 'Today, Year 9, you are going to incrementally, by practice, develop your observational skills.' That would be tough but you need to emphasize that today your lesson is primarily about 'practising working as a team player' or the 'sharpness of your observation' or 'considering the merits and demerits of your performance'. You are developing their skills and they need to know that.

Website

In lesson two, Paul takes the pupils down a path that mirrors the role of scientists. He gives them a hypothesis to test – are all metals the same reactivity? Might the pupils suggest their own hypothesis? He asks them to plan jointly and then offer suggestions as to the game plan. They measure, observe and collect data. They are involved in group work and health and safety aspects. I would like you to consider the benefits of getting 10 sets of observations on data reliability. How does this reflect how a scientist works in practice?

Finally I think it is worth mentioning that one of the main reasons for doing science is that it is fun and most children can enjoy science. What 12-year-old does not enjoy looking down the barrel of a microscope at a water flea or using a bunsen burner to burn metals and observe the colour of the flame. Who dislikes field trips? I once taught a particularly 'challenging' Year 8 group. I took them on a day trip to a science museum and among the rocks and insect specimens they were perfectly happy. One pupil who was always in trouble really appreciated the visit – he had never seen anything like it! He told me he was going to ask his dad to take him next week. Some months later I asked him if he had ever gone back to the museum. He said he had asked his dad but the dismissive look on his dad's face meant he would only ever go back on his own – in fact probably never. Is there a message for you as a teacher?

HOW HAS THE ROLE OF A SCIENCE TEACHER CHANGED OVER THE PAST 20 YEARS?

A teacher's role has evolved radically over the past 20 years, really since 1989 when the National Curriculum and its statutory framework was conceived. The social changes in England have put a greater emphasis on the teacher as a solution to many of society's problems. For example the rapid influx in recent years of pupils with English as a second language (ESL) has meant that all teachers have had to try to come to terms with more and more pupils in the classroom with low literacy and oracy. Progressive governments and departments have pushed for the inclusion of all but the most severely disabled pupils into mainstream schools. The current Every Child Matters agenda, precipitated by the recognition that schools, home and other support agencies were sometimes not working in unison has led to a more integrated approach to pupils' needs. Every teacher is now required to take a holistic approach to every child and have a full working knowledge of all the agencies that might provide a spoke in a pupils support network. We can see this development reflected in the Professional Standards for Qualified Teachers (2008, TDA, 2007c) where Standards Q20, Q21a, Q21b all emphasize the need for trainees to recognize, be aware, know the players involved in issues of support and inclusion and the Every Child Matters agenda. It is a theme that runs through the document and is a challenge to every teacher or trainee as well as tutors in initial teacher training.

The revised National Curriculum states as its overarching aims (and the aims are tied in with the Every Child Matters agenda):

- Successful learners who enjoy learning, make progress and achieve.
- Confident individuals who are able to live healthy and fulfilling lives.
- Responsible citizens who make a contribution to society.

Again teachers have had to find ways to include all in the classroom often with enormous challenges, and I feel it safe to say that many were not trained to cope with. It's not in the scope of this book, and certainly not in this chapter, to examine in a wider context the professional role of the teacher. Clearly the role of all teachers is changing.

WHAT ARE THE CHALLENGES SPECIFIC TO THE SCIENCE TEACHER?

You have seen that a major challenge to teaching pedagogy, the methods we adopt to teach, has been raised by the slimming down of the heavily content-laden National Curriculum. The 2004 version of the National Curriculum cut the statutory content detailed in the 1999 version (DfEE, 1999) from 158 items of learning to just 16 at Key Stage 4 (they conveniently fit all on one page). The emphasis is now on teaching how science works and scientific enquiry through the study of four key themes. This is an incredibly difficult transition for many practising teachers to make and for trainee teachers to engage with and build into their teaching. Yes, it has allowed scope for additional science courses to proliferate and gives freedom of choice to all pupils at school, but clearly an understanding of how science works is vital if you are to teach it.

In this section I examine specifically the changing role of the science teacher and draw on the experience of others who have had the task of coming to terms with the changes that happened as a consequence of the reorganization of the statutory content of the National Curriculum in 2004 and its implementation in 2005 resulting in core and additional science, new assessment modes and a proliferation of courses by all the awarding bodies.

The major challenge emerges on two interlinked fronts. The first I explored in some degree of detail in an earlier section – you will have to move away from the traditional role of the science teacher, with its emphasis on content, knowledge and understanding, to a role focused on skill development and developing in pupils an understanding of the nature of science.

The second aspect that will present massive problems is a natural consequence of the changes to the science National Curriculum at Key Stage 4 in 2006. Most children are studying the core science as defined as the statutory science that has to be taught. This is normally delivered in Year 10. In Year 11 there is a whole plethora of options for teachers to decide routes which individual pupils will follow. The awarding bodies publish a range of syllabi that schools can follow, all accredited by the Qualifications and Curriculum Authority. Some are traditional, some are vocationally linked and some purely vocational. Choosing these options, then familiarizing yourself with the multitude of assessment modes for the chosen courses and then adapting to the new content is mind boggling for many science teachers. The curriculum is rapidly being opened up so small groups of pupils and even individuals can mix and match the courses on offer to suit their individual needs. Personalized learning is upon us.

At this stage I consider the options open to the pupils in a large 11–16 school in the north of England. Remember the Assessment and Qualifications Alliance (AQA) and Oxford, Cambridge and the RSA (OCR) are both awarding bodies and that core science is the statutory science in the National Curriculum.

It is also worth while pointing out that a single award is worth one General Certificate of Secondary Education (GCSE) and a double award is worth two passes if successful. In this context most pupils in England will expect to achieve two GCSEs with core and additional.

The quote below is from a local science teacher and gives a fascinating insight into the differentiated curriculum that now exists (see acknowledgements):

AQA Separate Sciences: This is a course for the pupils with a proven track record in science who would be capable of studying science at a higher level. At the end of the two-year course pupils have a separate GCSE for biology, chemistry and physics.

AQA Core: This is a one-year course worth one GCSE, usually taken in Y10.

For the pupils that do very well in the year nine SATs it is a combination of two biology, two chemistry and two physics modules plus coursework. The type of pupil that would usually take this course will have performed reasonably well in science over the previous key stage. It is the first part of two GCSEs and some of the pupils would be expected to study Advanced level science. A small minority of pupils with a past performance profile that is not so strong in science will also take this course but over two years and therefore will only get one GCSE in science.

AQA Additional Science: This is a one-year course studied in Y11 and combines with AQA Core to give most pupils a double GCSE.

OCR Gateway Science B: This is a one-year course studied by Y10s for pupils who have not performed particularly well in science over the previous key stage.

It is quite a different course to AQA but the same types of pupils could still do it. Also it is a suitable course for pupils to move on to Advanced level with if they have got high enough grades. This is to be combined with the equivalent Year 11 course from OCR but we have not started to deliver this yet as we are only in the pilot stage with the first cohort of Year 10.

OCR Double Award Applied Science: This is a double award GCSE for pupils who have low past performance in science but pupils who work hard and have good attendance. The best pupils have high CATs and low SATs scores due to their poor performance during tests.

Clearly the logistics of implementing such diverse options is a huge challenge. Selecting and sorting children into diverse courses that will decide their future employability is a daunting responsibility. Becoming familiar with the differing content and changing pedagogy inherent in each course will be time-consuming and require extending your repertoire. The individual modes of assessment are, case studies, individual skills assessment, module examinations and, in some cases, terminal examinations. This is all being thrown at teachers by a government responding to the needs of a diverse and evolving pupil clientele.

The major challenge to all science teachers involved in delivering the demands of the revised National Curriculum is summed up quite succinctly by a work colleague of mine and an assistant head teacher of a north-west 11–18 comprehensive (see acknowledgements) who astutely and with some insight sees the future of your role and its changing nature.

> The stiffest challenge science teachers face is coping and adapting to change. All teachers must understand that the profession is never static and a permanent state of change is normal. In fact the only constant thing is that we are always changing. Sometimes change is trivial and transient, at other times it is more fundamental. The changes in the science curriculum at the moment are more fundamental. With far greater attention being placed on how science and society interact rather than pure science for science's sake, the science teacher needs new skills. There are many science lessons these days that could be taught well, (perhaps better), by English or Humanities teachers because the classroom skills necessary include group work, discussion, opinion, critical analysis etc. Certainly science teachers will need to have a greater repertoire of classroom techniques than they have had before.

Point for reflection

Consider your own experience at school. Did you do traditional chemistry, physics and biology at GCSE? Do you think everybody should study this type of traditional course? Go to the websites of the three main awarding bodies (EdExcel, OCR and AQA). Compare and contrast the traditional science, vocationally linked and vocational science courses. Can you fit a person profile and perhaps career to the particular course?

GETTING STARTED: FROM NOVICE TO EXPERT

In your teacher training course, certainly if you are training via a Postgraduate Certificate of Education (PGCE), I am sure you will notice a wide variety of science degrees. Trainees bring to the course a huge variety of qualifications and experiences. This is one of the reasons why the year is incredibly stimulating and rewarding both for trainees and tutors.

There will be the trainee that is 22 and straight out of university not having exited the educational system at all. There will be the career changers, who, having worked for 10 years and are dissatisfied with a job that does not excite them. There will be a fair share who have worked a sizeable part of their working careers in a variety of professions and who want a fresh challenge, in many cases expressing a wish to do something that they had 'always wanted to do but got sidetracked by life'. The split between male and female at secondary is roughly 60:40 in favour of females. That is not a problem for the Teacher Development Agency. What is a problem is that the cohort each year on postgraduate initial teacher training (ITT) courses breaks down to about about 80 per cent biology, 15 per cent chemistry and about 5 per cent physics as their subject specialism. This reflects the intake and output at undergraduate level for the science disciplines.

All trainees start with two fundamental anxieties.

- Will I be able to manage the pupils?
- Will I be able absorb all the knowledge and understanding that is in the National Curriculum? A fear of not knowing all the facts and having a lack of understanding of basic scientific ideas.

This second anxiety is a particular fear for the scientists because they have such a wide breadth of knowledge to work with. Science is a multidisciplinary theme. Science teachers are often expected to teach all three disciplines in school, and most scientists have only one specialist subject area. Studies of trainee teachers (for example, Deng, 2004) have suggested that subject knowledge is fragmented and in some areas week. If you want to explore the almost limitless misconceptions and alternative conceptions that exist both in children and adults, and I include science teachers in the adults' category, then look no further than Driver et al. (2002). What is comforting is that all specialist scientists are in the 'same boat'. It's been this way since science became broad and balanced in the National Curriculum in 1989.

Nevertheless on an 11–16 ITT science course you will be expected to know enough science to be able to teach at Key Stage 3 across all disciplines and at Key Stage 4 in your specialism. I think it's realistic to say that the more confident and competent you are in all the disciplines the more it will give you a boost in the job market where flexibility in an era of broad science across the key stages is required. Biologists appreciate that many schools will not have many specialist chemists and physicists and will need to step into the breach where required and teach both aspects of the physical sciences.

Schulman (1986; 1987) emphasizes the importance of teachers' subject knowledge in effective teaching. If you think about it, it is reasonable to suggest that the more knowledge and understanding of a science topic you have then the more adept and effective you will be at teaching it. He also suggested three components make up a teacher's holistic knowledge:

- Content knowledge – a knowledge of the underpinning scientific principles.
- Pedagogical content knowledge. This is knowledge of how to represent and transmit the science knowledge.
- Knowledge of the curriculum. What do the pupils need to be taught?.

I would suggest that the second strand that includes what activities, strategies and 'kit' I use to deliver my knowledge to the pupils, is the most demanding and can only be acquired over a period of years. Both experienced science teachers and trainee teachers learn many new ways to deliver the key concepts that are on offer every day. The first and third strands are more readily acquired but again take time. I think it is safe to say that the 'best' way to learn something is to be asked to teach it! All novice science teachers will buy science textbooks and revision guides to quickly acquire subject knowledge. You will make sure you are very quickly au fait with the key concepts, facts and ways in which pupils are tested. Apart from the textbooks you are working with, how else will you slowly acquire Schulman's 'three aspects' of your knowledge? McCarthy and Youens (2005), working at the University of Nottingham, provide an insight into both the ways you can develop your subject knowledge and trainee teachers' perceptions of the usefulness of the method of building subject knowledge on a postgraduate ITT secondary science course.

Trainee science teachers were asked, at the end of the ITT course, the question: 'What strategies did you use to develop your subject knowledge and how do you perceive the usefulness of the different strategies?' The results are shown in Table 1.1.

I include Table 1.1 for a number of reasons, not least because it illustrates that all trainees use a variety of strategies to develop knowledge where there is a gap and enhance existing knowledge and understanding when it is present. It must be said that I do think that the question focuses largely on what I have referred to earlier as Schulman's 'first strand', that is, what I call 'straight' subject knowledge of science. You will not get advice on how to teach something from a revision guide, although there are books that give advice and I have listed three such books at the end of the chapter in the further reading list. Knowledge of the 'art and craft' of the science teacher will be built up by interaction with experienced teachers, tutors at your training institution, who are often specialists with a wealth of hard-earned experience, and workshops with specialists such as Chris King and Peter Kennett from the Earth Science Unit at Keele. My message is read around science education, join the Association of Science Education (ASE), join the Institute of Physics (IOP) or the Institute of Biology (IOB). If you

Table 1.1 Frequency of use and usefulness of methods for development of subject knowledge, each in rank order.

Frequency of use		Usefulness	
Method	Mean	Mean	Method
Revision guides	1.16	1.19	School textbooks
School textbooks	1.20	1.20	Revision guides
Method workshops	1.46	1.47	PGCE colleagues
Websites	1.50	1.49	Lesson observations
Lesson observations	1.54	1.50	Reference books
Reference books	1.76	1.52	Websites
PGCE colleagues	1.84	1.57	Mentors/teachers
Mentors/teachers	1.88	1.68	Method workshops
Tutors	2.36	1.86	Tutors
Television/videos	2.38	2.07	Television/videos

are a chemist then join the Royal Society of Chemistry (RSC). All have websites that channel materials and courses for the practising teacher. Keep your eyes open for subject knowledge-based courses organized by universities, educational agencies and local authorities. Geology, astronomy, plant science, information technology (IT) in science and now an array of courses aimed at teaching you how to teach how science works – they exist and will act as a driver for your professional development if you want to develop as a teacher.

CONTINUING PROFESSIONAL DEVELOPMENT (CPD): SUBJECT KNOWLEDGE IS IMPORTANT

In 2000 a piece of research (Dillon et al., 2000) found that at Key Stage 4 the percentage of topics taught by teachers without a degree in the subject was 39 per cent in biology, 51 per cent in chemistry and 66 per cent in physics. Alarmed at such research, which clearly indicated a shortage of teachers with specialist qualifications in the physical sciences, the Teacher Development Agency (then the Teacher Training Agency) went into overdrive on plugging this gap in expert qualifications and funded a number of higher education institutions to organize a range of taught courses for prospective PGCE trainees. These ongoing courses include short subject knowledge booster courses for ITT trainees and lengthy six months long chemistry and physics enhancement courses. These have involved a large number of prospective science teachers, largely postgraduate scientists with an offer of a place on a PGCE course, enhancing their knowledge of the physical sciences. There is a move to place much of the materials generated by these courses in an online, interactive, blended learning environment in the next two years. These courses have been extremely useful in filling gaps in both subject and pedagogical knowledge. You could call them method workshops where prior to the start of your ITT course you can both enhance your subject knowledge and begin to acquire knowledge of pedagogy and the National Curriculum. The TDA also fund two-year PGCEs where the first year is subject knowledge enhancement and the second year is subject application (pedagogical and educational studies). Most lately we have extended PGCEs where applicants for PGCE science courses with a blend of science modules and non- science modules in their degree, for example, psychology, study a selection of physical science undergraduate modules to strengthen their subject knowledge and enhance their academic profile in science. These courses are organized by the local ITT provider and are bursaried.

For in-service teachers a number of higher education institutions have been funded by the TDA to deliver physics and chemistry subject knowledge/ pedagogy courses to practising teachers that are primarily biologists but find themshelves teaching physics and/or chemistry in schools. These courses have the support of the IOP and the RSC and a regional network of school- and university-based mentors to support teachers in school and assess the success of the schemes on the quality of teaching in the classroom. The 'additional specialism' courses have a bursary attached and many have master's-level credit awarded by the organizing institution. Booster courses, enhancement courses and additional specialism courses can all be accessed on the TDA website. Again as in the pre-ITT courses there is an ongoing development programme to get them online in the next two years.

A problem in some schools is the lack of enthusiasm sometimes shown by head teachers to fund subject teachers to refresh or enhance subject knowledge and pedagogical knowledge in 'work time'. This is understandable for a number of reasons. First, the children will have their regular teacher absent for a day or half a day, with possible supply cover – this breaks the continuity in terms of teaching. Secondly, it might not fit in with the school's developmental plan and this is crucial in terms of funding by school governors who are aware of budgetary constraints. It is worth mentioning here that I taught in three secondary schools from 1985 to 2000 and I cannot remember once where the management team invited in a subject specialist tutor/teacher to deliver science subject knowledge and application to any of the science departments I worked in. The attitude was that it was 'up to you' to keep your subject knowledge and knowledge of the craft of delivering it up to date. I think this is a shame as it lowers the status of subject knowledge below, for example, classroom management or teaching children with special educational needs. I seem to remember that I was frequently addressed by guest speakers and regularly popping into local professional development courses themed around these practical and relevant aspects of teaching – but not so many subject knowledge-based events were evident. Of course, the best CPD is organized by yourself and for yourself. Read around your subject. If all you know is what is in the curriculum you are teaching then you are at a severe disadvantage. Grab hold each week of publications like the *New Scientist* or *Nature*. Keep your university library card active and talk to other scientists about developments. If you do not adopt this constant engagement your teaching will suffer – if you do not progress you will regress. Join the ASE and visit regional and national conferences. In five years' time you will be presenting at one.

Point for reflection

Point for reflection

Get hold of the content, that is, the knowledge and understanding, contained in the Key Stage 4 GCSE separate sciences from the AQA. For your specialist science discipline make a broad list of the learning objectives specified in the booklet and try to identify your individual gaps in your own subject knowledge. Do this with the A2 and AS content in your specialism. Reflect on how secure you are. Consider the use of an audit like this with children. Is it useful as a teaching and learning tool?

WHAT IS PERCEIVED AS GOOD PRACTICE IN SCIENCE TEACHING? THE NOTION OF A GOOD SCIENCE LESSON

All of us are aware that there are science teachers out there who are enthusiastic, making the science relevant to the children, teaching with clear objectives and outcomes, and using a variety of different strategies in the classroom. Working in ITT and seeing both trainees and experienced teachers teach science, I know with some degree of certainty that this is the case. The Key Stage 3 Strategy, now the Secondary Strategy, has had a massive impact on science teachers. They now know what a tripartite lesson is. They also know that assessment must be integral if it is to be useful. The knowledge of what constitutes an Office for Standards in Education (Ofsted) 'good' lesson is common knowledge. What about the 'good' science lesson?

Recently the Science Advisory team for Sefton Local Authority (LA) in Merseyside produced a poster for science teachers to reflect on. It is a large glossy pin-up for your preparation room or classroom and attempts to define the characteristics of a good science lesson. I paraphrase and rework the English but essentially it suggests that you:

First set the scene – Show me what you've got

Find out what ideas they have on the concept. Don't knock any of their ideas if they are incorrect. Share the learning objectives with them without giving away any 'answers'. Then, tell them what activities they are going to do and with the timings. Check they know what to do. Explain why they are doing the activities.

Second – Let's do something

Get them working as groups to promote constructive discussion. Intervene only if you have to. Intervention should be directed at getting them to think – if you've given clear instructions then you shouldn't have to give task support.

Third – What have we got? Is it different?

Pull together the data, analysis and results and find out what they have learnt. Share the learning around the group by considering the evidence. Have any of their ideas changed? Have they gained any new knowledge or skill? Again get them to talk about what the task(s) have led them to alter or discover.

Fourth – Can we join it up?

Link the learning to relevant, everyday situations that will allow them to transfer the new knowledge into different situations. Give them homework that reinforces or extends the learning. It doesn't have to be test tubes and 'practical' work but if the hands are engaged then there is a better chance of the 'brain' being engaged as well. Can you see that this sequence, which is very prescriptive, links with many positive aspects of teaching and learning science.

- Observation
- Group collaboration
- Discussion
- Building on what knowledge the pupils have already
- Intervention only when necessary
- Making it relevant
- Having fun
- Engaged in finding things out that are not evident
- Using scientific pieces of kit
- Using what is learnt in a wider context
- Pupil reflection on their own learning
- Shared and clear learning
- Data collection
- Data handling
- Pattern spotting.

I explore more fully some of these aspects in Chapter 5 but I do think the poster is a thought-provoking piece of advice and sets a clear vision of the pupils as scientists and researchers. It goes without saying that a lesson like this is not possible without structured planning and a working knowledge of where the individuals in the class are at. The three-part sandwich proposed in the secondary strategy is a format that a lesson can be built around, which encompasses these aspects.

What the research says

There has been plenty of recent research into children's views of scientists. Many such research investigations into children's ideas about scientists use DAST (Draw-A-Scientist – Test).

Buldu, M. (2006) 'Young children's perceptions of scientists; a preliminary study', *Educational Research*, 48(1): 121–32.
Quita, I.N. (2003) 'What is a scientist? Perspectives of teachers of colour', *Multicultural Education*, 11(1): 29–31.

Both provide accounts of the nature of young children's views of scientists. They typically show that they hold stereotypical images of white, middle-class, ageing figures with glasses. Many children have no real notion of the way scientists work and the scientific process that is essentially observation, data collection and analysis to gain understanding. These images and ideas about scientists show no real signs of being revised. You might try a DAST test in you own classroom.

 Further reading

Driver, R., Leach, J., Millar, R. and Scott, P. (1996) *Young People's Images of Science*. Buckingham: Open University Press.
How pupils perceived scientists and science 12 years ago. Any change?

Kuhn, T.S. (1970) *The Structure of Scientific Revolutions*. Chicago, IL: University of Chicago Press.
Thoughts from a pivotal philosopher of science on how science works.

McDuell, R. (ed.) (2000) *Teaching Secondary Chemistry*. London: John Murray for ASE.
Ideas on how you might teach 11–16 chemistry.

Millar, R. and Osborne, J.F. (eds) (1998) *Beyond 2000: Science Education for the Future*. London: King's College London.
Definitive suggestions for a new direction in science education You can see the beginnings of core science.

Monk, M. (2006) 'How science works; what do we do now?', *School Science Review*, 88(322): 119–21.
Monk suggests that we need to develop our own views of how science works to effectively teach such a curriculum.

O'Brien, P. (2003) *Using Science to Develop Thinking Skills at Key Stage 3*. Materials for Gifted Children. London: David Fulton.
Useful ideas on developing pupils' higher level cognitive processes.

Osborne, J., Duschle, R. and Fairbrother, R. (2002) *Breaking the Mould? Teaching Science for Public Understanding*. A report commissioned by the Nuffield Foundation, London: Nuffield. Downloadable from www.kcl.ac.uk
Evaluation and commentary on the AS Science for Public Understanding course. A course which attempts to develop at Post–16 an appreciation of how science works, treatment in the media of science and how science impacts on people's lives globally.

Popper, K. (1959) *The Logic of Scientific Discovery*. London: Routledge.
Heavy reading but outlines how science moves on and up.

Reiss, M. (ed.) (2000) *Teaching Secondary Biology*. London: John Murray for ASE.
Ideas on how you might teach 11–16 biology.

Sang, D. (ed.) (2000) *Teaching Secondary Physics*. London: John Murray for ASE.
Ideas on how you might teach 11–16 physics.

Sang, D. and Wood-Robinson, V. (eds) (2002) *Teaching Secondary Scientific Enquiry*. London: John Murray for ASE.
Ways to develop pupils' skills of enquiry.

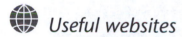

Useful websites

www.qca.org.uk
Documents relating to the National Curriculum and even obsolete previous versions of the National Curriculum can be found via the QCA website.

www.teachers.tv/video/22844
Lots of ideas to deliver How Science Works shown in moving images.

www.nuffieldcurriculumcentre.org/go/minisite/OtherScienceProjects/Page_148.html
Project on How Science Works from the Nuffield curriculum team.

www.sciencelearningcentres.org.uk
Any of the regional science learning centres will offer training courses to practising teachers giving ideas on how to teach how science works effectively.

2 WHAT ARE YOU EXPECTED TO TEACH IN A SCIENCE LESSON?

Matt Cochrane

This chapter:

- discusses how science teaching fits in to the Every Child Matters framework
- summarizes your responsibility for safeguarding children
- describes how to assess an activity for risk
- describes the background and structure of the National Curriculum
- discusses Science at Work and the place of practical work in the curriculum
- explores how pupils' thinking can be structured through the study of science.

EVERY CHILD MATTERS

When the government set a new agenda called Every Child Matters (DfES, 2003), all matters concerning the welfare of children were brought under one piece of legislation. The Every Child Matters (ECM) initiative places a unified duty of care on all children's services – education, childcare, social services. All these agencies have the same set of responsibilities, which includes an obligation to communicate effectively from agency to agency, because children, but particularly vulnerable children, have been found to be disadvantaged when important information is not shared by those who need it.

The Office for Standards in Education, Children's Services and Skills (Ofsted), now regulates care for children and young people, and inspects education and training for learners of all ages.

The government has also produced *Every Child Matters: Common Core of Skills and Knowledge for the Children's Workforce* DfES (2005a). This describes the skills and knowledge required by all professionals who work with children in schools, social services or children's support groups. All these agencies, and the people who work in them, now have an obligation to follow the ECM agenda.

This means that all schools have a legal obligation to operate policies which look after the welfare of the pupils. This is normally overseen by a single member of staff with responsibility for child protection, and you will be expected to work within this policy. If you witness something in school which causes you any concern about the welfare of a pupil, you are not allowed to keep it to yourself. You *must* report it to the senior member of staff – if a child is suffering abuse, do not attempt to deal with it yourself – indeed you are not allowed to.

Abuse takes a number of forms – physical, emotional and sexual abuse or neglect – and may be carried out by children, family members and other people known to the victim. The evidence is not always obvious, and may manifest itself in very different ways; for example, in the form of aggressive or inappropriate sexual behaviour or unexplained bruising. A pupil exhibiting these symptoms may or may not be the victim of abuse, but if you have any suspicions, you must always report them to the school's child protection officer. If a child confides in you, take this seriously and always remember that a child's evidence is as reliable as an adult's. Do not make promises you cannot keep about maintaining secrecy – but try to help the child see that you are trying to keep control of the situation with them.

EVERY CHILD MATTERS AND THE SCIENCE CURRICULUM

There are five 'outcomes' for the ECM agenda:

- staying safe
- being healthy
- enjoying and achieving
- making a positive contribution
- achieving economic well-being.

It is a whole-school responsibility to ensure that the curriculum of all subjects covers these five outcomes appropriately, and all departments will have audited their schemes of work to make the best use of opportunities to reinforce them. Some of them, as we shall see, lend themselves very well to the science curriculum.

Staying safe

Your school will have a policy which expects all members of the school community to respect one another – this means refusing to tolerate or condone bullying and discriminatory behaviour for example, and the way you establish the environment in your classroom is very important in promoting an atmosphere in which pupils feel safe and comfortable. And not just in the classroom – everywhere you go in the school, you should calmly and quietly challenge antisocial behaviour. Children should be taught that personal safety is also a personal responsibility, and in the science laboratory we have an almost limitless opportunity to promote an appropriate attitude to working safely.

So do not waste this opportunity by telling the pupils what to do – when you first meet them, discuss safety with them and find out what they know already, and develop an agreed code of safety for the laboratory. Before you carry out your first experiment with them, challenge them to define the safety procedures. And then stick to these procedures at all times – never give in to the temptation to take short cuts to save time. You may teach many hundreds of pupils in your career, and you never know just when something unexpected is going to happen. Be alert (and ask the pupils to do this as well) not just to the obvious issues such as eye protection, but to long hair dangling too near a Bunsen flame, or to somebody sitting down while working with apparatus (spilling a chemical in your lap is far more serious if you are seated).

Some teachers copy the idea of a bathing red flag on the beach – if the flag is flying, then safety procedures must be observed. This works well, as it is important to remember that the greatest danger to a pupil is the experiment at the next bench – a fragment of glass or a drop of acid can travel a long way if dropped on the floor.

All the experimental procedures you use will have to be assessed for risk using a form like the one in Figure 2.1.

In fact the school will already have done this and will be able to advise you, because the Health and Safety Executive requires employers to control substances hazardous to health under the COSHH regulations. Remember that a risk assessment is not a device to try and prevent you from doing something interesting – it is a procedure to help you find a way to do it safely. Indeed the organization CLEAPSS, which exists to advise a consortium of local authorities on safety issues, published a booklet in which they 'investigated alleged bans on the use of various chemicals or particular procedures that were commonly used in the past' (CLEAPSS, 2005). They list about 60 activities and procedures which some teachers have refused to carry out, wrongly believing them to be banned.

There are two questions you need to ask every time you make a risk assessment: 'How likely is an incident?' and 'How serious would it be?' Let us take a look at an example for a neutralization experiment in Year 7. The normal procedure involves adding acid to a measured amount of alkali through a burette. The use of stronger solutions and a burette allows for an accurate determination of the volume required for neutralization. The resulting liquid can then be evaporated to reveal common salt. So Table 2.1 shows the substances and procedures placed in the first table on the form in Figure 2.1.

The next step is to decide on the likelihood and severity of the various mishaps. We have to be realistic here – pupils in Year 7 have been known to drop things – and we have to say that even with the best organized and most

School Practice Risk Assessment Form

Title of practical activity: ....

Teachers and pupils involved: ....

	Substances hazardous to health – Chemicals regulated by COSHH*		Hazardous procedure or item of equipment
1		1	
2		2	
3		3	
4		4	

Risk estimator: A score of 10 or more means the risk is unacceptable

Likelihood of occurrence	'L' score	Severity of outcome	'O' score
Highly unlikely	1	Slight inconvenience	1
May happen but rare	2	Minor injury	2
Does happen but rare	3	Medical attention required	3
Occurs from time to time	4	Major injury leading to hospitalization	4
Likely to occur often	5	Fatality or serious injury	5

Hazard	L score	O score	Total (L × O)	Control measures

* Control of Substances Hazardous to Health

Figure 2.1 School practice risk assessment form

Table 2.1 Examples of hazards

	Substances hazardous to health – chemicals regulated by COSHH		Hazardous procedure or item of equipment
1	Sodium hydroxide (Molar)	1	Fill burette via funnel
2	Nitric acid (2M)	2	Use of burette to control flow into flask
3		3	Use of mixture for evaporation
4		4	Preparation of salt by evaporation

Table 2.2 Scoring hazards

Hazard	L score	O score	Total (L x O)	Control measures
Spillage of acid on clothing or skin	4	3	12	Use of weaker acid reduces O score to 2
Spillage of alkali in eye protection	3	4	12	Use of weaker alkali reduces O score to 2; use of eye reduces L score to 2.
Danger of upsetting burette due to height	5	2	10	Use alternative apparatus – bulb pipette and measuring cylinder – L score reduces to 3, O score is 1 if reactants are weaker
Boiling using evaporating basin to form crystals – spitting	5	2	10	Use of eye protection reduces O score to 1
Burns from hot apparatus	3	2	6	Warn pupils, leave time for apparatus to cool

careful of groups, sooner or later someone is going to tip something over. So the risk estimator for these procedures might look like that in Table 2.2.

Nearly all the scores are above the limit – therefore we *must* reconsider. Fortunately, this is quite easily done – use of much weaker solutions such as 0.25M for the acid and alkali means that spillage now becomes an inconvenience – there is time to rinse the spill away before it does any harm. Use of a pipette to transfer the acid avoids the use of a burette – many Year 7 pupils will simply not be tall enough, and we cannot have them clambering onto stools! Liquid will spit from the evaporating basin, and eye protection and an instruction to stand well back will cover this risk.

In reality you are not going to fill any risk assessment forms with risk estimator tables like the one above – the aim is to work out the control measures which ensure the score is below the limit, and then to fill in the form, which then demonstrates that you have taken appropriate measures to control the risk.

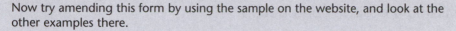

> **Website**
>
> Now try amending this form by using the sample on the website, and look at the other examples there.

You will also take pupils out of the classroom from time to time – either for fieldwork in the school grounds, or further afield. Do not take this upon yourself without seeking advice first. Your colleagues at the school will not take kindly to groups of children banging bin lids together outside their room while you measure the speed of sound! Trips outside school involve a whole extra level of organization – parents and carers must be informed, permission sought, payments made and taken, and so on. Your school will have a policy for this, and you should follow it.

Being healthy

Once again, science lessons offer a wide range of opportunities to encourage pupils to develop a healthy lifestyle, whether this be physical, mental or sexual.

We can encourage children to eat healthily by teaching them what foods contain and what effect overindulgence can have. We can encourage them to make good decisions relating to sexual matters and drugs by teaching them the consequences of abuse. We can encourage them to discuss these issues openly so that they are able to argue a viewpoint and resist temptations provided by others.

In your lesson planning, you should be aware whenever these issues of health and safety crop up, and make good use of them.

Enjoying and achieving

We hope it goes without saying that you will try to make your science lessons interesting and enjoyable, for example by putting plenty of varied experiences into your teaching and by giving pupils active things to do, because the essence of science teaching is to enable learners to observe, describe and explain the things they see around them. If you can challenge pupils' thinking sufficiently, their sense of achievement will come from overcoming these challenges. There is a bit of a balancing act here – make the challenges too hard and they may give up; make them too easy and they will get bored. Absorbing science lessons will encourage pupils to attend regularly, and while they are attending regularly, their personal and social development will be supported positively. This sort of approach is designed to help learners recognize and take responsibility for their own learning – once they have determined a need for their learning there will be no stopping them. It is fair to say that this section would fit into a textbook for teaching any subject – all of the above skills you would expect to see in the best lessons, where teachers are aiming to get the best out of all their pupils by target-setting, monitoring, and providing support when the going gets difficult. If you can achieve all of these, then the pupils will leave your room with a sense of fulfilment, good examination results and a liking for your subject.

Making a positive contribution

Pupils need to leave school with a good sense of what it takes to be a responsible citizen – are they able to take an active part in their community? We can mirror this in school – for example when there is a general election, schools will organize a parallel event, selecting candidates to represent the parties (some of the best actually choose to represent a party they do not particularly support, but are able to develop the arguments anyway!), and arranging for voting and counting on polling day. It can be surprising just how the results conform to national trends. Many schools run councils of one form or another, and when these bodies are involved in real decision-making, it is interesting how responsibly most of them act – they are aware that halving the school day and abolishing homework are not options, and they set about looking for ways to improve the school environment. We want them to develop a sense of perspective about life and a positive attitude to school. It is surprising how the little things can help here – do not fall into the trap of talking yourself and your subject down. Perhaps there is one part of the syllabus you are not particularly fond of – make the effort to take a special interest in it – if you present it with enthusiasm, the pupils are far more likely to be enthusiastic themselves and to take an active interest in the lesson, and will volunteer for the tasks you set them. Then you are likely to find the whole experience more rewarding yourself.

Other opportunities will present themselves – most schools will enter challenges of one sort and another, and good schools will have pupils involved in a whole range of projects – perhaps there is a science club providing an opportunity to build a more informal relationship between pupil and teacher. Generally it is the enthusiasm of individual teachers that drives these initiatives forward, and invariably it is the successful and dynamic departments that get involved this way.

Achieving economic well-being

Research shows that pupils in the early stages of their secondary career are often unable to recognize the link between education and employment – they are often unaware of the opportunities that an interest in a particular subject can open up.

The curriculum at Key Stage 4 and beyond has developed considerably in the last few years, with the introduction of a wider range of subjects which involve an understanding of the relevance of subject knowledge to the world of work. The new 14–19 diplomas being introduced over the coming years are an example of this: they aim to bring together a blend of specialist learning in the relevant subject, along with functional skills in English, mathematics and information and communication technology (ICT) and a key element of work experience, which is now compulsory for all pupils in Key Stage 4.

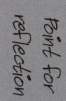

Point for reflection

Make sure that you are familiar with the five Every Child Matters outcomes. In this section we have given examples of how you can use your science teaching to work with the agenda. Consider each of the five aims, and think of other ways you can develop the way you approach ECM. Compare this with how the schools you observe have tackled the ECM agenda. What should the lessons contain, what materials and approaches can you prepare?

THE STRUCTURE OF THE NATIONAL CURRICULUM IN THE SCHOOL

English, mathematics and science were established as the core subjects which must be taught to all pupils from Year 1 to Year 11, and National Tests were developed at each of the key stages to monitor progress. The tests established an expectation for pupils at each stage of the National Curriculum (Table 2.3).

Table 2.3 Expected attainment at key stages

Age	End of key stage	Expected level
7	1	2
11	2	4
14	3	5–6

Naturally, there is considerable variation from pupil to pupil and from school to school, but there is an underlying expectation that children will advance by about two levels in each key stage. How to recognize the level of a child's learning is the subject of Chapter 6.

The establishment of a common curriculum for all took place against a background of accountability and the belief that market forces would drive out failing schools, since parents would choose to send their children only to successful schools. Successive governments therefore provided more and more guidance for schools in the form of the Key Stage 3 (and later Secondary) National Strategy. This specified not only the subject matter to be taught, but also the order in which it should be taught, and even went down to the detail of how the individual lesson should be structured.

It must be said at this point that the guidance provided by the National Strategy is sound advice, and you will see that the lesson planning we tackle in the next chapters follows closely the National Strategy.

Since 1989, the science content of the school syllabus has been prescribed by the National Curriculum. From the perspective of the science curriculum, this was a response to an imbalance in the teaching of biology, chemistry and physics as three separate subjects. There was a tendency for boys to study the physical sciences, and girls often opted for biology, and to address this issue it became compulsory for all pupils to study a balanced programme covering all three subjects equally. It soon became the norm for schools to provide at Key Stage 4 what became known as 'co-ordinated science' – a blend of the four strands of the National Curriculum delivered in the time allocated to two GCSE subjects. There were rules which allowed for some pupils to opt for a single award, the original intention being for someone gifted in, say, music to be able to spend extra time on the subject. In practice, it became common to offer the single version to less able pupils as they often found the full curriculum too demanding and many lost interest.

Since then, a greater variety of courses has been developed, with vocational courses, and applied science in addition to the 'traditional' course.

THE STRUCTURE OF THE NATIONAL CURRICULUM IN SCIENCE

The science National Curriculum aims for all young people to become:

- successful learners who enjoy learning, make progress and achieve
- confident individuals who are able to live safe, healthy and fulfilling lives
- responsible citizens who make a positive contribution to society. (QCA, 2007a: 207)

You will see how this matches the Every Child Matters agenda, but it also means that the science curriculum must provide more than simply subject knowledge. The programme of study gives a set of key concepts which underpin the teaching of science:

- *Scientific thinking.* Summarizes the way scientists approach phenomena: develop theories and models to explain them, and use creative thinking to devise ways of testing them. This is followed by critical analysis and evaluation of the results.
- *Applications and implications of science.* How does the creative application of science affect the way we live? What are the moral and ethical implications of this?
- *Cultural understanding.* Recognizing that science has origins in many cultures, and draws on a variety of methods.
- *Collaboration.* Sharing developments with others.

In order to get these key concepts across, pupils need to become skilled in a range of key processes, listed in the programme of study as:

- Practical and enquiry skills.
- Critical understanding of evidence.
- Communication.

The practical skills will be those which enable pupils to use appropriate methods and equipment accurately and safely, assessing risk as they go along. They should be able to plan and carry out investigative work individually and with others. Using these techniques, they will gather and record data using ICT where appropriate, and analyse the data. The analysis of the data gives evidence for scientific explanations of phenomena, and in order to understand the evidence fully, they will need to have a critical awareness of the validity of their evidence and methods. Finally, pupils need to be able to communicate these ideas to an audience, again using ICT as appropriate.

So as you will see in the next chapter, planning to teach science is not a case of lining up a number of topics and taking the class through them one by one. The pupils themselves are to play the part of scientists exploring and testing the world around them.

The programme of study now begins to specify the subject matter to be taught, by listing them under four attainment targets:

- How science works.
- Organisms, their behaviour and the environment.
- Materials, their properties and the Earth.
- Energy, forces and space.

You will recognize the last three under the traditional labels of biology, chemistry and physics, and most schools still divide their teaching under those labels.

At Key Stage 4, the programme of study is worded somewhat differently:

During the key stage, pupils should be taught the *Knowledge, skills and understanding* (original emphasis) of how science works through the study of

- organisms and health,
- chemical and material behaviour,
- energy, electricity and radiations, and
- the environment, Earth and universe. (QCA, 2007b: 224)

Now the subject boundaries are less obvious, with a significant proportion devoted to the environment. In devising a timetable, schools tend to share out subjects like geology between the chemists and physicists, though more and more, there is an expectation that as a science teacher you will be expected to deliver the National Curriculum at all subjects confidently to the end of Key Stage 4.

Each document then goes on to specify the actual subject content required, but the difference at Key Stage 4 is that this is all within the framework of Science at Work. Therefore, with the study of Science at Work at the centre of the National Curriculum, it is vital that all our teaching incorporates an understanding of how scientists plan, observe, describe and explain evidence. This focus on scientific enquiry from the start of the National Curriculum led to the development of a very different approach to the teaching of practical work to replace the idea of providing pupils with activities on the lines of a recipe, with 'experiments to prove … ' in which the outcome was effectively predetermined. Now pupils are given the task of defining the problem for themselves and undertaking an investigation divided into four distinct areas:

- *planning*, which involves setting the scene, making predictions about the outcome, and planning a strategy to collect data
- *observation* – the collection and presentation of data with appropriate precision and taking into account the need to ensure that measurements are accurate
- *analysis* of the results, providing an explanation of the outcome
- *evaluation* of the investigation, looking for flawed results, improvements and possible future developments.

This means that experiments can be devised to engage pupils while still covering basic science knowledge. Consider the example in Figure 2.2, in which a trainee provided the pupils with a letter, apparently from the local football club (insert your team here!) asking for assistance with the surface of their training pitch. The pupils took part in the investigation with gusto, and in the process learned a great deal about friction and forces.

The example in Figure 2.2 probably leads to a fairly traditional 'fair test' investigation which will compare the properties of different surfaces under controlled conditions. Watson et al. (2006) suggest that there are six categories of enquiry and suggest examples for each:

- Classifying and identifying (for example, What chemicals are in this green rock? How can we group these spiders?)
- Fair testing (for example, What is the effect of exercise on heart rate? How does the rate of reaction of sodium thiosulfate solution with an acid change with different concentrations of the acid?)
- Pattern seeking (for example, What causes the variation over time in levels of air pollution? What affects how far people can throw a tennis ball?)
- Exploring (for example, How does the size of the hole in the ozone layer over the Antarctic change over time? Is there a pattern in hourly measurements of the concentration of nitrogen dioxide in the air in central London?)
- Investigating models (for example, Why does the population of ladybirds in the school nature trail change? Why do the bubbles in a fizzy drink get larger and faster as they rise in the glass?)

Dear Ms Teacher

My new player (name of latest signing here) is having trouble on the training pitch. He keeps falling over because his trainers do not grip on the grass. Can you ask your pupils to investigate the problem and tell me which type of surface would be best for us to train on? This is very important to us, as we want to win the European Champions League again, so please help.

Yours sincerely
Football manager
(They change too quickly to use the real example!)

Figure 2.2 Putting the subject into context

- Making things or developing systems (for example, Devise a way of retrieving pure salt from salt that has been spilt on the soil. Design a regime to improve your fitness and to evaluate its effectiveness).

Website

What other ideas can you provide to stimulate pupils' thinking? The website has some suggestions ('Stimulus and Support' sheets) written by trainee teachers to start you thinking. It helps pupils if their scientific study is put into a familiar context. Watch the video of the start of lesson 2. How could you devise an introduction to the lesson which might involve pupils' experience of metals reacting (rust, tarnished metal, and so on)?

From the 1990s, investigations became a significant part of the GCSE syllabus, but there was a problem: some schools were highly successful in coaching their youngsters to complete their investigation with high marks, but some observers felt that learning was not always evident, particularly for the less successful candidates, who felt unable to see an investigation from start to finish. In particular, the concept of evaluation was particularly difficult to grasp.

Now that this attainment target has developed into Science at Work, there is a much broader brief in which investigative work is still taught, but without necessarily requiring pupils to demonstrate a holistic approach. Pupils must now also study the work of scientists past and present, and show an understanding of the development of scientific knowledge and understanding.

SCIENCE, NUMERACY AND LANGUAGE

Included in the National Strategy is a rationale for teaching children key skills – particularly in the early stages, literacy and numeracy. We cannot separate science teaching from the need to construct clear and precise language – for if the purpose of teaching science is to enable pupils to observe, describe and explain the phenomena they see, how can this be achieved without language and an understanding of number? Therefore it is worth considering how pupils are to develop this understanding of science thinking through language, and Fisher (2005: Ch. 7) provides a useful commentary on our understanding of how children learn. Traditionally, teachers have regarded knowledge as a body of ideas which they must transfer into their pupils' heads (the transmission model) Alternatively, and perhaps more recently, the 'discovery model' suggests that children can uncover hitherto hidden truths which will become fixed in their minds by the very process of discovery.

The reality is more complicated than this, and we need to be aware of children's modes of thinking as they learn. For example, a child with a misconception (for example, the belief that there is no gravity in space), must first of all see how the misconception raises a conflict (why the moon does not fly off into space) before resolving it with a revised conception (there is no weight in space where there is nothing to stand on).

The development of understanding of the way children think has passed through a number of phases described by McGregor (2007). Behaviourism, in which children's responses can be trained, suggests that pupils learn through involvement in didactic procedures with the whole class, resulting in rote-learning. Piaget recognized that pupils are able to adapt when they meet a new experience, and are able to construct new meaning to situations as they compare their existing knowledge with the latest encounter (constructivism). Piaget also recognized that children follow a hierarchy of cognitive processes which inhibits understanding of a given concept until they have achieved a stage of maturity to cope with it. Vygotsky takes this a stage further into social constructivism, in which 'learning can be influenced by social, historical and cultural factors' (McGregor, 2007: 54).

Thus we return to the need for language and the 'Literacy Across the Curriculum' training received by all schools from 2002, and a summary of the ways in which children use language.

Thinking out loud

Children need to be given time to try out ideas. They are often highly reluctant to do this, as it places them in a vulnerable position through the completely understandable fear that they might be wrong. We can provide them with the space for this type of thought by lowering their feeling of exposure – talking to them individually, inviting them to talk to their classmates and knock ideas around. Concept cartoons are particularly good for this, as they offer familiar situations with a range of plausible explanations provided by the children in the cartoon thinking aloud.

Talking

Children need *time* to think. If we ask them a question in the heat of the moment, and when a child is obviously struggling with the question you have just given them, it is all too tempting to supply the answer too soon. Fisher (2005: 158) suggests five ways in which we can encourage the child to talk:

- Pausing – allow the child 'think time' during question-and-answer or discussion. Waiting for an answer demonstrates a trust in the child's ability to answer, and expectation of thoughtfulness even if the silence sometimes seems to be interminably long!
- Accepting – do not 'rush to judgement' on a child's response; give the child time and give yourself time to reply in a thoughtful way. Ways of accepting a child's idea are to restate it, reapply it, recognize it, compare it to another idea, or simply to acknowledge her view. Passive acceptance can be the non-verbal nod of the head, active acceptance will show understanding, or perhaps elaboration of the idea.
- Clarifying indicates that the teacher does not understand fully what the child is trying to say. Instead of 'rushing in' to explain to the child what he is trying to say, the adult requests more information and invites the child to elaborate on his idea. 'Can you explain what you mean by … ?' 'Tell me again, I couldn't quite understand … '
- Facilitating means sustaining talking and thinking through feedback and response. The teacher needs to provide opportunities for the child to check her ideas to see if they are correct. 'Are you sure?' 'Let's check it and see.'
- Challenging – to be understood by others is part of the stimulus a child needs, but children also need challenge and should be encouraged to challenge each other and adults. 'Do you agree with what I/another child says?' 'Can you see any problems?' 'What do you think?'

Website

Watch lesson 1. Here the pupils are given an opportunity to discuss a problem without too much intervention from the teacher. How many of the above points are covered by this approach? It is useful to listen to Paul's discussion of his planning – also on the website.

Table 2.4 Using different writing styles

Writing style	Context	Rationale
Concept map	Acids and alkalis	Helps to link ideas
Cartoons	Digestive system	Allows pupils to revel in the 'yuckiness'
Newspaper article	Thermit process	Reporting a spectacular incident in the classroom
Science Fiction story	Earth in space	Enables speculation about conditions beyond Earth
Love story	Bonding	How the rakish Mr Aluminium stole Miss Sulphate from Mr Copper
Letter	Photosynthesis	Describing a difficult concept to one of their friends

Writing

There are so many different ways of putting ideas onto paper, so many of which are fun, and we should make use of them as often as possible. Traditionally there was only one way to describe an experimental procedure: ('Diagram, method, results, conclusion' from the behaviourist school of thought!). Why do children need to write? Who are they writing for? What are they writing for? Does it need to be writing?

The range is huge, and we should make full use of it. Table 2.4 is just a small example. For each one, consider the possible audience(s), and work out some alternative contexts.

Numeracy

Numeracy was defined in the National Strategy as follows:

> Numeracy is a proficiency which is developed mainly in mathematics but also in other subjects. It is more than an ability to do basic arithmetic. It involves developing confidence and competence with numbers and measures. It requires understanding of the number system, a repertoire of mathematical techniques, and an inclination and ability to solve quantitative or spatial problems in a range of contexts. Numeracy also demands understanding of the ways in which data are gathered by counting and measuring, and presented in graphs, diagrams, charts and tables. (DfEE, 2001: 9)

Numbers and measures

We should expect children at the age of 11 to be able to measure and estimate force, and to describe the weight of an object in terms of the gravitational pull upon it. Yet the definition of weight is rooted in an arcane system of units and sub-definitions which would be almost impossible to explain to most 11-year-olds. So to ask them to use the newton scale presents a challenge – what does '1 newton' actually mean?

Mathematical techniques

All the numeracy skills exist in a hierarchy, none more significantly than when children attempt to use mathematical formulae. Being able to calculate the moment of an object when we tell them to multiply force by distance is a very different proposition from the question 'Where must Alfie sit on the see-saw to make it balance?' Bloom's taxonomy (see Chapter 3) will be useful here: at the earliest level, children will be able to 'use a mathematical formula to make a calculation' through stages to 'manipulate a mathematical formula to solve a problem'. What are the stages in between?

Quantitative problems

Not all quantitative problems are solved by mathematical formulae. Chemical equations provide another hierarchy of skills – ranging from the simple statement in words, to the balancing of equations with a number of compounds on either side. Before you use the higher-level skills with your class, you need to be sure they can handle the lower-level concepts first.

Graphs and charts

There is not just a hierarchy of skills associated with producing an illustration of the way numbers behave, there is also a sequence to it, and this sequence can be time-consuming. Write down a list of the steps you must go through in order to produce a line of best fit on a graph. Starting with 'identify the variables', the list is very long. So if you are planning to teach a lesson involving graphs, be clear about the focus – if they need practice in plotting data onto a graph, then the process of collecting and tabulating the data becomes less important, and can be done by the class collectively or using a computer and data logger, or by yourself.

What the research says

Patricia Murphy and Elizabeth Whitelegg (2006) describe research that has been undertaken to look into reasons why more boys than girls choose to study physics. This is quite a serious problem, since there is a general decline in the number of students who wish to study physics, and if girls were better represented this would

(Continued)

(Continued)

help to halt the decline. The authors discuss differences in interests, motivation and aspirations between the sexes; 'teacher effects' such as question technique and feedback, and go on to recommend strategies for schools and teachers to overcome the imbalance. In a follow-up booklet to the one above, a team from the Institute of Physics (Hollins et al., 2006) provides practical guidance on the encouragement of girls in physics. It draws on the research to identify the barriers encountered by girls, and suggests strategies to overcome these barriers. There is a great deal of literature on gender influences in education, and these two books provide a very positive and practical approach. A further book in this series reviewing the impact of this work in the classroom was published in 2008.

Further reading

Corry, A. (2005) 'Mentoring students towards independent scientific enquiry', in S. Alsop, L. Bencze and E. Pedretti (eds), *Analysing Exemplary Science Teaching*. Maidenhead: Open University Press. pp. 63–70.
Alex Corry describes an 'apprenticeship' approach to developing pupils as scientists who use their existing knowledge to explore and enquire about science. He follows this with a helpful reflection on the process.

Useful websites

Live links to these websites can be found on the Companion Website www.sagepub. co.uk/secondary

Documents relating to the National Curriculum can be found via the QCA website at www.qca.org.uk/

The CLEAPSS website is at www.cleapss.org.uk/startfr.htm

3 PLANNING TO TEACH A SCIENCE LESSON

Matt Cochrane

This Chapter looks at how to:

- place a sequence of topics into a long-term plan
- divide a topic into a sequence of lessons
- write appropriate learning outcomes for a lesson plan
- link assessment to the learning outcomes
- plan a lesson taking into account the needs of the whole-school curriculum.

If you have ever made a presentation to a group of people (at an interview for your teaching course perhaps), you will be aware that the task is made much easier by good preparation. Some teachers will say that there is no substitute for experience, therefore, until you have gained that experience, detailed and focused planning is an essential part of preparing a successful lesson. It is important to develop an understanding of all the different elements that constitute a lesson – and for this we have supplied a template for lesson planning which covers all the aspects you are likely to encounter. Do not be daunted by its complexity – we will discuss how to focus on key strategies and how to provide a balanced curriculum which addresses all areas of the National Strategy such as literacy, numeracy and citizenship, and also takes account of the Every Child Matters (ECM) agenda.

For that reason, we start not with planning in the short term (the single lesson), but with the long term – everything that needs to be taught in one school year. Medium-term planning follows, showing how the school year can be broken down into topic-based chunks (typically 5–12 lessons).

We illustrate this chapter with an example of a short-term plan to help you see how the sequence of events you see in a lesson is built up through a careful consideration of the needs of the pupils. The planning template we use here is for illustration – there are many ways of putting a plan together, and you will encounter different versions on your training course and in your school. But you will recognize the basic elements, and we would contend that they all need careful consideration in every lesson and scheme of work that you plan, however they are laid out on paper.

LONG-TERM PLANNING

Your start point here is the National Curriculum (DfEE, 1999; DfES, 2004b). At Key Stage 3, the National Strategy organizes the entire curriculum into a series of coherent units, so really the purpose is to sort out the order of teaching. A suggested list has been published by the Department for Children, Schools and Families (DCSF), which publishes examples on the Standards site (see 'Useful websites' at the end of this chapter). When the new National Curriculum came into force in September 2008, this list was not replaced – it will remain for a time as a guide and while the remaining two cohorts move through the system. Schools are no longer expected to follow the same programme of study from year to year, but will be able to choose their own route instead. However, it is instructive to look at the way these topics were organized so that learning could be supported.

As an example, consider the concept of the cell as the building block of life. Early in Year 7, pupils will use microscopes to observe and describe cells. They cannot do this until they have learned to use microscopes. They will later learn about specialized cells used in reproduction and photosynthesis; they will learn that cells group together to form tissues, and that organs are made of tissues. Later still, they will describe the processes involving whole systems of organs (for example, the circulatory system, but not until they have learned separately about the gases involved and the way gases behave). So the whole process has to be planned first in the long term so that it fits together as a jigsaw puzzle, with all the right pieces being prepared at just the right time. Schools are encouraged to develop their own models of long-term delivery, because they will have local reasons for covering topics at a certain time (perhaps they have a particularly rich pond which becomes available only in the summer months).

At Key Stage 4 and beyond, the various examination boards have developed specifications for their awards at GCSE level and at post-16. These are approved by the Qualifications and Curriculum Authority as being compliant with the needs of the National Curriculum. They can be found at the various websites (see list at the end of the chapter) of the boards concerned.

Many publishers now produce materials which have taken over some of the tasks of long-term planning, and many schools subscribe to these materials. The publishers produce a handbook dividing the curriculum into topics, and providing order and resources for delivery. Used considerately, resources help to keep pupils 'active and goal oriented' according to Petty (2006: 214). Even so, most of these schemes provide a great deal more material than you can use, so it is still necessary for each school to break it down in their own way according to facilities, staff expertise and time available, and taking account of the particular cohort of pupils. We will return to this latter point when we discuss how to move from medium- to short-term planning. Therefore a feature of long-term planning is the coverage of all the bases – the plan needs to cater for the most able pupil and the least able, the gifted, talented, disabled, and so on. Every pupil has a special need of some sort, and these must all be included in the plan.

The use of published schemes of work has taken a new turn with the introduction of new specifications at GCSE from 2006. The National Curriculum at this stage was revised, with a smaller compulsory core and a wider range of optional topics. This was done to provide the alternatives to the 'traditional', 'academic' course as found in grammar schools since 1948, and to the 'vocational' courses which have become popular in the past 20 years or so.

Point for reflection

Some observers regard 'traditional' and 'academic' courses as necessary to safeguard the quality of education, and that 'vocational' courses are of lesser value. Explore the range of courses available, and consider whether they cater for all needs.

The aim is to provide courses which will as far as possible carry out the seemingly impossible task of catering for pupils of all abilities and tastes – disaffected pupils who need to be inspired by interesting and exciting lessons; pupils who want to pursue courses and careers involving science as a thoughtful discipline; pupils who will use science in a practical context. This development is continuing in the post-16 sector, with the government setting out plans for a wide range of courses to be developed over the coming years.

MEDIUM-TERM PLANNING

A curriculum is often set out in a spiral form, so that as we cover each topic we are aware of both what has been covered before, and what will be covered later. While the long-term plan has put topics into an appropriate order, and is in some ways merely a logistical task, medium-term planning is where the needs of the whole curriculum must be considered. The National Strategy specifies for example that numeracy and literacy must be embedded into the whole- school curriculum. This is a task for management and subject teams across the school to get together and ensure that all the needs of the National Strategy are met. Work schemes from each subject will need to be scrutinized so that no elements of the strategies are missed, and so that all elements are spread evenly and coherently across the school curriculum. In this chapter, we aim to demonstrate how various elements of numeracy, literacy and so on can be incorporated into lesson plans without too much repetition ('Oh, Miss, not another word search'), and in a way which inspires pupils to uniformly develop their wider skills at the same time as learning some science.

Figure 3.1 shows the sort of information that needs to go into a medium-term plan. It provides the link between the long-term plan, which might indicate simply that this topic is about 'cells', and the day-to-day lesson planning. By scanning a medium-term plan, you will be able to identify at a glance the coverage of numeracy, literacy, citizenship, health and safety issues. In the section on short-term planning we discuss the inclusion of these in the individual lesson plan.

One physics teacher had this to say on the subject of medium-term planning:

> It's important to have a view of the whole topic – you need to know where it's going. Generally, in any given topic, there will be a small number of favourite activities that experience tells me will provide good learning, and I try and fit these into the pattern. I like to use starters which introduce the lesson and lead into it. For example for a Key Stage 4 section on the Electromagnetic Spectrum, I would start with a display of examples from each part of the spectrum to provoke discussion – the pupils are interested in the X-ray pictures and ultra-violet security pen, and want to study further. This helps to break the topic down into lesson-sized chunks.

SHORT-TERM PLANNING

Website

Go to the companion website www.sagepub.co.uk/secondary
First, have a look at the interview given by Paul, the teacher in our video lessons. He gives a description of his thoughts on planning lesson 1.

The lesson plan in Figure 3.2 is for a one-hour practical session where pupils will make a microscope slide of a sample of onion and observe the cells. They will see the 'brickwork' arrangement of cells, and be able to identify clearly the cell wall and nucleus. Other details are quite hard to see, and it may be helpful to have a projecting microscope showing some sample slides on the whiteboard. (Many schools have one of these microscopes, but not every classroom has the facility to project onto a screen.) The lesson follows the 'three-part' model favoured by the National Strategy. This is examined further in the next chapter.

Module title/topic: *Cells*   **Timing:** 4 lessons   **Year Group:** 7

Cross-curricular opportunities:
Numeracy: measurement of scale
Literacy: research; comprehension

Title	Aims	Learning outcomes	Suggested activities and resources	Assessment
How can we see small things more clearly?	Using a microscope to observe small things	• Use a microscope safely • Estimate the size of objects under the microscope	Use of microscopes with prepared slides and a range of sample objects (newspaper, string, graph paper, etc.)	Use of microscope Sketches of objects viewed through microscope Estimation of scale
What are plants made of?	Observation of plant cells under microscope	• Prepare microscope slide • Describe plant cells as viewed through microscope • Observe a variety of plant cells • Label a diagram of a plant cell	Preparation of onion cell: Microscopes, slides, onion Prepared slides of other plant cells viewed via ICT	Quality of slides Labelled diagrams of plant cells
What are animals made of?	Describe the functions of parts of the cell	• List the parts of animal cells • List the differences between animal and plant cells • State the function of different parts of the cell	Start with a basic cell model and adapt it for use in different parts of the organism; write a story about the journey of chemicals through the cell	Comparison of plant and animal cells; identifying and describing cell wall, vacuole and chloroplasts
Different cells for different jobs	Researching different types of animal and plant cell	• Describe an adaptation to a cell • Explain the purpose of the adaptation	Using text/Internet resources, research various animal and plant cells: palisade, root, cilium, cheek, nerve, sperm, ovum, etc. Pupils describe cells to each other and draw them from the description. Try to work out the purpose of the cell	Written and verbal descriptions of cells and their adaptations

Figure 3.1   Secondary science scheme of work pro forma

Lesson Title
Observing Cells with a microscope

Group: Y7 set 3 (of 4)   **Location:**   **Date/Time:**

Learning objectives
Pupils will learn how to use a microscope to observe plant cells

Learning outcomes
1. Prepare a microscope slide
2. Draw a labelled diagram of a plant cell
3. Use the terms cytoplasm, vacuole, nucleus, chloroplast, cell wall, cell membrane

---

National Curriculum/syllabus references (incl. reference to previous KS)
Science at Work: reviewing the work of Robert Hooke

Links to other areas
Numeracy – measurement and scale

Previous assessment details informing this lesson
Pupils were able to use microscopes in the last lesson, but some needed close supervision to avoid damage to the slide. Some were able to count the number of graph squares in the field of view but many didn't understand how to use this information to measure size.

Differentiation
Worksheet to help with slide preparation – weaker groups will need step-by-step support. Challenge stronger groups by getting them to estimate the size of a cell

---

Health and safety
Eye protection while using iodine; use of sharp instruments; care with glass slides and cover slips

---

Figure 3.2   Secondary science lesson plan framework

It is fundamentally important to see the link in the planning process between the intended outcomes, the activities and the assessment; because, as Ireson and Twidle point out, 'teaching should be a logical and intentional activity' (2006: 6). Otherwise the lesson will lack direction and any outcomes will be either accidental or not linked directly to the intended learning. Look at the lesson plan in Figure 3.3 and see how the pieces fit together. Then we will work through the plan in stages and see how it builds up.

Timing (min)	Teacher activity	Pupil activity	Resources	Assessment Items
0–5	Supervising entry to room	Starter activity: '3 things that can go wrong with a microscope'	Class exercise books/jotters	Class discussion to reinforce learning from last lesson
5–10	Lesson overview – WALT and WILF	Share outcomes in 'pupil speak'	Whiteboard	
10–15	Activity 1– Introduction to Practical	Listening to instructions; observe techniques	I set of equipment to demo.	LO 1: Q&A
15–20	Organize into appropriate groups	Collection of apparatus	Worksheet	
20–35	Support pupils	Preparation of slide and observation under microscope	Worksheet	LO 2: Pupil feedback
35–45	Demonstration with classroom microscope – variety of plant & animal cells to view	Pupil slides viewed on screen	Electronic microscope, computer, projector	LO 3: Q&A to identify parts of cell
45–55	Identify parts of cell – show how to interpret microscope view	Draw labelled diagram of plant cell	Pupil books	LO2/3: diagrams
55–60	Summarize key learning points	Finisher activity: 'spot the difference'	Projected image of plant & animal cell	LO3: correct use of terms

Figure 3.3   Lesson development

LEARNING OBJECTIVES

These are the broad aims of the lesson and are concerned with what the lesson will cover. It is quite helpful if they follow on from the phrase 'We are learning to … ' (WALT). So with this example, which is the second in the medium-term plan described earlier in this chapter, we could use 'We are learning to use a microscope to observe plant cells'.

The number of objectives should be small – you are going to share these with the pupils, so they need to be worded in a pupil-friendly way. 'Pupil-friendly' means that the pupils will not be intimidated by them – that is, no big words (except scientific terms they need to learn, and not too many). When you attend a lecture, you like to know what it is about, and so do pupils. It is now a requirement of the National Strategy that objectives are shared with the pupils before, during and after the main body of the lesson, and many schools specify how this should be done (often through the acronyms WALT and WILF).

LEARNING OUTCOMES

The outcomes define *precisely* what the pupils will be able to do by the end of the lesson. It is difficult to stress just how important and central they are to the whole business of teaching. With carefully worded outcomes, you will have a clear idea of what the pupils are expected to achieve and how you are going to assess it. You will be able to plan activities which will give pupils the opportunity to demonstrate individually and collectively that they have mastered them. With carefully worded outcomes (and a well-planned lesson built around them), the pupils will be focused and motivated, your confidence will increase, and behavioural problems will diminish.

With vaguely worded outcomes, your activities will lack purpose and pace, pupils' minds will start to wander, and your confidence will drop as they drift off task. The worst thing is that the pupils will see your dwindling confidence and begin to take advantage – you are then at risk of entering a descending spiral where behavioural problems begin to increase.

It is not true to say that all your problems will disappear with good-quality planning – you will still need to work on this; see Chapter 6 – but it cannot be stressed too highly that classroom management begins with sound lesson planning, and sound lesson planning begins with well-worded learning outcomes. The acronym to accompany WALT is 'WILF' (What I'm looking for). In other words, outcomes are statements which you or the pupil should be able to look at and say 'yes, I (they) can do that'.

- I can draw a labelled diagram of an animal cell.
- I can draw a labelled diagram of a plant cell.
- I can name/describe/explain the job of the nucleus/cytoplasm/membrane.
- I can name three things in a plant cell that are not in an animal cell.

And so on.

Note that it is important to specify *which* parts the pupils should learn. The statement 'knows the parts of a cell' could be included in the specification for any course up to and beyond degree level! And what do we mean by 'knows'? Do you want pupils to be able to say/spell the word (nucleus)? Or use it with understanding in a sentence ('the nucleus controls the cell')? Or use it to describe a concept ('the nucleus contains genetic information')? Each of these outcomes describes a more sophisticated learning process than the one before.

Table 3.1   A hierarchy of cognitive function

Knowledge	Simple recall of factual information	*List* the parts of a cell *State* the differences between plant and animal cells *Label* the cytoplasm in this diagram
Comprehension	Describing	*Describe* the function of the nucleus *Select* the plant cells from these diagrams *Classify* the following cells
Application:	Applying knowledge to a different context	*Sketch* a cell from my situation description *Draw* a cell which could waft particles along the windpipe
Analysis	Subdividing a topic into components	*Compare* and *contrast* these groups of cells *Calculate* the size of the cell in this picture
Synthesis	Creating new information	*Design* a cell which could waft particles along the windpipe *Predict* what would happen if an organism was not made of cells
Evaluation	Asking questions about evidence	*Assess* the accuracy of this diagram compared to the photograph *Estimate* the size of a cell under the microscope

This is where Bloom's (1956) taxonomy comes in useful. Bloom identified a hierarchy of six levels of cognitive function. Table 3.1 describes how the hierarchy might apply in the cells example we've been working with in this chapter.

The complexity of the task increases down Table 3.1. Pupils need opportunities at all levels of the hierarchy, but it is important to give a balance. If you concentrate too much on activities at the top of the table, you will not challenge them. Too many activities towards the bottom and you will lose them. Note that similar activities can work at different levels – if you have spent some time discussing the different adaptations that cells exhibit, and pupils have seen a variety of cell design, then being able to draw a cilial cell will be a matter of *application*. It becomes *synthesis* if they have to use their imagination to construct a new type of cell.

Now you can start to develop a sense of the evidence you will be looking for that the pupils can achieve or have achieved the outcomes you specify. This evidence takes many forms, and is covered in Chapter 6. But suffice to say at this stage, you are not just looking for a test with questions like 'What is a nucleus?'. If the pupils are working on a display where they will collaboratively produce a large-scale diagram or model of a cell for the laboratory wall, and if they are talking to one another and using accurately the terms you have specified, then those pupils have achieved that outcome.

Now that we have a list of learning outcomes, and an idea of how we can assess the pupils' achievements of the outcomes, we can start to plan one or two main activities that will develop and demonstrate this achievement of learning. How will we introduce the lesson? How will we lead into the main activities? How will we review learning at the end of the lesson? We now start to discuss the lesson plan in more detail. In this chapter, we discuss the mechanics of putting together a coherent lesson which (we hope) will work well in most circumstances. In the next chapter, we cover *why* the particular methodology has been selected in this case.

Point for reflection

The lesson plan in this chapter will not be suitable for all pupils. How can you change the outcomes to provide more challenge to both the able and less able pupils? How can you adapt the lesson to provide more support to weaker pupils? Use the hierarchy from Table 3.1 to help you.

COMPLETING THE LESSON PLAN

Now we have covered the crucial topic of setting achievable outcomes, we will see that the remainder of the lesson plan constantly refers back to these outcomes – whether we are planning the activities, the assessment or considering cross-curricular themes – all parts of the lesson build around the outcomes. The headings in this section refer to the headings on the lesson plan pro forma in Figure 3.2.

Previous assessment informing this lesson

We need to ask the question: 'How do you know these outcomes are realistic for these pupils?' In this example, it is assumed that pupils are able to use microscopes – do not wait until the lesson starts before you find out that they have never even seen a microscope before! To what extent are they able to deal with problems of scale? You need to know so that you can decide whether to include using the microscope to measure size. We have assumed that this particular group have used these microscopes before, and the class has been able to estimate the size of a millimetre square of graph paper in the field of view.

National Curriculum area covered by this lesson

Enough information is needed here so that it is possible to cross-reference to the medium-term plan and check that all parts of the National Curriculum are being covered.

Links to other areas

All schools need to audit the work they do, to ensure that all aspects of the National Curriculum are delivered. Each school will have a different way of recording this, but it is helpful to label those lessons which cover some aspect of the wider curriculum. By using the opportunity in this lesson of estimating the actual size of onion cells, we are covering an important part of the Numeracy Strategy – that of measuring scales and dealing with small numbers. So record the fact at this point. By looking at the whole curriculum in this way, the school is able to check that all the parts of the numeracy strategy are being met. Note that it is not enough to put just 'numeracy' at this point. Nor is it necessary to attempt to cover numeracy (or any of the other areas) in every lesson. Just include those which are clearly supported by the topic in hand.

Differentiation (see also Chapter 7)

All pupils will be able to recognize that cells are very small, because they cannot actually see them on the slide, and yet they are visible under the microscope. Many will recognize that they are much smaller than a millimetre across, because they know that the field of view is approximately 1 mm, and they can see a number of cells within this. Some pupils will actually be able to estimate the size of a cell because they will be able to count the number of cells across the field of view and express this as a fraction. But this will not be accessible to pupils who are unable to deal with fractions. This section is used to describe the strategies you will employ to support and challenge *all* the pupils. In this case, open-ended questions can help to provide this challenge – for example the question 'How small is a cell?' can elicit legitimate responses from 'very', through 'too small to see' to 'about 1/20 mm across'.

Website

It is worth having a look again at lesson 1 and the interview given by Paul. He has used an interesting approach to differentiation, and applied it from two different angles. First, he has made sure the groups are well briefed and contain pupils of varying ability. Second, he chooses topics for them appropriate to their abilities.

Health and safety

As mentioned in the section on Every Child Matters (Chapter 2), there must be a risk assessment for every lesson involving a practical procedure. Is it safe to use sharp instruments to separate the onion skins? Is there a risk of getting iodine in an eye? You must follow the school's safety policy both in the production of risk assessments and in carrying out procedures. Note that the head teacher of the school has the ultimate responsibility for health and safety within the school, and therefore has the final decision. If your mentors, or the head of department, offer you specific advice or instructions about the use of certain equipment, then you have to comply. That is not because science is a dangerous subject to study (it is not) but they have the legal responsibility for any damage, not you.

> **Website**
>
> A risk assessment for the lesson is supplied on the website, but note that it applies to a particular time and place, and you will need to adapt it to your circumstances.

Lesson development

At this point you are in a position to prepare a timed plan of how the lesson is to proceed. By now you have decided on the outcomes for the lesson, and will have an idea of the activities which the pupils will use to learn these outcomes and to demonstrate their achievement. Focus first on the main activity – in this case the preparation of onion skin slides and their observation. How long will this take? You will only know if you carry out the procedure yourself. If it takes too long, how can you cut it down to save time (for example, prepare the bits of onion yourself).

Now, how can you introduce this activity? I am assuming there has already been a lesson using microscopes, and that the pupils are able to use them competently (but there is a differentiation issue here concerning those pupils who find it difficult to manipulate them). There are many starter activities in all sorts of contexts. The best activities are chosen because by awakening the child's natural curiosity they lead them into the next stage of enquiry. Which starter activity would you choose? Are you prepared to recite a nursery rhyme about sugar and spice? Will they respond to a story about Robert Hooke? What is a house made of? To a large extent this is a matter of personal choice, but it should be something which attracts the pupils' interest and enthusiasm. The worst starters are simply activities to keep them quiet while you take the register.

Exactly how much detail you put in the timed grid is up to you – it will not help to put it in the form of a script because that will tie you to the front desk and make your performance wooden. Try to give rough indications of the timing of each part, but recognize that these are just indications subject to circumstances. Be prepared to change the timings according to circumstances – the pupils may be enthusiastic about one particular part of the lesson and want to take extra time on it. This is fine, but you will always need to be aware of the time so that you can bring the lesson to a logical conclusion.

Assessment

Assessment is covered fully in Chapter 6, but note the range of assessment activities: it is not just a case of marking pupils' work when they have finished the lesson – there are opportunities for assessing them at every stage of the process, and many different forms of assessment. Notice how the suggestions below link together the activity, the outcome and the resources so that assessment becomes an integral part of everything you do.

Some of these strategies can be used to measure the progress of individuals, while others keep track of the whole class. The pupils will also be encouraged to measure their progress if you tell them what they are going to learn. And if you return to this for the plenary, you will be able to judge their confidence in their learning ('traffic-light' activities work well here).

- *Pupil engagement.* How many pupils are engaged in the starter activity? Have they identified the key points you were trying to make? For example, here you would want them to remind you to rack the microscope upwards while focusing. But do not expect them to say that straight away – only a few will realize what you are looking for at first and the rest will need prompting to remind them. So give them time (and gentle hints!) to come up with an answer. This first assessment item establishes the learning from the previous lesson and gives you the opportunity of judging which pupils will need close supervision and which will be able to get on with the experiment quickly.
- *Pupil response.* While you are demonstrating the procedure for preparing the microscope slide, you will be asking pupils questions about the procedure ('What's the iodine for?' 'Why do we need a cover slip?'). Their answers will tell you a lot about their understanding – are they using scientific terminology? Are they staying on the task?
- *Enthusiasm.* The first time they see something startling down the microscope, they will want to share it with you: 'Hey, Sir/Miss, come and look at this!' Are all the groups responding this way, or do some need support and help in making progress? By the end of the activity you should have a good idea of which pupils were able to complete the task unaided, and which would need further help if the activity were to be repeated.
- *Games.* Quiz games, like the spot the difference finisher activity suggested in the lesson plan, provide an informal and enjoyable way for pupils to demonstrate their understanding.

Resources

When you need specific equipment for the lesson, such as microscopes and slides, the school technicians will prepare them for you. Every school has a different system for this, and you need to be very clear what that system is. In many cases, the technicians are solely responsible for setting equipment out, and will not take it kindly if they find you rummaging about in the preparation room. It is normal to expect teachers to make requests for equipment one week in advance. This gives time for staff to identify and resolve clashes, and for you to practise the activity in advance. Never underestimate the importance of this practice for even the simplest of procedures! You need to know how much to use, how long it will take, how many slides you can make from one piece of onion. You will very quickly lose the attention (and respect) of the pupils if you are floundering around trying to get the experiment to work.

In addition, you will need to consider what other resources you need – the class textbook might not cover the topic in quite the way you want, but there may be a worksheet available. For your course you will be expected to demonstrate the ability to make your own materials for use in class, so look for opportunities to do this.

Evaluation

No lesson is complete without an evaluation. All teachers evaluate their teaching whether they realize it or not. Sometimes they come out of a lesson glowing with satisfaction because it 'just felt right'. Occasionally it has felt like a futile struggle and a wasted hour. By working on the planning, we trust that you will experience many more of the former. If a lesson has been difficult, avoid the temptation of focusing on behaviour issues, but examine the limitations in pupil learning – how might they be mitigated? At the end of the lesson, you will consider all the assessment information you have gathered together during the lesson and evaluate the *learning* that has taken place. It is all too easy at this stage to focus on classroom management issues ('they didn't achieve the outcomes because they wouldn't use the microscopes properly'). By focusing on using pupils' learning behaviours to evaluate learning, you will have a clearer picture of where the outcomes have been embedded and where they will need further reinforcement next time. We return to this theme in Chapter 12.

Points for reflection

Points for reflection

Write a list of outcomes for a one-hour lesson based on the objective 'We are learning to....measure current in series and parallel circuits'.

What activities will you use to develop these outcomes?
What activities will you use to assess the outcomes?
How will you introduce the lesson?
How will you close the lesson?

Now fill in the rest of the details on the template. Compare it with the example on the website.

What the research says

McWilliam et al. (2008) discuss how the downturn in interest shown by pupils on science courses in recent years can be addressed by a change in pedagogy. They suggest that planning creative activities into science lessons will engage pupils more without necessarily losing the scientific rigour that some might see as a consequence of allowing creative thinking.

Further reading

McGregor, D. (2007) *Developing Thinking, Developing Learning: A Guide to Thinking Skills in Education*. Maidenhead: Open University Press. pp. 7–24.
By encouraging the cognitive development of children through thinking skills, we can accelerate their learning. Chapter 1 of this book provides more information about the taxonomy of learning terms.

Sotto, E. (2007) *When Teaching Becomes Learning: A Theory and Practice of Teaching*. London: Continuum. pp. 190–4.
Eric Sotto includes a chapter on lesson planning which summarizes many of the points above, and also draws the link between assessment and objectives.

Useful websites

Live links to these websites can be found on the companion website www.sagepub.co.uk/secondary

DCSF Standards website available on www.standards.dfes.gov.uk/schemes2/secondary_science/ (accessed March 2008).

Hackney Schools e-learning portal can be accessed at www.learninglive.co.uk/ (accessed March 2008).

http://www.aqa.org.uk/

http://www.ocr.org.uk/index.html

http://www.edexcel.com

4 ELEMENTS OF A SCIENCE LESSON

Matt Cochrane

> *This chapter discusses how to:*
>
> - identify the different parts of a science lesson
> - observe science teaching in action and critically reflect on it
> - compare your own ideas on lesson planning with those of an experienced teacher.

> **Website**
>
> In this chapter we refer often to three recorded lessons on the website www.sagepub.co.uk/secondary. These were taken from actual lessons recorded at a secondary school, and show classroom activities as they happen. The recordings show well-organized lessons led by an experienced teacher. But feel free to view them critically, and be ready to pick out points you would wish to improve on – nobody's perfect! On the whole, though, you will find these clips instructive and helpful.

A brief summary of the three lessons is given below. Use Tables 4.1, 4.2 and 4.3 to navigate through them and to choose the clips you want to watch.

THE STRUCTURE OF A LESSON

The National Strategy has invested a great deal of time and effort in developing a model of lesson delivery that was described in the last chapter as the three-part lesson. We will break that down into its components in this chapter and see how the parts of a lesson fit together coherently by referring to video clips

Table 4.1 Lesson 1

Lesson 1: Group work and pupil presentations

Segment	Start time	End time	Stage	Content
Part 1 (duration 18:31)				
1	0:00	6:05	Entry and starter	Organized entry, starter activity, feedback on starter
2	6:05	7:42	Objectives	Sharing and explaining objectives
3	7:42	10:16	Organization	Briefing for activity Grouping has been planned in advance – lead learners have been briefed ahead
4	10:16	13:00	Main activity	
5	13:00	18:31 (end)	Main activity	Further instructions, reinforcement Success criteria shared with class – reinforces objectives shared earlier Teacher constantly monitors groups
Part 2 (duration 17:57)				
6	4:28	7:30	Main activity	Further challenge – groups who have finished have extension activity which is complementary to lesson
7	7:30	9:37	Conclusion of main activity	Prepares class for presentations
8	9:37	12:28	Presentations begin	This is really the plenary
9	12:28	13:28	Feedback	Reinforces objectives again, positive feedback; reinforces purpose of lesson
10	13:28	17:57 (end)	Plenary	Does the plenary really begin here? Conclusion – praise for class at end, final review of objectives

of live lessons. In the simplest model, the three parts fit together in sequence like this:

However, there is no reason why you should not alter this a little:

or

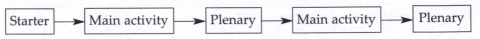

Table 4.2　Lesson 2

Lesson 2: A practical lesson

Segment	Start time	End time	Stage	Content
Part 1 (duration 18:36)				
1	0:00	2:30	Entry to room	Review of marked books – read improvement points 'next-step marking'
2	2:30	4:10	Starter activity	Groups working on how to test hypothesis
3	4:10	6:15	Class discussion	Pupils offer suggestions for experiment
4	6:15	11:20	Instructions for practical activity	Consideration of safety points; setting challenge (pupils select own method) Organization of collection and return
5	11:20	12:30	Practical activity	Collection of apparatus
6	12:30	18:36	Practical activity	Identification of metals; practical proceeds Continues to offer advice to groups
Part 2 (duration 11:22)				
7	0:00	3:30	Practical activity	
8	3:30	6:30	End of activity	Apparatus tidied away; accounts written
9	6:40	11:22	Written activity	Reminds class of main points of account
Part 3 (duration 11:31)				
10	0:00	1:21	Mid-lesson	Account writing continues
11	1:21	4:30	Sharing results	Pupils group together to compare results
12	4:30	11:31	Demonstration	Organization, demo Question: alternative name for gp 1 metals – leaves open Safety discussion; reaction of Li, Na, K with water (could have used Periodic table to guess the next metal)

Table 4.3 Lesson 3

Lesson 3: A starter for a lesson in imaginative writing

Segment	Start time	End time	Stage	Content
1	0:00	4:30	Entry and introduction playing	The class enters to music (from the film 'Hannibal'); generating an emotional response to words relating to volcanic eruption
2	4:30	7:35	Quiet time	Story-telling by teacher
3	7:35	8:40	Writing activity begins	

and so on. There is no prescribed pattern to this, except that there is a starter at the beginning and a plenary at the end, and we will discuss the reasons for that. In between each section of the lesson, we need to identify and mark a 'transition point' to enable pupils to progress smoothly and logically through the activities – terminating one before moving to the next.

Point for reflection

These are suggestions, not rules! Consider situations where you might want to suspend or modify this model.

Point for reflection

This way, each part of the lesson has a purpose, and the lesson as a whole tells a story, which we hope the pupils will comprehend. Otherwise, why are you doing it?

As we go through this chapter, we will look at sample extracts from live lessons to illustrate these points. But please note that these are examples only, and your task is to identify the strategies which will work for you. As well as looking at these basic components of a lesson, we will also focus on the variety you can (and must!) put into your teaching, along with some of the reasons why.

Starter

Lesson 1: start to 6:05
Lesson 2: start to 6:15
Lesson 3: start to 4:30

This is normally a short activity to set the scene for the lesson, typically lasting no more than 5 minutes. There are many, many ideas available for good starters. Try putting 'starters and plenaries for science' into a search engine and you will see what I mean. The best are often the simplest and require very little preparation. Avoid the trap of using them simply as exercises to keep the pupils occupied while they enter the lesson. A well-planned starter whets the appetite for what is to come in the lesson, and helps the pupil construct meaning from the rest of the activities. How about a word search containing words learned in the last lesson (for example, parts of a cell) – when they have found the words we can say 'in this lesson we are going to learn where these cell parts fit into plant and animal cells'. You could ask the class to make as many new words as possible out of the word 'neutralization', so long as at the end of the exercise you focus on the spelling and meaning of the word, because the activity will help them to become familiar with a new and difficult word.

Website

Watch lesson 1, part 1, clip 1 (0–6:05).

The class is brought into the room, given a short starter activity, which is followed up by some question and answer to reinforce the previous learning.

Notice how further questioning is used to test understanding – when pupils give a correct answer, can they justify it?

Teacher: 'Tell me all you know about ethanol.'
Pupil: It's an alcohol.'
Teacher: 'How do you know that?'

Further information from the pupil now confirms that he understands the principle, but this also has the advantage of giving the class time to consider for themselves – rather than a simple 'Yes, well done, that's the right answer.'

The starter in lesson 3 shows a completely different approach to starting a lesson. There is music playing as the class enters the room, and they are given some time to just sit and think at an emotional level. They are then led on to a writing exercise about volcanoes where they will use the scientific ideas they have been working on to describe what it would be like to experience an eruption at first hand. This links in with the suggestions for creative writing discussed in Chapter 2.

Sharing outcomes

This might or might not be part of the starter. You might want to do this before the starter if you are following on from a previous lesson, or your starter might well provide the background which explains the reasons for your lesson outcomes.

Whichever way you do it, the learning points need to be shared with the class early in the lesson to help the pupils recognize their own progress. For this reason, the objectives and outcomes (described as WALT and WILF in the previous chapter) need to be phrased in clear terms that the pupils can understand. They will need to be repeated at intervals throughout the lesson ('if you understood that explanation then you have achieved the first WILF'), and reinforced at the end. If we want our pupils to become good learners, then they really have to grasp the importance of working to objectives and outcomes. We all need to recognize when we have achieved a goal so we can move on to the next one.

For outcomes to work well, they need to tempt pupils out of their 'comfort zone' – not too easy or they will not be interested, and not too hard or they will not want to take the risk. Always remember that learning involves a significant amount of risk – 'what if I start the journey and don't make it?' For some pupils this prospect of failure is a common feature of their lives, and is a huge disincentive for them. They will not like to contemplate learning objectives which give promise of yet more failure.

Website

Watch lesson 1, part 1, clip 2 (6:05–7:42).

Why did the teacher (we will refer to him as Paul) introduce the objectives and outcomes *after* the starter? How did he distinguish between objectives and outcomes? As you watch the rest of the clips of this lesson, you will see the objectives being revisited again and again – sometimes quite subtly, at other times it will be more explicit.

Main activity

As the model above suggests, and as the lesson plan in Chapter 3 illustrates, there is likely to be more than one main activity in a one-hour lesson. The main activity provides the chief learning opportunity for your class, and needs to be carefully chosen to help them achieve those outcomes. I hope it goes without saying that the activities should be as varied as possible – your pupils will soon get bored with a one-dimensional approach. There is a good deal of literature about preferred learning styles, and much which recommends that we should cater for visual, auditory and kinaesthetic (VAK) learners (watchers, listeners and doers). However, as Price (2007: 139) points out, 'there is little research evidence to support the effectiveness of this in terms of increased performance'. Unfortunately, this has not stopped a great many schools taking the theory of learning styles very seriously indeed, and devoting considerable resources to developing teaching programmes which focus on VAK learning in the belief that it has scientific grounding. We have suggested some reading at the end of this chapter for you to follow up the research on this area.

On the other hand, it is likely that if you spend time and effort presenting your pupils with a variety of learning styles, your lessons will be more interesting and you will be more enthusiastic about them. Most pupils are enthusiastic about 'doing' science, but they will not learn much without a fair bit of 'listening' and 'watching' to help them along.

The main activity of a lesson can take many forms and, in keeping with the suggestion above that you try and vary styles of learning, make sure that every lesson has variety. The list of possibilities is very long; this sample is by no means complete:

- Practical activities
  - demonstration
    - by teacher
    - by pupil(s)
  - investigation
  - circus of experiments
  - single experiments
  - procedures (for example, aseptic technique)
  - designing
  - modelling
- Written work
  - formal
  - journalistic
  - story style
  - display work (group or individual)
  - presentations
- Reading and research
- Role play
  - scientists at work
  - modelling
- ICT
  - data logging
  - presentations
  - graphs
  - data handling
  - research
  - modelling

and on and on.

Website

Watch lesson 1, clips 2–6.

A group activity
In clip 2, it is clear that Paul has planned this lesson carefully and thought about the grouping of the lesson – 'lead learners' have been chosen to work with each group and briefed in advance. How does this help the lesson to progress with pace?

Each of clips 4–6 shows Paul interrupting the lesson to give some positive feedback and some additional guidance. Again, how does this help the pace of the lesson?

Lesson 2 contains a number of parts which could be labelled as 'main activity'. The starter for this lesson is less obvious as Paul does not inform the class that they are doing a starter. Why should he? The class is given time to consider ways in which they might test a hypothesis. By the time they start the first main activity (an experiment) they have already been thinking about what to do for some time and are thoroughly immersed in the lesson.

Plenary

Very often, the plenary will in some way summarize the learning points in a way that helps the pupils to recognize the progress they have made, again generally taking only a few minutes. As with starters, there are many helpful suggestions available on the Internet and through various publishers. If you are ever lucky enough to have your lesson inspected by Ofsted, you will be keen to demonstrate how your pupils have progressed. What better way than for them to compare what they could do at the beginning of the lesson with their achievements by the end?

Website

Watch lesson 1, part 2, clips 8–10.

Clip 8 shows the pupils giving their presentations; in clip 9 Paul is giving feedback on those presentations; and finally he declares, in clip 10, that the plenary is about to begin. Where do *you* think the plenary begins? At what point do the pupils start to get the chance to review their learning and pull the themes of the lesson together? (The meaning of the word 'plenary' refers to the fact that the whole group comes together for the session.)

Point for reflection

Bearing in mind the discussion above, it is still constructive to be able to devise a range of approaches to teach one point. Look at the lesson plan in Chapter 3. The plan uses a largely visual style to explain the preparation of a slide (though unless you mime it, the style is also auditory!). In the next section of the lesson, pupils will carry out the procedure, so the kinaesthetic style will be used as well.

Transition

Even with the simplest three-part model for a lesson, there will be two points in the lesson when you need to move the pupils from one activity to the next. This is called a transition point, and in well-organized classrooms this is an apparently effortless and seamless process. It serves a very important function in transferring pupils' concentration from one task to the next, and also offers a chance for a breather. This last point can be very important. Put the words 'brain gym' into a search engine and you will find just as much material as you will on VAK learning. Some of it is based on bad science, but broadly speaking we all need to get some more oxygen to the brain from time to time, and often we do that by getting up and having a stretch. So let the pupils do the same. There are exercises to do which involve scratching your head while patting your stomach. These work very well in providing a break to the routine and waking us up a bit, so go ahead and use them. It is also quite good if the pupils need to get up and move around to collect things, as this has the same effect. Alternatively, as in lesson 2 clip 11, the class is invited to move over to the next table to discuss results with their neighbours. This enables both groups involved to relax a bit and refocus.

The other important thing to note about transition is that we need *all* the pupils to be ready to move on. If they are working at different speeds, they will not all have reached the same point. So give a summary of where they should be up to (a good opportunity to refer back to the learning outcomes), make it clear that however much of the previous activity they have completed, you feel they are ready to continue, and then start the next activity. You will see throughout the clips that Paul frequently reminds the class of the task in hand, monitors their progress, setting extra little challenges as he goes along (for example, as mentioned above, the quick finishers in lesson 2, clip 11, are moved on to discussing results with their neighbours), and then brings the whole class together for the start of the next activity.

Point for reflection

Look at the beginning of each of the video clips in Tables 4.1–4.3 at the beginning of this chapter. They are *all* transition points! They have a positive influence on many aspects of the lesson, including maintaining pace, discipline, and a positive learning environment. On the website you can watch Paul discussing lesson 1 making further points about this in an interview.

MANAGING THE CLASSROOM

Watch lesson 1 again. Count how many interventions Paul makes as the lesson progresses. Confrontation is avoided because he approaches the pupil in question and gives a quiet reminder about his expectations. This cannot happen overnight – these expectations have been built up in the period of weeks and months Paul has been working with this class. In the next chapter we cover this in more detail, and you will learn techniques which help you build this understanding. Look in particular early in clip 7 – is it entirely coincidence that Paul is standing in that position just as the pupil starts to talk? Also observe how he is constantly moving around to keep an eye on each group in turn, and how he never seems to spend too long with them before moving on.

When Paul does ask for quiet from the class, his body language makes it clear that he is waiting until they are ready, and they respond. This type of body language is well worth observing and emulating.

One of the more obvious aspects of classroom management for the science teacher concerns arranging practical sessions safely and effectively. 'Safely' does not just mean avoiding injury – we want to avoid damage to the laboratory and its equipment too. Paul's instructions to the class fall into three categories:

1. Safety information. He makes it clear that the pupils have a responsibility for their own safety by giving them time to consider what precautions they need to take before summarizing them with the class.
2. How to perform the experiment. Here he is working with a class he knows well, and so the detail is left up to them – for example how much acid to add to the test tubes, exactly what to look for, how to compare and record results. Beware of giving too much information at this stage, and talk to the class about possibilities, asking plenty of open questions: 'What do you think will happen?' 'How do we know a reaction is taking place?' 'How can you tell if something is reacting more strongly?'

3. Distribution and collection of apparatus. Again, because he knows the class well, Paul is able to show the apparatus they need, confident that the class will collect it and use it appropriately. However, you will not find this happening the first time you try an experiment! There is a strong tendency for pupils, in their enthusiasm to get started, to rush out, collect one of everything and then arrive back at their place without the least idea what to do next. Returning the apparatus at the end of the experiment is another aspect often neglected. It takes *time*! Hot apparatus needs to cool, the slower pupils need to finish. Plan your lessons so that the practical activity is not the last part of the lesson, and that time is specifically given to tidying up. Paul's class do this efficiently because they have done this many times before. Develop a routine (Paul identifies three pupils who will have the job of monitoring the clearing) so that pupils will know what to do once you give them their cue.

In lesson 2, Paul knows that he can give the instructions for the lesson without having to write them down and repeat them. The exercise is differentiated because pupils of different abilities will operate at different levels of accuracy (some will carefully measure the amount of acid for example). With many classes, and particularly early in your practice, you will find that pupils need step-by-step guidance, otherwise they will be easily confused. But avoid turning the session into a recipe, because then the pupils will be working without a clear understanding. There are several ways you can give these instructions:

- detailed (or brief) points on the board
- worksheet
- PowerPoint presentation, revealing steps as you go
- pupil notes.

These instructions should always be developed through class discussion ('How shall we go about this?') even if you are going through a worksheet you have already prepared.

Finally, note that some pupils find it very difficult to visualize the whole experiment, and need the activity to be structured in some way. If they are encouraged to complete each step before moving on to the next (and some will need guidance on recognizing when they have completed a step), then they are less likely to miss an important detail, or pick up the wrong piece of apparatus.

CRITICAL REFLECTION

Let us have a critical look at lesson 2. If we were sitting as an observer in this lesson, what feedback would we give to Paul? It is important to start with positive points, just as you would with your pupils, and there is plenty in this lesson to praise. But no teacher has all the answers. We will look for areas which we can highlight for further development.

Clearly, Paul's relationship with his class is strong – he treats them with respect, and deals with problems very calmly and quickly. Early on in the lesson he is talking, and you can see that he notices that several in the class are talking over him. He pauses, waits until the class is quiet again, thanks them (that is important!) and then continues. He is sending a very clear message that he expects the class to listen while he speaks. It is all too easy at this point to raise your voice and battle on, but this will only teach the class that it is acceptable to be noisy.

The Standards for subject knowledge include *professional* knowledge – how well does Paul present the topic in an engaging manner? He is doing this by giving the pupils a practical activity where they are asked to investigate on their own terms, though you may feel the experiment is a little limited? What is the purpose of the investigation? By discussing their own experiences of metals reacting, for example through rusting, they might see that investigating the reactivity of metals is a worthwhile pursuit.

Health and safety are dealt with explicitly in the lesson and Paul spends time discussing the need to wear eye protection – but look more closely. Pupils are sitting down while pouring acid, and tops are left off acid bottles. Safety issues need monitoring throughout the lesson – we cannot assume that agreeing on the use of safety equipment at the beginning of the activity is enough – we must keep reminding pupils, because they will not normally notice when hazards are nearby. Do not forget that the biggest hazard is often from the neighbouring experiment.

The timing of the lesson is good – generally the activities take the time expected, and there is good variation as we move from activity to activity. Pupils are required to move around a little, and this helps them to stay active and engaged. While pupils are carrying out the various activities, they are clearly engaged on the tasks virtually the whole time. There is a good positive working environment for the pupils.

Paul shares the objectives with the pupils at the beginning, and refers to them during the lesson, but is the objective in this lesson in a 'WALT' or 'WILF' format? The question on the board suggests 'We Are Learning To test metals to see if they react the same way'. But 'What I'm Looking For' is left out. Remember, this is about what the pupils will be able to do at the end of the lesson that they could not do before it.

We might spend a little time asking questions such as 'How can we tell if a metal is reacting?' and 'What will happen if the reaction gets stronger?' Then we might put a short series of outcomes on the board:

I will be able to

o   plan a fair test to observe metals reacting with acid
o   describe the reaction of a metal in acid
o   observe differences in the way metals react.

Now we can revisit these outcomes as the lesson progresses. After the discussion about how they will do the experiment, we can say 'We've covered the first outcome – let's move on to the next one.' As we patrol the class during the practical we can again refer to the outcomes. The end of the lesson should be an opportunity to review the outcomes so that pupils can leave the room satisfied that they have achieved what they set out to do. This is done briefly just before the final demonstration, which is used to confirm the hypothesis given at the beginning.

Other issues you might like to consider are the organization and management of the lesson. They enter in an orderly fashion and collect their books – this could present a bottleneck, and you might want to look for alternatives. The practical activity is well organized – equipment is collected by one individual from each group, and three pupils are assigned the task of monitoring one part of the equipment. There is clearly a system in place here – the class is used to the idea that the apparatus will be in one part of the room for them to collect. This did not happen overnight! Do not assume that your first practical lesson will go as smoothly! Plan that first activity with military precision and give yourself plenty of time to do it.

Website

Teacher interview

Let us give the last word to Paul, the teacher in the video clips. He discusses in a short interview the planning decisions he has made in preparing lesson 1. Notice that the preparation started well before the lesson (he briefed some of the pupils in advance), and that the behaviour management is part of the planning. He also explains how the groups were chosen, how he maintains a positive learning environment, and how the work was differentiated.

What the research says

Can you find evidence that a visual learner will learn best if provided with a diet of visual learning? Or does the evidence suggest that visual learners need more auditory input to help them learn in a variety of styles? Petty (2006: 30–9) mentions a number of styles, referring to 'whole brain learning', and 'left-brain' and 'right-brain' learners, without mentioning VAK learners. Ireson and Twidle (2006: 22) briefly mention VAK in the context of multiple intelligences. Sharp and Murray (2006: 43) review the origins of VAK, and offer a number of criticisms. Sharp et al. (2008) in a Department of Industry (DoI) report, strongly criticize the unorthodox claims made by those who promote VAK and other types of learning, claiming that it trivializes the complexity of learning.

Further reading

Cooper, H. and Hyland, R. (2002) *Children's Perceptions of Learning with Trainee Teachers*. London: Routledge.
This book looks at things the other way round – what do primary school children think of being taught by trainee teachers?

 Useful websites

Live links to these websites can be found on the companion website www.sagepub. co.uk/secondary
If you want to take the subject of self-evaluation a stage further, access this website, which suggests a number of ways of collecting information about your teaching – student surveys, peer feedback, action research, and so on: www2.warwick.ac.uk/ services/ldc/resource/evaluation/teaching/ (accessed September 2008).

5 MANAGING LEARNING IN SCIENCE

Bernie Kerfoot

> ### This chapter:
>
> - gives a brief overview of some influential theories of learning and examines how individuals learn
> - considers the implications of these learning theories to the National Curriculum in England and also your classroom practice
> - focuses on the role of collaborative work and discussion in the science laboratory and suggests approaches that can result in effective learning
> - offers some advice on the logistics of organizing practical work in the school laboratory
> - explores one project that aims to develop pupils' thinking skills.

WHAT IS LEARNING? HOW DO CHILDREN LEARN?

A number of years ago a trainee teacher near the end of a one-year initial teacher training course asked me 'What does it mean when someone learns something?'* Surely you would think that by the end of a PGCE course the trainee teachers might have some conception about what this thing called 'learning' is. Perhaps some blame goes to the teacher trainers!

The problem lies in the fact that teachers often travel a route that means they assume fundamentals and do not often reflect on some important aspects such as what learning really is. Nevertheless I think it is fair to assume that most practising teachers realize that without a knowledge and understanding of what we are about in terms of developing the learners that we work with, there cannot be solid foundations for you as a teacher. An appreciation of the way that children learn is essential for effective teaching.

*Incidentally the trainee teacher was for all intents and purposes really quite competent by this stage.

If this situation describes a trainee teacher with a vague concept of what constitutes learning then in a similar vein, and around the same time, I had an interesting conversation with a school-based mentor who was having a crisis of confidence and even identity. They questioned out loud the necessity to spend time, effort and resources on allowing pupils the opportunity to play with the kit that allows 'practical work' and investigation. 'Why am I doing all this practical work, letting them discover bits of understanding, pulling concepts from them by questioning when I could just simply tell them it?' It is sometimes not obvious.

Teachers talk about critical incidents and I guess these two scenarios suggested that an appreciation of the underlying beliefs about how children learn and what can be learnt are important in science teaching.

Both the scenes described are bound up with an enfolding drama that is played out time and again by science teachers who become extremely frustrated at children not grasping key concepts despite, in their perception, good teaching. Why is this? A child can be taught about, for example 'What a plant needs to grow' at Key Stages 2, 3 and 4 and yet, when they come to sit down in an end of Key Stage 4 test and are asked to 'list the factors a plant needs to grow', they simply cannot list them. You know this happens in examination halls all over the UK. The saddest part of the scenario is that even if they can list the four things as light, carbon dioxide, water and chlorophyll they do not really believe it!

Let us start at a basic level. Can we define what is meant by knowledge, skills and understanding? Jon Scaife, in Wellington and Ireson (2008), refers to knowledge as 'something that a person has'. A neuroscientist would argue that the facts and chunks of learning that stick permanently in a pupil's brain are a result of neuro-connections and synaptic junctions. Scaife goes on to describe understanding as 'a capacity to apply knowledge and skills appropriately in various contexts'. He describes understanding as the degree of 'connectedness of their knowledge and skills' – it is this idea of joining up the facts and the skills and applying it. As a teacher can you see that the commodity we are trying to 'sell' is not that easy to define.

Defining learning is rather less complicated and controversial. Learning involves change in any one of a number of 'aspects of learning'. These aspects of learning will include knowledge, understanding, skills, beliefs, attitudes and values. You know that pupils can pick up some changes in their knowledge and understanding from their interaction with you. Aside from this, they can also develop a whole raft of skills. These include key skills, thinking skills, science procedural skills and motor skills, and in many of these aspects they will do this by practice. They can also develop beliefs, attitudes and values from you. They might begin to develop an attitude to fast food because of your attitude to it. They might also develop a value system that means they do not drop litter because you have explained the impact of pollution on our lives. They will almost certainly believe the world is getting hotter because of greenhouse gases – that is because you probably believe it! They will also develop an appreciation of how scientists work and how science as a movement advances and regulates itself.

Can we start to unravel some insights into how children learn through the work of others? If so can we make learning more meaningful and longer lasting for the children we teach? The children we teach become adults and it is worth reminding yourself daily that your primary role as a teacher is to educate children to function as autonomous adults.

Early work on how learners acquire learning was characterized by a behaviouralist tradition. Some well-known behaviourists are Pavlov, Watson, Skinner and Thorndike. It has to be said that they did some of their work with animals! Their work into how learners acquire knowledge and behaviour was centred on reinforcing behaviourial responses through rewards and sanctions linked to specific stimuli. The learner, through positive or negative feedback, develops a conditioned response. Historically in our schools there is a behaviourist tradition. We can still see this in many of the assertive discipline regimes that are common in many schools. You can also see aspects of this rote learning in many examination revision classes where learners are asked to repeat and sometimes recite stock answers to well-worn questions. The pupils learn through seeing examples, doing test questions, considering answers to questions and learning the required response 'parrot fashion'. This can be effective in helping the pupils to pass tests. The danger in the classroom is that it is boring and can lead to classroom management issues – the pupils need to be fairly well motivated to accept the ritual. In addition the learning is almost always superficial. If you put the pupil into a situation where they have to transfer the rote learning into a different context they will struggle. Nevertheless given a stimulus most pupils can be taught to perform a particular response.

Teacher:	'What colour does Benedicts solutions turn when warmed with a reducing sugar?'
Pupils altogether:	'Orange/brick red.'
Teacher, again:	'What colour does Benedicts solution go when warmed with a reducing sugar?'
Pupils altogether:	'Orange/brick red.'

This is not an unusual situation and as a strategy for the straightforward acquisition of a 'factlet' it can be effective. But we know that there is far more to teaching and learning than this scenario.

A CONSTRUCTIVIST APPROACH

Can Jean Piaget (1896–1980) offer an insight into children's learning? Piaget was a Swiss philosopher, natural scientist and developmental psychologist. He was Professor of Psychology at the University of Geneva from 1929 to 1975.

During his career he wrote more than 60 books and several hundred articles. Piaget suggested that children's cognitive, development moves through a series of four stages and that as children grow physically so they develop cognitively. Piaget's observations and research led him to the following conclusions:

- Young children's thought processes are inherently different from those of older children and adults.
- Children pass though a number of developmental stages and each stage is an understanding of a 'reality' at that period.
- Children develop an understanding of a key concept by slowly realizing that their current understanding is flawed, that things cannot be explained. Errors build and they experience 'cognitive conflict'. I always think of the child saying 'Hang on, that can't be right' at this point. Thought structures are reorganized and learning occurs.

Piaget suggested four developmental stages that most children need to pass through in order to develop the capacity for abstract thought:

1. Sensorimotor stage: from birth to 2 years. Children learn through movement and senses.
2. Preoperational stage: from ages 2 to 7. Acquisition of language and the use of language to represent their sensory motor discoveries.
3. Concrete operational stage: from ages 7 to 11. Children begin to think logically and develop the ability to classify and organize. Such a child might be able to sort out a group of words or photographs into solids, liquids and gases but he would not be able to explain the rules of how he had done it. He or she could measure a spring's extension and link this to the load on the end but would have trouble relating the results to a direct proportion relationship.
4. Formal operation stage: after age 11. The development of abstract reasoning with the ability to conceptualize scientific concepts such as sustainability, interdependence, energy, validity, proportionality and the ability to manipulate multi-variable problems – for example, what factors affect a pendulum? What are the best conditions for a seed to germinate?

Piaget's analysis suggests that a child constructs knowledge based on experiences. When a child encounters a new experience it might or might not fit in with their current understanding. If it fits then the new experience is assimilated into the existing cognitive structure. If the new experience does not fit in with previous understanding then the child has to make some adjustments in order to accommodate the new information. Piaget uses these two words *assimilation* and *accommodation* to describe the processes that build learning, be it knowledge and understanding or skill-based learning in individuals. Piaget describes this mismatch between the existing understanding or knowledge and the new experiences that are forcing the learner to readjust their framework as *cognitive conflict.* It is worth noting that Piaget recognized three important aspects of the process that are vital for any teacher to recognize:

1. Cognitive development is not linear – children can develop slowly then suddenly 'shift gear'.
2. Although he suggests a chronological time line for progressing through the stages of development, it is not always the same time frame for all children.
3. Some children and adults will never attain fully the ability to reason in abstract terms.

Piaget suggested that children actively make meaning for themselves. Conceptual understanding is actively constructed. This learning theory is called *constructivism*. Piaget's ideas about how children learn have been interpreted, refined and given a fresh 'slant' by other notable constructivist thinkers such as Glasersfeld (1995) and Vygotsky (1978) but it is this constructivist viewpoint of learning that certainly has influenced the way that science teachers, and indeed teachers of other aspects of the curriculum, view learning in the UK classroom. Science teaching in recent years in the UK has adopted a constructivist approach. A belief in a constructivist methodology forms the basis of much of the advice that you will receive about what constitutes good practice and effective science teaching in the classroom. These ideas have a clear influence on the way you will teach science. Although you will be for the most part a class teacher with maybe 33 in your Year 8 middle set, you will try as much as possible to differentiate for the individual needs of the children in your class.

Constructivism underpins this practice. You cannot build on and change perceptions unless you initially find out where the pupil is 'at', that is, what they already know. We operate in an inclusive classroom: individual needs analysis and personalized learning is the order of the day and rightly so.

SOCIAL CONSTRUCTIVISM

If Piaget's views on the way children develop cognitively have influenced the way science teachers go about their business then Lev Vygotsky has been almost as influential. Vygotsky's work lay relatively undiscovered until 1962 when *Thought and Language* (1934) was published in English. Later, in 1978, a major compilation of his work was published titled *Mind in Society: The Development of Higher Psychological Processes*, and a recent interpretation of Vygotsky's work from the 1930s was published in 1986, by Kozulin (1986).

Piaget really laid very little emphasis on social interaction in his research methodology and this is often used as a criticism of his work, but for Lev Vygotsky this was an important factor in learning. Vygotsky was born in Russia in 1896 and died in 1934 of tuberculosis. He worked at the Institute of Psychology in Moscow between 1924 and 1934 and did extensive research into the relationship between language and cognitive development. Vygotsky suggested that higher cognitive functions develop through social interactions with significant people in a child's life. Through these interactions a child acquires the habits of mind of his or her culture. When a child first picks up a pencil the child has no idea about how to use it. The role of the pencil is 'outside' his or her experience. The child gets better with the pencil as a result of interaction with significant persons. Eventually the child can use the pencil for his or her own ends. Vygotsky emphasizes a number of important aspects of children learning:

- the role of imaginative play in developing higher-order cognitive skills
- speech as a tool for social interaction
- the crucial role of language in cognitive development. Vygotsky suggested that key concepts were in essence 'inner speech' and develop from an internalization of external speech. Thinking can happen without language but through language it develops to a higher level of sophistication

Both Vygotsky and, more recently, the American psychologist Jerome Bruner (1915–) are educationalists that believe in the power of effective instruction. Vygotsky suggests that a teacher can move a child on from their current level of understanding by offering assistance and guidance with tasks. This might be a formal adult teacher in a structured classroom experience but it might also be a more capable peer. I remember a Year 9 child looking at me quizzically from the front row and hurling the bombshell at me, 'What are you talking about, Sir?' At the time, I had spent 5 minutes warbling on about the formation of coal. His friend then took 10 seconds to explain my key points and the painfully honest little chap settled back happy in his new-found knowledge. Similarly if you watch a group of Year 7s assembling an electrical circuit from a circuit diagram and the coaching and prompting going on then you will recognize what Vygotsky knew – that peer teaching is an extremely powerful tool. Vygotsky coined the term 'zone of proximal development' (ZPD)'. Each child has an individual ZPD. This represents the difference between the tasks the child can do or the understanding he has on his own and the level he can achieve with a teacher or peer assistant. An effective teacher works through knowing where the pupil's current level of development is and moving him or her on through guided learning. Bruner coined the term *scaffolding*. By this he meant that an expert teacher could provide learning tasks that would allow the learner to climb from one level of performance to the next. As every individual has a unique set of life experiences and so has a unique internal learning environment so it follows that all children have their own unique ZPD. Finding what they know, understand and can do before attempting to develop a strategy to move them on is vital in targeting instruction. Bruner is more optimistic than Piaget insomuch as he dismisses the limiting factor of stages of development. For Bruner it is the effectiveness of the teacher that is the factor in the success or not of the learning.

IMPLICATIONS FOR YOUR TEACHING STRATEGIES AND ACTIVITIES: ARE THEY READY?

In 1981 Michael Shayer and Philip Adey published *Towards a Science of Science Teaching: Cognitive Development and Curriculum Demand*. This was in response to a drive for 'science for all' by the Inspectorate in 1980 and an Association for Science Education policy discussion document that originated in 1979.

In it they took a large sample of secondary school pupils and analysed them in terms of Piagetion stages of development. Was the child at the Piagetian stage of concrete operations or at formal operations? They proposed that in secondary school populations there are two major types of thinking in pupils, concrete and formal operational, based on Piaget's classification. They asked the question, 'Is the level of demand embedded in the curriculum objectives for science appropriately matched to the level of cognitive development of the clientele?' Was the learning on offer too difficult for many children to access? Even though the initial Piagetian evaluative model is a rather simple analysis, and like many such tools is a crude measure, this was the first time this type of analysis had been done. 'Younger and less able pupils will be limited to the use of concrete operational thinking, while older and more able pupils will have available a facility for abstract thought and multi-variate problems which is characteristic of formal operations' (Shayer and Adey, 1981: 7).

Did the concepts on offer at the time match the level of cognitive development that the population was at? Shayer and Adey developed science reasoning tasks (SRTs) to measure the stage of cognitive development of the individuals in their sample. They also analysed the various science curricula at the time for Piagetian level of demand. One of the conclusions they arrived at was that in the average comprehensive school in an average Year 9 class only 20 per cent of the pupils would be at the Piagetian stage of formal operations. What does this mean at the chalkface? Is it a similar situation in 2009?

First, let us link our Piagetian stages, concrete and formal operational to National Curriculum levels and a pupil profile from the UK. At the back of the current National Curriculum we see a section that informs teachers what the pupils should achieve at a variety of hierarchical levels. They are called attainment targets and are essentially level descriptors, statements about what the pupil should demonstrate in order to be at a particular level. We can see much evidence of formal operational thinking emerging at level 5 and firming up through level 6. If you look at the website linked to the book you will see a Word document that details the attainment targets that describe what a pupil can demonstrate at level 5. It is worth noting that level 4 is rooted in concrete operations.

Can we analyse some learning objectives described in the new 2007 Key Stage 3 National Curriculum for cognitive demand? Are they difficult? Are they easily accessible for the pupils you are teaching? What is on offer? On page 210 of that document we see:

3.2a the particle model provides explanations for the different physical properties and behaviour of matter.

This is built on and extended at Key Stage 4 where we see, on page 224, a more complex model being used to explain different phenomena:

6a chemical change takes place by the rearrangement of atoms in substances.

Can you see that 3.2a provides an incredibly difficult challenge to you as a science teacher working with the 11–14 age group? The pupils have first got to accept the kinetic theory and the model it represents. This is a type of snooker ball model. When trying to teach this model I used to have 200 table tennis balls all in an open shoebox arranged closely packed. I then picked it up and moved it about gradually with more shaking, shouting 'Getting hotter, Getting hotter' as I and the balls got more violently energized. As some popped out of the box I shouted 'starting to boil' then, and this was only ever done at the end of the lesson, I chucked them in the air shouting 'Gas, gas, gas!' The pupils who had not done homework or had been awkward in the lesson used to help me pick them up. I'm sure some thought I was mad and the physical model had its limitations but you could work off lots of stress using the balls and the box! Can you see that underpinning 3.2a are the assumptions of the kinetic theory?

- Matter is made of particles.
- Particles are constantly in motion.
- The particles in solids are close together and vibrate about a fixed point.
- The particles in liquids are close together but have a freedom to drift about.
- The particles in gases are far apart from each other and move faster than in a solid or a liquid.

What state in which we find many substances, such as water or lead, depends on temperature. But it is not obvious to children when they observe things like paper or coal that certain solids do not melt when temperature starts to rise but, rather, a rise in temperature will cause them to chemically react. Pupils can use this model to explain all kinds of things like evaporation, expansion, change of state, heat movement and, even, convection. Convection is a real nightmare!

'A localized rise in temperature causes a volume of fluid to become less dense than its surrounding fluid and as we know less dense fluids will rise up through the more dense fluid. As it rises it will cool and return to its former density and so fall again.' I was never quite happy with this explanation and, of course, the Year 8 never really understood the sequence of events. Even so, if they were asked 'What is the process by which heat moves through liquids and gases?' they could write or say 'convection'. In examinations this was often enough.

Shayer and Adey in their original research in 1981 analysed such learning objectives in terms of the level of demand – a curriculum analysis taxonomy. My short account is merely a synthesis of some of the major points which are as relevant today as they were in 1981.

Children in the stages of early concrete operations will be able to tell you that a 'liquid can turn to a gas'. By late concrete they can recognize that heat causes the melting or freezing. There is also the recognition that particles in substances can be a close together or far apart.

By early formal the child will realize that all materials might exist as solids, liquids and gases. Also they might suggest that melting involves particles moving around faster with more freedom. By late formal they can explain how the particles in, for example, steam can be far apart and yet the steam can be easily compressed. Some may view melting and vaporization as equilibrium processes. There is a spiral cognitive hierarchy of demand.

In the past 20 years we have been trying as science teachers to push abstract concept after abstract concept to all children in the hope that they will simply acquire the higher-level cognitive thinking that the curriculum demands.

Can you see that if only 20 per cent of your pupils are not yet at the stage of formal operations then the majority cannot think in the abstract and begin to understand the sorts of problems in investigations containing more than one variable to manipulate? Even the pendulum investigation is a real cognitive challenge for many and pushing the limit of their intellectual capacity. Philip Adey (1992) comments that only 30 per cent of 16-year-olds show the ability to use higher-level thinking skills, that is, levels 6 and 7 of the National Curriculum.

As a postscript to this brief analysis it is probably worth noting that when trying to analyse curriculum content, level of demand and pupil profiles the *Guardian* (24 January 2006) picked up on a piece of research that Michael Shayer will leave us as his final chapter before he retires. Again he uses a Piagetian model to analyse both the cognitive level of the pupil profile of a large sample and the level of curriculum demand. He claims in the *Guardian* that pupils 'are now on average between two and three years behind where they were fifteen years ago' in terms of cognitive development. Using data from a large sample, the research suggests that as a population the cognitive ability of our secondary school children has not advanced in the past 15 years. He suggests that as a group the recent cohort is now less able to tackle formal operational thinking than the corresponding group of pupils was almost two decades ago. It's interesting that this research resurfaced in the *Daily Mail* (27 Oct 2008) in a similar article by Laura Clarke. It made front page headlines and on page 6 a commentary claiming pupils have lower attainment in terms of higher level thinking skills than in 1976 is played out by the author based around several of Michael Shayers's remarks. It is worth while noting why such research keeps on making national headlines. Education has a political agenda.

Point for reflection

Focus on the evolution of the science curriculum in the past 20 years. Get hold of the first incarnation of the National Curriculum in 1989 and compare and contrast it with the 2008 version. How has the learning described changed? Consider Adey's recent comments. Why do you think these changes have happened? In your opinion have the changes been a good or bad move?

DEVELOPING THINKING SKILLS

In Chapter 1 I argued a case for the inclusion of science in the core curriculum as a vehicle that was necessary to develop what have recently been termed thinking skills – those aspects of 'intelligence' that allow the pupil and, of course, future adults to go beyond the absorption of facts. They are in fact aspects of formal operations. In the Key Stage 3 Strategy materials, now the Secondary Strategy, we see the use of Bloom's taxonomy used as a guide to framing learning objectives/outcomes. Factual recall is at the bottom, and analysis and synthesis are at the top along with the ability to 'use models to explain'. In Chapter 1 we looked at Patrick O'Brien's list of thinking skills. These were:

- the ability to synthesize information and represent in a creative way
- grouping and classifying
- modelling
- evaluation (recognize strengths and weaknesses of a performance)
- pattern spotting
- recognition of validity and reliability of data.

Lists of thinking skills are often different. If you go to the DCSF Standards website (see 'Useful websites') you will see the mention of Edward De Bono. For nearly 40 years, since he published *Lateral Thinking* in 1970 De Bono has pushed a number of strategies to develop aspects of intelligence such as creativity, organization, information processing and action. Some schools are taking on board his methods and he is often featured on television shows. Other lists include reasoning, observing, comparing.

Both you and I know, often from bitter experience, that children and adults will not learn if they will not listen and participate. Learners need to be alert and attentive if they are to learn. I have to say it does not help when the learner is up all night watching television, playing on PS3 or listening to noisy parents! You also know that if a child gives up or simply lets things slip past him or her without asking for advice, then the learning can be lost. Being determined, enthusiastic and motivated is probably equally as important as the level of cognitive development the pupil is at. Any teacher that works in a tough inner-city school for any length of time will be able to tell you that the single biggest obstacle to learning is the lack of self-motivation inherent in a large proportion of the pupils. Long term this is destructive and debilitating for staff and it is one of the major reasons staff turnover is high in such 'challenging' schools.

You will regularly teach pupils who at the end of the lesson seem to be able to demonstrate learning, for example, 'list the characteristic of an insect', but one day later when asked again they will not be able to reiterate these facts. There are many reasons for this but I believe that one of the major reasons for this loss of learning is the fact that they have not really 'thought' about what they have acquired. A word is used to describe this process of 'thinking' about what you have learned – *metacognition*. When the pupil leaves the room with these little facts about an insect it is crucial that he or she reflects on the facts and contextualizes them. Next time the pupil sees an ant and a beetle he or she has to think with some depth about what you gave him or her and the structure of the two creatures. He or she has to think 'Yes that fits in – the ant fits the same bill. But does the beetle?' If the pupil does not do this it will be lost – recognition is required. Very often teachers do not give children this time to reflect, contextualize, scratch their heads and apply. Consequently, they will not transfer or bridge from one context to the next.

THE MATERIALS OF THE THINKING SCIENCE: CASE PROJECT

Cognitive Acceleration through Science Education (CASE) was a project funded by the British Economic and Social Research Council from 1984 to 1987. As part of the research a number of activities were devised and taught through science aimed at enhancing pupils' thinking skills and so assist their learning as they progress though school. Pupils are tested before and after the CASE intervention lessons, and added value, that is, gains in cognitive development, analysed.

The project has subsequently given rise to the *Thinking Science* course which is now in its third edition (Adey et al., 2001). The original CASE materials consist of a range of activities, 32 lessons that are designed to intervene in secondary school children's cognitive development and accelerate the higher level cognitive processes over usually two years. You can also buy a set of pupil textbooks called *Thinking Through Science* (2004) which is designed to develop children's understanding of key science principles, develop thinking skills and examine how scientific understanding has changed with time.

The CASE activities are designed to familiarize pupils with the language and apparatus (concrete preparation); provide events which cause the pupils to pause, wonder and think again (cognitive conflict); encourage the pupils to reflect on their own thinking (metacognition); and show how this thinking can be applied in many contexts (bridging). Adey and Shayer (1994) describe these features.

So what does a CASE lesson look like? Let us look at one described in the *School Science Review* by Shirley Simon in June 2002. In this case she is working with two groups where, because of setting, the normal distribution in terms of cognitive performance is different; in fact one group is considered more cognitively advanced in general terms than the other.

The theme of the lesson amuses me because I once had the misfortune to be teaching next door to a class of Year 7 pupils led by an ambitious, but ill-advised, young science teacher. To coin a well-worn teaching term, the pupils went 'ballistic' when the intended creatures under investigation, 40 or so woodlice, went 'absent' in the laboratory. All staff in the vicinity were called to arms to calm the terrified children down, and in some cases lift them off benches and window ledges. We also had to track down the missing arthropods when true to form they scuttled into the darkest moistest crevice they could find after breaking out of the confines of a petri dish.

In the CASE approach a number of elements must be present, and I use Simon's article closely to guide my account:

- Group work and class teaching is mixed to allow new ideas to be constructed.
- The child needs to view other learners being successful at the task. The child can then find what they need to be successful from the performance of others.
- Cognitive conflict or challenge is present where the pupil has to revise prior knowledge in the light of new experience.
- Group energy is apparent where children talk about their ideas.
- The pupils construct new understanding and models from the assimilation of new experience and discussion.

CASE trainers identify four 'acts' that characterize CASE lessons.

1. Concrete preparation – introduction to the activity.
2. Construction – pupils discuss ideas to resolve cognitive conflict.
3. Metacognition – pupils express their solutions to the cognitive conflict.
4. Bridging – where the class apply their new ideas to new and different contexts.

Simon sets up the activity for two different teaching groups with a discussion about the pets they have. She asks the pupils to list the pets they have, things the pets like, what they eat and where they like to sleep. At the end of the discussion Simon then draws a table on the board with two columns: 'values' and 'variables'. This gets the pupils talking in a real-life context and brings in two key terms. She calls this stage *concrete preparation*. The tank with the woodlice is then introduced and the children are asked, 'In what sort of conditions are woodlice most likely to be found?' The variables and values that relate to the conditions that woodlice live in were again listed: these being light, dark, dry and damp. Simon assists the pupils in thinking about combining variables for testing. As this is a 'one-off' lesson she is unsure about their ability to do this successfully so she shows the children the kind of container used to set up choice chambers and asks them to discuss in groups how to set it up to find which conditions woodlice like best. In a mixed-ability set-up, and with two different groups, the amount of intervention and time is different. Some pupils found the task of combining the two variables (that is, the amount of light and the amount of moisture) in a test set-up difficult. There were different degrees of pupil talk involved. She refers to groups that talk constructively as 'high energy'. She labels this stage *construction 1*. Cognitive conflict is apparent at the design and consideration of the variables stage. She then adopts a class teaching approach where the limitations of the single variable design are commented on by the teacher. She then asks the groups to pool their ideas and work out the varied conditions. She lists six sets, of which two were collectively disregarded, and four sets of test conditions a settled on. This stage she labels *metacognition 1*. With her as a guide, the pupils think about what they have designed. In fact she draws a design for the choice chamber on the whiteboard. This cycle of concrete preparation, construction and then metacognition based around group discussion and teacher intervention is essential to CASE lessons. The cycle is repeated again with both teaching groups. They are set questions that ask them to collectively consider such issues as probability and are then asked to predict, for example 'If they don't have favourite conditions and I let 20 free where would you expect them to be after 5 minutes?' Some listened to others; some could explain why they had concluded this. They then did the investigation and tabled the results. Conclusions are drawn again, group energy is apparent and construction is enabled as pupils decide on how best to organize their results and determine which was the dominant factor – dampness or darkness. Simon concludes that an awareness of group dynamics, social skills and individual learning styles all contribute to the success of CASE lessons. In short, the teacher has to use prior knowledge to inform the lesson.

Can you see that the lesson is all about using scientific investigation to develop in the pupils an understanding of how to recognize and combine variables, how to consider probability and use this to hazard an educated guess – a prediction? Higher-level thinking skills? Is this a common scenario in science laboratories around the country? I leave you to consider this.

ACTIVE LEARNING IN SCIENCE

Children come to you with a myriad of ideas that are sometimes in conflict with commonly held scientific ideas about the world. They also find it incredibly difficult to amend and refine these ideas – it really takes cognitive conflict to develop another view. This is a real 'eye opener'. You will see that the alternative conceptions, naive conceptions, and misconceptions, whatever you want to call them, which are apparent in all children and adults are extremely hard for teachers to correct in learners. Children have to actively really 'violently' release these naive conceptions. It is your job to help them to do this and you will not achieve success by simply talking at them. For additional reading on the 'common misconceptions and alternative conceptions' pupils cling on to, read Driver et al. (2002) in the further reading, where the chaos that exists in young minds is fully explored using extensive global research.

All active learning techniques have one thing in common. They insist, indeed force, the pupils to *think* about the materials, resources and activities they are asked to engage with by you. Active learning has activities and strategies that take the pupils' prior conceptions by the 'scruff of the neck' and ask them to test it against real-life observations. The pupils are given time to play with a new idea and revise what they know. Some units of work in school science readily lend themselves to hands-on practical investigation. I really could not see any science teacher teaching 10 lessons on chemical reactions without getting the pupils fiddling with glassware and the powders, grains and liquids that inhabit the preparation room shelves. Likewise topics such as enzymes as catalysts, heat and temperature and current electricity give the pupils many opportunities to observe phenomena and test their understanding against observations they might make and have to try to explain. The other facet of active learning is that the pupils have to play with the concept and test it out in the real world – it is important then that the pupils link any school science to everyday experience. When an inconsiderate pupil pushes a large chap then does the same thing to a smaller chap he instinctively realizes that for the same push the smaller guy moves away 'quicker'. Can you see that this experience and intuitive understanding gives you the ideal opportunity to build on, extend and refine in the school laboratory? Get them pushing a variety of objects like model cars and larger vehicles and ask them to roll them down a variety of inclines. Now this can start off a whole range of explanations and discussion. Predictions, fair testing, observing, measuring, pattern spotting and graphing even before they ever reach a conclusion and attempt an explanation that examines the relationship between force, mass and acceleration. Can you see that this type of reflection can initiate an overhaul of ideas?

Sometimes you will meet a unit of work where you might feel that it is difficult to weave too much in the way of investigative 'practical' science into it. How do you make it active? English and modern foreign language teachers have never had Bunsen burners to amuse pupils – they do it in different ways.

One way is to get them *actively talking*. Staples and Heselden (2001; 2002a; 2002b) in a series of *School Science Review* articles (see further reading list) describe a number of ways to get pupils 'actively' talking.

- Discussion: the more structured the better.
- Jigsawing: ask a group to split up and research different parts of the learning then regroup and recount to each other.
- Snowballing: a pupil researches a piece of science then tells two others. They in turn tell more and the information 'snowballs'.
- Role play: give each pupil a role in a simulation. Displacement reactions are a classic!
- Mantle of the expert: ask a pupil to become the expert on a particular piece of science and ask the others to ask the expert.
- Hot seating: *à la Who Wants to be a Millionaire*?
- Plays: mining for oil? The eco warrior, the oil company director, the local residents, the man from the environmental agency.
- Debates.
- Piece together the evidence. Give each one of the group a snippet and then ask the group to come together and guess the whole (I have seen it work well with bits of information about a particular element).
- Poetry: do not underestimate the power of a creative and imaginative piece of poetry with some good science at its base.
- Rap: pupils with a beat box can both entertain and educate if it is structured but be careful with explicit use of certain words!

Alternatively ask the pupils to *actively listen*.

- Multimedia: use a writing frame.
- Sequencing exercises: they listen to talk and sequence a series of cards.
- Labelling: they listen to talk and label as they listen.
- Cloze activities: they fill in missing words as they listen.

Organize some *active reading*. You will soon realize that a packed classroom of 30 children is not conducive to reading. Davies and Green (1984) suggest a number of activities that by their nature insist that pupils engage actively with the text or opt out of the lesson. They are often referred to as '*directed activities related to text*', or DART, activities. DART activities are grouped into two categories:

1. Pupils reconstruct modified text.
2. Pupils analyse straight text.

In terms of reconstructing modified text the pupils can use the reading to, for example, label a diagram or complete a table. They can complete activities with disordered text (and you might think about why this is a valuable learning strategy). The pupils might also be given a chunk of text and asked to predict what section or line comes next.

Analysis DART activities include simply underlining or labelling parts of text which deal with different aspects. They can turn text into diagrammatic representations such as flow charts. For example, 'What happens when a fuse blows?' can be a flow diagram. They might also read text and convert it into a table, or vice versa. For a good example of such DARTs in action go to the Nottingham Schools website (www.nottinghamschools.co.uk/eduweb/uploadedfiles/apples.doc) and reflect on the 'apples' piece of text and the DARTs that are used to engage pupils with the text.

Activities such as those described above that are designed to promote group talk and group energy on the basis that talk, listening, reading and writing, are an excellent melting pot for ideas and the subsequent reformulation of ideas. It also gives you a break from the front of the room!

I suggest that along with your practical work groups that we see in science laboratories, you also think about setting up 'discussion and reading groups'. This should happen more often in science classrooms.

Point for reflection

Watch the BBC video *Simple Minds: Education Special*. In this Phil Scott and Louis Wolpert, among others, give a frighteningly tense description of the nature of the difficulties involved in developing real scientific understanding and changing alternative conceptions. Did you realize it was going to be as violent a struggle as this to move pupils to a 'scientifically accepted' view?

USING RESOURCES

In this section I comment very briefly on the issues and problems of resource management. I believe that teaching is all about organizing and managing two things: first, learners and, secondly, resources. This is why the best teachers are always good managers and organizers as well as being creative and enthusiastic.

A science teacher in 2009 has more resources at his or her fingertips than ever before. We can use resources from 1926 if we want. Sometimes old books are useful in pointing out the way ideas have altered – although beware of politically inappropriate commentary in a book over 20 years old.

In recent years heavy emphasis has been laid on the visual, auditory and kinaesthetic (VAK) analysis that can be observed in the '*learning styles inventory model*' proposed by Dunn and Dunn (1984). Some schools analyze pupils' learning styles, sometimes called learning preferences, and can 'set' pupils on the basis of a VAK questionnaire. Although there is some evidence that in some learning situations pupils and adults have a preference for a particular mode of learning, the crude VAK questionnaire and analysis in my opinion should not distort the obvious – that in any learning situation people pick out a way forward if they are sufficiently motivated and that the nature of the task should define the instruction. Most of us would rather be physically shown how to put a flat-packed wardrobe together by an expert rather than read the non-verbal instructions on a piece of paper. Unfortunately expert guidance initially comes at a cost.

Nevertheless, what VAK analysis has done is create in the classroom an atmosphere of the 'catch all' lesson where visuals, talk and pieces of kit are very often on offer to the pupils – without exception this is a good thing because it means variety in a lesson. As a consequence, you will be expected to bring into the classroom a variety of resources to engage and allow learning to happen.

Any science department will have a preparation room full of the paraphernalia that science teachers use to make complex ideas become a reality and also allow pupils the opportunity to explore and investigate. An Ofsted report in June 2008 entitled *Success in Science,* picked up by the BBC and the tabloids, bemoans the quality of science teaching. It rattles on about 'poor subject knowledge' in science teachers, resulting in children not being allowed to investigate using the science kit that sits in schools' preparation rooms. As a science teacher you have got to make the link between the key scientific concept you are trying to share with the pupils and the resources that you have in a preparation room to help you deliver it. If you are teaching a topic such as 'enzymes', then be aware of the presence of amylase, catalase and so on in the preparation room and the glassware and indicators that will allow you and the pupils the opportunity to do hands-on investigatory work and 'go for it'. Give out clear instructions, set the scene and organize your class practical or even your circus of investigations. It is not by accident that the science laboratory has gas taps, electricity and running water – use them, because if ever science teachers neglect the use of laboratory space then you can be sure the decision-makers will decide we do not need them. Science is funded at present as a 'practical' subject, rather like design and technology. Neglect the laboratory and the status will disappear.

Early on in your teaching you will find websites that offer ideas for both teaching and resources. You could spend hours on them and I have listed some of them in the 'useful websites' at the end of the chapter. These are all good and you need to explore, download and pick up on as much as you can, but beware of spending too much time wandering around in them and then forgetting what you actually want the pupils to learn and the nature of the group and individuals you are teaching. Please do not become 'resource driven'. This is where you say 'Oh, I like that. I'll use it' without really thinking if it is suitable for the pupils you are teaching – in short you have got to be critical, evaluative, discerning and astute in what you use. Think about what you want the pupils to learn, then decide on the activities that are most suitable for these objectives. Try to include some visual aids because not only do they focus the eyes of some pupils, they can also guide you through the lesson. A slide display can help organize and sequence you as well as the pupils. Do not spend too much time talking. Many times you might put in a lesson plan 'discussion' and it is not really discussion; it is actually 'teacher exposition'. Beware of too much teacher talk. Most pupils do not want to listen to you for more than about 5 minutes at a time. They will drift off or, worse, play up and your voice is one of the most precious resources a teacher has, so limit it.

Do not get wrapped up in a presentation. Many teachers overdo the slide show and you need to use presentational software smartly. I once watched a Year 9 lesson with 23 slides and you can guess what happened – the pupils got bored and fed up. Beware of the university-style lecture/presentation at Key Stage 3. If you can do your slide show with acetates and projector then is reliance on ICT necessary?

Moving images such as film or animation need to be relevant, linked to tasks and short and sweet. A generation weaned on Keanu Reeves and *Blade* might not appreciate 20 minutes of the 'life of plants' or the infamous 'the blast furnace' sequence without material to force them to engage.

You have to get to know all the resources that are in the preparation room you spend so much time in. Seek advice from the laboratory technician who sees teachers trying things out every day, get the props out and let the pupils use them to explore what science is about – investigation of phenomena, spotting patterns and trying to explain them.

If you become adept at spreadsheet modelling, database interrogation and databasing then use it when it enhances the science and really gives you an option that would be impossible to do without the computer in front of you. Please do not show the pupils a simulation of an acid/alkalis titration when they could be doing it themselves. Yes, by all means use the simulation to compare and contrast its data with your own, but remember the important thing is they create their own. We expand on the use of ICT and computer-mediated resources in Chapter 10 on 'innovations'.

We also provide a useful commentary on taking science 'out of the classroom' (see Chapter 11). You may think that organizing a school trip to the local nature reserve is more work on top of what you are doing already, but do not ever underestimate the value to children of getting out of the classroom and engaging with the world outside the school. Sadly, for some pupils the classroom is nightmarish and going out for a visit gives them some respite. It will also make your job more varied and get you out of the classroom, which can sometimes be a lonely place where you are often without other adults.

In short, use resources that get pupils 'doing', out of their seats, measuring and observing.

MANAGING A SCIENCE LESSON

When I was training to be a teacher in the mid-80s my tutor gave me a piece of advice that registered and struck home. He said 'Teaching is all about staggering from one crisis to the next' (Bob Wilson, science tutor Edge Hill College of HE, 1983).

In this section I will try to give you, hopefully, some solid advice about making some attempt to ensure your teaching and the pupils' learning does not stagger from one crisis to the next – although sometimes it will seem Bob was right!

Classroom management

There are a number of books that offer advice on classroom management. Peter Hook and Andy Vass both work with various local authorities (LAs), individual institutions and the secondary strategy team to advise on managing the challenging classroom environment. Both go down well in schools as does Jason Bangbala, another well-known education consultant, specializing in classroom management (see website in the 'Useful websites' list). If you can get hold of Peter and Andy's book *Creating Winning Classrooms* (Hook and Vass, 2000) you will find helpful and practical advice on the 'art' of classroom management. *The Challenging Behaviours Pocket Book* by Fintan O'Regan (2006) will also give you an insight into the reasons for disruptive behaviour and some practical advice on coping with pupils with specific problems such as attention deficit hyperactivity disorder (ADHD). I think it is fair to say that one or two children with ADHD in your class can create a real challenge when you are trying to manage the learning of another 32 who can and will happily focus. Sue Cowley (2006) *Getting the Buggers to Behave* (what a great title) is another good read. They all focus on *you* as a leader in the classroom and stress the way *you* can influence the way individuals in your classroom respond to your *leadership*. Your expectations and the way you interact with individuals is the key to management in the classroom. All these books with their pages of advice focus on the need to establish positive, human relationships with the pupils in your classroom. Obviously, like all relationships, a positive one can only be built over time and this is why supply teachers and trainee teachers may struggle initially until a relationship has been built. Interestingly, over time it is almost inevitable that a positive relationship will be built – most children respond to a consistent, even-handed teacher whom they can see respects them and will give something of themselves to him or her.

All these books suggest the need to focus on the positive behaviour by the pupils who are in your classroom and use them as models to pressure others to behave the same way. All advise a consistent use of rewards and sanctions, with the emphasis on rewards rather than sanctions. All advise a use of escalating sanctions, with the pupils fully aware of what will happen if they break your rules. All advise an avoidance of confrontation if possible. All advise assertiveness rather than aggression. Some schools that have felt classroom management was becoming an issue have implemented some basic classroom rules for all groups and, although pretty simple, they seem to help in large mainstream classes – they might not be a suitable tactic when pupils show behaviour that is more disturbed than disruptive.

1. Boy/girl/boy/girl seating plan.
2. Silent starter period at the beginning of every lesson.

Just these two tactics can both settle the group initially and avoid the unfocused chatter and low-level distractions that are always going to crop up when friends are sitting next to each other. Pupils may not initially like it but they will soon get used to it, especially if it is a whole-school policy. In one school I know of, teachers are severely reprimanded by the school management if they do not follow these two simple rules.

Classroom management is an aspect of teaching, like lesson planning, that can be learned with a reflective approach and some clear evaluation of what works for you and what does not, but I always feel that there is an element of personality that impacts on a teacher's ability to implement leadership in the classroom. There are lots of intangibles that affect the human interactions in a classroom. Your sense of humour and 'mood' can affect, certainly in the short term, what goes on. We expect pupils to show some emotions, but for the practising teacher our own personal level of emotional maturity is vital to our dealings with pupils in the classroom.

Pupils will pick up very quickly on the teacher that apologizes for boring work or seems disorganized. They will act on first impressions and often hold on to those first impressions. It is important when meeting a class for the first time to act confidently even if you are inwardly not. It is exactly like a big football game or acting in a play – you need the correct balance of adrenalin. Too much and you get stage fright, too little and your performance can be 'downbeat'. It is obvious that you need to get to know names and what makes a child 'tick' as quickly as you can. Personalize the relationship as soon as you can – teachers that do not learn names quickly are at a serious disadvantage. Also, have the highest expectations of children. If you do not want the children 'effing and blinding' at each other, and you, then this type of behaviour, which is essentially disrespectful in its nature, will need to be stopped before it can take a grip in the class. Sometimes pupils will 'let slip' an obscenity – you might tactically ignore this depending on the context but let the pupil know, perhaps one to one, that you know he or she 'let slip' and you are not happy and neither is the person on the receiving end.

All this, of course, needs to be linked with interesting, well-planned lessons. In my opinion the single biggest factor in having a reasonably well-ordered lesson is getting the pupils hooked into the learning and involved in the activities. Boredom is responsible for many disruptive situations that crop up in the classroom. If the lesson is flat and tedious then problems occur. If the flat and tedious lesson is also linked with tasks that are not demanding enough or are too difficult for the pupils, then you have a recipe for disaster. They will play up – so would you!

Have a read of the extensive work on classroom management tactics by the likes of Vass, Hook and Bangbala. Also read Bill Rogers's *Cracking the Hard Class* (2006). He advocates a protocol when threatened with a challenge to your authority:

- Tactically ignore the behaviour initially – if you can!
- Rule reminder or restatement, 'Do we push and shove in here?'

- Give pupils a choice – 'If you choose to do this then … will happen.'
- Sanction – 'OK. You've chosen this now you will spend 5 minutes during break … .'

Two points you must always remember:

1. All teachers have pupils that they have reached an impasse with and things break down. For some reason the child just simply does not like you and thinks you are the worst thing on two legs. It could have been a chance remark you have made that they will not forget, the colour of your tie or dress, or the fact they see you as 'posh' – in short, anything. Do not treat it personally because it is not meant that way
2. Remember that, as the song goes, 'you are not alone'. There will be a pastoral system in place that should be a back-up, allow reinforcements and give advice and support. Get to know the system and work within it.

Managing pupils in a science laboratory

In this section I give some advice on the managerial problems linked specifically with the science laboratory and organizing pupils in the unique confines of a science laboratory. In particular:

1. How to manage specifically the unique environment of the science laboratory.
2. How to keep a laboratory relatively safe.

In 1974 the Health and Safety at Work Act came into being. As science teachers we have a responsibility to take reasonable care of ourselves and our pupils while at work. The 1989 COSHH (Control of Substances Hazardous to Health) regulations give statutory rules on how to deal with any hazardous materials. A number of bodies such as the ASE and CLEAPSS provide advice and produce Hazcards summarizing information about materials and activities you might consider using in school with pupils.

Website

Observe and reflect on the online video files of Paul teaching a lesson on reactivity of metals with Year 9.

A number of key points of laboratory management techniques and strategies are apparent. Paul actively involves the pupils in the recognition of health and safety aspects and the precautions they will use to keep safe and healthy. The pupils write two points at the back of their books. Although the points are only really about wearing goggles, the children are made to accept that acid is a potential hazard. In Chapter 2 we introduced a risk assessment form. Laboratory coats are optional at Paul's school, although I would recommend that if you are doing work involving acids then a laboratory coat is essential. Even weak or dilute acids and alkalis will take the colour out of pupils' clothing as well as irritate the skin. Many teachers operate a red and green flag system for wearing glasses and goggles. When a red flag is flying then goggles are to be kept on. After the practical activity is finished the teacher shows a green flag and they all take the glasses off. Some teachers have red and green flags on sticks in the room stuck into a blob of Blu-Tack – an effective strategy as many pupils get liquids on them when clearing up. Can you see that even in Paul's well-run lesson the children that finish early take their goggles off and the pupils who are still working are moving acid about. This might potentially be a hazard so red and green flags mean this is avoided. As a rule, assume all liquids on benches are hazardous. The class coming into a laboratory can be injured by the acid or alkalis left in a puddle on the desk so it is important to clear all spillages.

In Paul's lesson we also see the pupils standing up when manipulating hazardous liquids. This, of course, avoids the nightmarish scenario of a pupils spilling acid over their lap – although one pupil appears so tired he slumps over the bench! You also see Paul delegate collection to one person in each practical group – this attempts to avoid a scrum when he sets the group off on the practical work and it can also allow a rota of monitors to share responsibility for kit. Paul also gives very clear verbal instructions on the technique they will need to show in the lesson – he does not give out paper-based instructions. I find that written instructions are often overlooked or not read. Many schools have banks of risk assessment forms completed generically, but health and safety awareness can be inconsistent in schools. You need to take personal responsibility based on informed common sense.

Paul shows good movement when the practical activity starts and seeks to offer advice and guidance as the task moves on. Even in a relatively simple procedure like pouring dilute acid into a boiling tube with a measuring cylinder you can see that it is not straightforward for some pupils. Indeed, group work offers the best solution. We can see this group approach in the form of three pupils who work coherently as a team.

- One pupil pours.
- One holds the glassware steady.
- One observes very close to the acid and metal mixture.

This is good but you need to be aware of the fact that children will fall into defined roles if you do not mix and match the groups or at least change the dynamics every so often. In a group of three one will turn into the hands-on person who fiddles with the glassware and so on. Another will be the observer and one will do nothing but write down the results as they come in. Beware!

In terms of organizing practical work like this you have a number of options:

1. Class practical. This is the where you plan for a large number of groups of children all doing the same activity, as in Paul's reactions of metals main activity. For example, 10 groups with three in each group.
2. A demonstration. At the end of Paul's lesson he spends a few minutes demonstrating the five reactions to consolidate and clarify the learning. This is teacher led, but good demonstrations get the pupils involved in the delivery. Only one set of kit is used by the teacher, and the group observe (the use of the van de Graaff generator is a classic demonstration).
3. A circus of practical activities. In this format a variety of practical activities usually linked to a theme such as light or enzymes are set up and pupils work through each one.
4. Long-term project work. This format is used very often for assessed coursework. In this type of organization the pupil is set a wide-ranging question to investigate and investigates the question over a long period of time setting new targets and formulating new tests allowing expansive data. It is rather like a dissertation at university.

Point for reflection

Consider the four common ways of organizing practical work/investigation and construct a cost–benefit analysis of each. Are there different learning objectives that the organizational structure allows and lends itself to? Talk to experienced teachers and ask their opinions of each format. Which format is the most common?

On our ITT courses we advise all our trainees, and I think this applies to all teachers, to observe as many teachers as they can working in the classroom. It is crucial you reflect on good practice and weak practice. Filter out the things you think will work for you with individuals and groups. The overwhelming majority of teachers I have worked with are hardworking, astute and committed, although they can have a bad day or a bad lesson. You can learn as much, if not more, from weak practice – and you will see some. There are some things you have to find out and try to do. The list is long but mentors in schools will assist in your integration into the school and the department. After all, they want you to do the best you can – they will not want the pupils' learning to 'suffer'.

1. Get all the schemes of work, set lists, textbooks, homework timetables and individual educational programmes (IEPs) for the pupils you are going to teach. You cannot begin to teach without the pieces of the jigsaw.
2. Find out the school's assessment policy. You will need historical data on all the pupils you are to teach, that is, what they have achieved in the past, and you will need to build up your own contemporary assessment profile on each child.
3. Familiarize yourself with the school's discipline policy. Many schools run assertive discipline linked to a rewards and sanctions system. This necessitates the learning of names.
4. What are the safety procedures in place in the science department? Who is the nearest first aid person? What is the safety policy? What do I do if a child gets acid in his or her eye?
5. What is the system for ordering equipment? Upsetting the laboratory technician can be deadly.
6. Familiarize yourself with the layout of the laboratories. Gas taps, fume cupboards, gas and electrical isolation 'cut offs'; where the Bunsen burners are kept and what is in the other cupboards. Many laboratories contain specialist kit in the storage benches and cupboards. Where do coats and bags go? Do the pupils line up outside the laboratory or are you to get them in as quickly as you can? Have the laboratories got a master key? Have you got one?
7. Make some attempt to fit into school life and, most importantly, the culture of the science department. I am sorry but you get more out of people in any walk of life if they have an affinity to you and a positive relationship with you – an easy relationship with other professionals is crucial.
8. Try all experiments out beforehand and count equipment in and out. If a scalpel goes missing with Year 7 then you have real problems.

The concept of 'professionalism' is a difficult one to define but I always feel that it is bound with the practice that a 'professional' does not just come in and do the job – they give more than is the minimum required. Staff will want to see the trainee teacher or newly qualified teacher (NQT) doing this. This means doing constructive work in your non-contact time. There are opportunities here to do some assessment and also try out the demonstrations and practical activities that you are going to do.

Point for reflection

Make sure you know what the difference is between a hazard and a risk. Find DfES (2002c) *Safety in Science Laboratories*. Read the advice about safety glasses and goggles, and in what circumstances children must wear them. Make a list of advice that surprises you.

Point for reflection

What the research says

Recent research into how both children and adults learn suggests that for any learning to be long term and meaningful the learner needs to be both active and engaged, and not placed in a passive role. Spoken instruction can be missed, ignored or easily lost after the event. Pupils need to accept additions to their under-standing and be allowed to play with the fresh idea, often in other contexts, if they are to move on towards a scientific view. The implications for science teachers are obvious. The first reference in the further reading section will allow reflection on this model of learning.

Further reading

Adey, P. (1992) 'The CASE results: implications for science teaching', *International Journal of Science Education*, 14(20): 137–46.
If there is a mismatch in pupils and content then what are we to do?

Adey, P.S. and Shayer, M. (1994) *Really Raising Standards*. London: Routledge.
How cognitive intervention and an emphasis on higher-level thinking skill development can raise achievement across all subjects.

Adey, P., Shayer, M. and Yates, C. (2001) *Thinking Science – The Materials of the CASE Project: Third Edition*. London: Nelson Thornes.
Activities designed to develop higher-level thinking skills.

Association of Science Education (ASE) (2001) *Topics in Safety*. 3rd edn. Hatfield: ASE.
Definitive advice on health and safety in the science laboratory. Everything from how to handle radioactive isotopes through to what micro-organisms you might culture.

Davies, F. and Green, T. (1984) *Reading for Learning in the Sciences*. London: Oliver & Boyd.
DART activities specifically for the sciences.

De Bono, E. (1992) *Teaching Your Child to Think*. London: Penguin.
Can you teach your child to think more astutely and coherently?

Driver, R., Squires, A., Rushworth, P. and Wood-Robinson, V. (2002) *Making Sense of Secondary Science: Research into Children's Ideas*. London: Routledge.

Hook, P. and Vass, A. (2000) *Creating Winning Classrooms*. London: David Fulton.
Ideas on how you might turn around even the most recalcitrant group.

O'Regan, F. (2006) *The Challenging Behaviours Pocket Book*. Alresford: Teachers Pocketbooks.
ADHD, ODD and CD pupils. Good advice on managing three types of pupils.

Office for Standards in Education (OfSTED) (2008) *Success in Science*. Report reference 070195. London: HMSO.

Rogers, B. (2006) *Cracking the Hard Class: Strategies for Managing the Harder than Average Class*. London: Sage Publications.

Shayer, M. and Adey, P.S. (1981) *Towards a Science of Science Teaching*. London: Heinemann Educational.
Was the curriculum too difficult for the pupils we teach? Is it still?

Shayer, M. and Adey, P.S. (2002) *Learning Intelligence*. Buckingham: Open University Press.
Can you develop higher-level thinking?

Staples, R. and Heselden, R. (2001) 'Science teaching and literacy, part 1', *School Science Review*, 83(303).

Staples, R. and Heselden, R. (2002a) 'Science teaching and literacy, part 2', *School Science Review*, 83(304).

Staples, R. and Heselden, R. (2002b) 'Seience teaching and literacy, part 3', *School Science Review*, 84(306).

Useful websites

www.jasonbangbala.co.uk
Classroom management expert.

www.teachingideas.co.uk/more/management/contents.htm
Loads of advice and strategies linked to management issues, all from experienced teachers.

www.teachingexpertise.com/
Guidance and advice from Optimus Education.

www.standards.dfes.gov.uk/thinkingskills/
See what the DCFS/DfES think of the way forward in terms of developing thinking skills.

www.ncl.ac.uk/ecls/reserch/education/tsrc
Can thinking skills be taught or are they innate?

www.aaia.org.uk/think.asp
Issues largely to do with assessment practice but succinct treatment of thinking skills and how to develop them.

6 MANAGING LEARNING; MEASURING LEARNING

Bernie Kerfoot

> **This chapter:**
>
> - examines the educational theory that underpins assessment practice and considers why assessment is important to good science teaching
> - presents an overview of national testing for pupils at the end of Key Stages 3 and 4 science and reflects on the implications to practice for science teachers
> - reviews the roles of questioning and testing in science teaching
> - suggests ways in which teachers can record assessment data in a format that assists the learning process
> - reflects on the ways parents are informed of the nature of their child's relationship with school.

WHY, WHAT AND HOW MIGHT WE ASSESS?

Assessment has become a 'buzz word' in recent years. Almost every interviewee for a teaching post will be asked a question by the interview panel on the role that assessment plays in learning. Perhaps right at the beginning it is worth looking at a simple definition of assessment and a number of key terms that are linked with assessment practice.

Deale (1975) has described assessment as 'an all embracing term, covering any of the situations in which some aspects of a pupil's education is, in some sense, *measured* by the teacher or another person'. This definition is broad and most importantly it emphasizes the fact that assessment is about *measuring learning*. You might, as a teacher, give pupils a worksheet or a series of written questions as a task to do after or during an investigation or a discussion. The worksheet or the written questions only become an *assessment item* when you collect it in and *measure* the degree of success for individuals or the whole class.

Alternatively the pupils may self-assess the learning implicit in the task – again a measurement is taken. The drive to raise performance in Key Stage 3 national assessment has led to a clear recognition that teachers can use assessment, and especially feeding back assessment information to pupils, as a driver to move along individual learning.

It is worthwhile explaining a number of terms that you will undoubtedly meet as a teacher at this point. Education is full of jargon and the vocabulary of assessment is the most 'jargonized'. The terms are useful because they demand an understanding of purpose. As science teachers you need to be aware of what you are doing and why you are doing it – if you are not then your clarity of purpose becomes 'fuzzy'.

Educationalists talk about *summative assessment*. This is the type of measurement that happens at the end of a teaching unit, course or module of work. For example the GCSEs at the end of Key Stage 4, the AS and A2 examinations in Key Stage 5 and the national tests sometimes referred to as standard assessment tests (SATs) at the end of Key Stage 2. In these formal assessments a pupil is given a mark, grade or level. Pupils are judged on this grade, departments in schools are applauded or criticized on this basis, schools are placed in special measures by Ofsted because of this measurement and newspapers thrive on the data. In some cases schools are closed on the basis of this performance. You will see this summative assessment referred to as *Assessment of Learning* (AoL) in material produced by the authors of the National Secondary Strategy.

Alternatively the strategists at the Qualifications and Curriculum Authority have been at great pains, and rightly so, to point out that good teachers have always been involved in what is now termed *Assessment for Learning* (AfL). This is the assessment practice that informs both teacher and pupil of the gains they have made in learning.

You will also meet the terms *diagnostic* and *formative* assessment in the literature that informs practice. Like a diagnosis by a doctor, what is healthy and what is unhealthy, the purpose of diagnostic assessment is to find out what the pupils know before you start to each them and also what they have picked up while you are teaching them. This information should inform and form what you do with each child and each group of children. It is obviously important that *you* know what the pupils already know before you start to try to build on it. While you are teaching a sequence of lessons you need to find out what they have acquired as a result of your teaching – this informs what you do with the pupils. The terms diagnostic and formative assessment are interlinked in so much as you need to diagnose before you can use the information to inform what you do. The Professional Standards for Qualified Teacher Status require you to 'know a range of approaches to assessment, including the importance of formative assessment'. Since the arrival of the Key Stage 3 strategy, which has rolled out the secondary strategy, the words formative and diagnostic have been linked with the label Assessment for

Learning (AfL). This differentiates between Assessment for Learning and Assessment of Learning (AoL) although as we will see formal tests can be used as a very good AfL tool.

You might also meet the term *evaluative assessment*. This is the assessment linked to performance that happens when a teacher teaches a group or an individual and then reflects on the success of the teaching and learning in the particular unit of work. Likewise a department, a school, a local authority and even national planners reflect on the strengths and weaknesses of the performance they are responsible for. Any form of evaluation is normally linked to a target.

Finally you may meet the term *ipsative assessment*. In education, ipsative assessment is the practice of assessing present performance against the prior performance of the person being assessed – this is a measurement made about the learning level of an individual at a point in time. Targets are set for a point of time in the future when the learning is again assessed and 'value added' is measured, that is, how much the individual has gained in terms of the desired learning outcomes. How much more has been learned? Has the pupil shown enough progress?

THE ASSESSMENT AUDIENCE

Assessment information is required by a number of different persons and organizations. I would argue that it is the nature of the audience that receives the assessment information that defines it as AfL or AoL.

Let us consider an example – the Year 9 national tests known as SATs. These are formal, externally marked national tests that are designed to measure a child's knowledge and understanding of key scientific ideas and assign a National Curriculum level based on attainment targets sitting at the back of the National Curriculum. Once they are sat in May each year they are bundled up and sent to a marker employed by the Qualifications and Curriculum Authority (although this year a new government quango termed the Office for Qualifications, OfQUAL, now leads the assessment and qualification side of things). The school then gets the results back early in July. The results of the national tests are crucial to a school's progress, and indeed survival, along with the End of Key Stage 4 examinations. School league tables will be published both locally and nationally that comment and rank schools in order of achievement and performance. In short the Department for Children, Schools and Families (DfCS) and newspapers collate performance tables. Historically schools with a profile of children skewed towards the lower end of the performance scale have contested this raw data and insisted that these tables are not a true reflection of the quality of teaching and learning that goes on in the classroom. Now we have 'value added' league tables where schools are ranked according to the gains pupils have made in the three years at the school given their past performance in the Year 6 national tests that they will have completed in primary school. Departments in schools are compared against each other by head teachers and governing bodies. Questions are asked if science is substantially underperforming relative to mathematics. Individual teachers are assessed against the targets that were set for them for their classes via the head teacher and these targets will have originated in the local authority offices given pupils' past performance data. National testing has become a political and educational bone of contention and is undergoing revision in pilot schools in 2008–9 at Key Stage 1 where schools can ask pupils to take the national tests when the school thinks they are ready for them, and not necessarily at the end of a the key stage. In fact, as this book goes to press, we have just learned that the KS3 SATs are to be scrapped!

For some schools the national test papers sit dormant on the floor of someone's office for years and the audience is a single test marker. Other schools see this as an opportunity to get them out of the stock cupboard and spend lots of time auditing each pupil's test and building a profile of questions that were done correctly and questions that were done incorrectly. A matrix is drawn up that allows analysis of individual pupils' needs and gaps in knowledge and understanding and pupils are given back the paper. They can see for themselves where they lost marks for incorrect answers, and they can see what type of response is credited. They can even relate their own answers to national levels. They can then begin to form a learning strategy working closely with the teacher who might point them in the direction of a range of curriculum intervention activities. Some schools link this intervention with the folder 'Science Intervention Materials' which was published as part of the National Strategy for Key Stage 3 materials (DfES, 2004d, ref 0077–2004). In this file you see novel revision exercises some of which work on developing not only missing subject knowledge but also the individual's thinking skills. Now can you see how this summative test can be the most useful tool to diagnose and evaluate performance in a whole list of ways and to use formatively. This information gleaned from a summative assessment becomes a powerful formative tool in the teacher's armoury.

So who, what and why do we assess? A list of participants that form the assessment audience might include:

- parents
- teachers
- local authority advisers
- Ofsted inspectors
- head teachers
- school governors
- pupils
- newspapers
- further and higher education admissions tutors.

Can you see that assessment information is not always about the teacher and the pupil?

Point for reflection

Reflect on the list of individuals and agencies that might want assessment data. Try to link the list with a reason why they might want the data, and whether the data is to be used for AoL or AfL? For each player in the assessment audience try to analyse why they are active in the assessment forum?

NATIONAL ASSESSMENT AT KEY STAGE 4: CAN WE ASSESS A PUPIL'S SKILLS AS A SCIENTIST? CAN WE ASSESS THEIR UNDERSTANDING OF HOW SCIENCE WORKS?

It is relatively simple to assess knowledge and understanding – you just place an objective test in front of a pupil and they either know the answer or do not know it! What about the 'How science works' section in the 2004 National Curriculum? Pupils should be taught and, you would hope, learn a vast array of scientific skills as well as an understanding of how scientists and science works. This needs to be assessed as it is now a major part of the learning in science and about science.

Up until the 2004 revisions to the Key Stage 4 National Curriculum, teachers could view four sections at both Key Stages 3 and 4 in the statutory programme of study. The first section was linked to pupils developing an appreciation of scientific enquiry and developing their *investigative skills*. There were four skills identified in this section called investigative skills and teachers had to assess how well a pupil was doing in developing these four skills both at Key Stage 3 and at Key Stage 4. They needed to measure how well the pupil could:

- plan an investigation
- observe within the investigation
- analyse data from the investigation
- evaluate both procedure and data.

All pupils needed an overall level, grade and score attached to attainment in these skills at the end of a key stage and it was left to the awarding bodies working under the scrutiny of the QCA to deliver a model for the assessment of these skills. Level descriptors were to be found in the back of the National Curriculum document and at Key Stage 4 it became known as *Sc1 coursework.*

As the National Curriculum redefined itself, evolving from 'scientific investigations' to 'how science works', we saw additional sections that asked us to develop in pupils an understanding and application of data, evidence and theories. Also we were asked to develop and subsequently assess communication skills including presentational skills. The practical and enquiry skills have been rethought as well. We see that pupils should now be taught to:

- plan to test a scientific idea
- collect data
- work accurately and safely
- evaluate for validity and reliability.

As the skills you are required to teach have broadened, so has the assessment. If it can be taught and learned, then it can be assessed!

The changes to the National Curriculum for science at Key Stage 4 were implemented in schools from 2006 with the introduction of a slimmed down statutory core linked to additional science courses that schools could offer. This resulted in a proliferation of Key Stage 4 courses in addition to the statutory core. Different access routes gave rise to different assessment modes. If we take a practical example from one school I am familiar with, then we see a number of different courses with different summative assessment modes.

The school has a Key Stage 3 profile that has a high percentage of students in Year 9 with level 4 and 5; 60 per cent of pupils reach level 5 or above in the Key Stage 3 End of Year 9 national tests. The school runs GCSE core modular science in Year 10 validated by the awarding body Edexcel. This organization has teamed up with the commercial publisher Pearson to develop '360 Science' – an incredibly well-resourced package. The assessment of this core and the additional science consists of:

- end of module tests on each module studied – multiple choice to measure the pupils' grasp of scientific knowledge and understanding
- internally assessed practical tasks. These tasks attempt to assess the pupils' ability to follow instruction, collect data and present their results. To achieve this they will need to take readings and measurement. They are also asked to make observations and use information technology. The assessment is criteria-based so if the pupil can do a procedure or read a meter accurately then he or she gets a tick in a box.

In Year 11 the pupils who study the 360 Science again face module tests and internally assessed practical tasks in the additional science modules they study. Some pupils can actually study additional modules and gain three GCSEs in the separate sciences (physics, chemistry and biology). They must gain level 6 or above in the national tests in Year 9 to have this opportunity. They can gain the equivalent of two GCSEs with grades that range from A to U, where U is unclassified.

Alongside this relatively content-laden course the school offers 75 per cent of its Year 9 cohorts Edexcel Business Technology Enterprise Council (Btec) First Certificate in applied science in Years 10 and 11. This is a vocationally linked course in which the assessment model is a portfolio of assignments linked to the content. There is no formal, summative end-loaded testing, and the port folios are internally verified. Samples are sent for external verification to assessors. If they are of a satisfactory level of demand and standards are met they are verified as being of a 'fit for purpose' assessment sample. The assignments measure the pupils' understanding of 'how science works' in the National Curriculum but there is heavy onus on literacy, and especially writing, to produce the goods. In this vocationally-linked course the grades are Fail, Pass, Merit and Distinction. A pass is equivalent to two grade Cs at GCSE.

Can you see that, as the awarding bodies increase the number of Key Stage 4 options for study, the options have increased in terms of assessment? Schools are now using the mode of assessment contained in a particular syllabus to determine what course to offer particular pupils. A 'horses for courses' strategy has been adopted by schools based on the best fit assessment for particular groups of pupils.

Many schools have chosen at Key Stage 4 the 'Twenty First Century Science' suite designed by science educationalists at York University in conjunction with the awarding body Oxford, Cambridge and RSA (OCR) and the publisher, Oxford University Press. Again this offers core science for all and additional science for pupils wishing to pursue a traditional academic route. It also offers an applied route with a vocational bias labelled 'Applied Science'. In the core science we see an assessment model that relies on a *case study* for the school-based coursework component. Case studies assess research skills, planning and organization, data representation and presentational skills, with a heavy emphasis on literacy. Pupils also perform a data analysis task situated in the case study. This accounts for one-third of the overall marks for the course. The knowledge and understanding is assessed via modular tests to measure pupils' knowledge and understanding of key concepts.

In the additional science we see almost a traditional Sc1-style investigation. It tests the pupils' ability to plan an investigation, collect data accurately and interpret the data. They then evaluate the data and present their findings. The data should be primary data and invites the use of laboratory space and kit. Secondary data can be incorporated. This accounts again for a third of the marks on offer for the course.

In Applied Science we also see some laboratory space being utilized for assessment purposes. The pupils do six standard procedures which attempt to assess the pupil's ability to follow instructions, work safely and make measurements and observations. They also perform a suitability test were they examine, test and compare the suitability of material, device or procedure used in the workplace. Alongside this they do a work-related report. These three pieces of coursework represent 50 per cent of the total assessment of the course. The rest is end of module tests which again test knowledge and understanding of scientific concepts.

Can you see that the formal assessment of the skills linked to science and how science works is now more varied and expansive than ever? Internal assessment is here to stay and investigative skills are still being tested but there is now a wider context in which large rafts of skills that were not formally tested in a science education are also on the assessment agenda. Can you see also that schools are now in an assessment 'minefield' with the method of formal assessment and the pupil profile influencing heavily the choice of learning offered to pupils at Key Stage 4? I point you in the direction of the websites of the three main awarding bodies. You will need some time to evaluate the various assessment routes a pupil might wander down!

Point for reflection

Talk to an experienced teacher who was involved in the assessment of practical skills up to 2005. Ask him or her if the Sc1 model assessment with its levelling of investigative skills was valid and accurately made a measurement of the scientific skills of the individual pupils. Now talk to the head of science in your school. Ask them why they chose the particular course at Key Stage 4 for a group of Years 10 or 11? Reflect on their responses.

THE ASSESSMENT FOR LEARNING (AfL) DRIVE: WHAT IS THE CONTEXT?

Since the implementation of the National Curriculum in 1989 the relationship between teaching, learning and assessment has been controversial. Originally an assessment framework was suggested to the then Secretary of State for Education, Kenneth Baker, that a system should be set up that married together a moderated, standardized system of external testing and moderated tests. This system could be used to inform both a local and wider audience, and provide a vehicle for good teacher/pupil-led assessment practice in the classroom. This has been the format of the assessment model since then.

The original working group that advised Kenneth Baker in 1987 was called the National Curriculum Task Group on Assessment and Testing (TGAT) and it was chaired by Professor Paul Black from King's College, London. Many of the TGAT recommendations were implemented and we have seen national testing linked to nationally accepted levels of attainment, and we see end of key stage tests allied to teacher-based assessment in schools, although this is changing.

In recent years the Assessment Reform Group (ARG) has been influential in forming the basis of the assessment strategy pushed so forcibly as a strategy to raise standards and improve learning by the recent Key Stage 3/Secondary Strategy consultants. The ARG consists of a small core of eminent educationalists with a focus on assessment, and in particular the use of assessment, as a driver in the learning process. Again Paul Black sits on the ARG core group and I give a web address in the list of useful websites at the end of this chapter.

If you acquire the large white, purple and yellow folder *Assessment in Science: Resource Pack for Tutors* (DfES, 2002b, and you can get this by phoning 0845 6022260) you will find it contains lots of training material for the science consultants and LA advisers that went into schools to advise practising teachers, and how to put this Assessment for Learning model of practice into reality in the classroom. Much of this material has been developed through recognition of the principles espoused by the ARG group. The assessment strand of the Key Stage 3 strategy, for the past two years termed the Secondary Strategy, reflects the ARG's key assessment principles. What are they?

The ARG group suggests that improving learning through assessment depends on five key factors:

- giving effective feedback to pupils
- involving pupils in their own learning
- teaching in a way that responds to the results of assessment
- recognizing that assessment has an important effect on the motivation and self-esteem of pupils
- pupils having the opportunity to assess their own learning, and know how to improve and set targets.

These characteristics of good classroom-based formative assessment have been organized by the ARG into a short concise leaflet. You will find it downloadable as a poster/leaflet from the ARG website. Ten attributes of good classroom assessment practice are given:

- Assessment for learning should be part of effective planning of teaching and learning
- Assessment for learning should focus on how students learn
- Assessment for learning should be recognized as central to classroom practice
- Assessment for learning should be regarded as a key professional skill for teachers
- Assessment for learning should be sensitive and constructive because any assessment has an emotional impact
- Assessment for learning should take account of the importance of learner motivation
- Assessment for learning should promote commitment to learning goals and a shared understanding of the criteria by which they are assessed

- Learners should receive constructive guidance about how to improve
- Assessment for learning develops learners' capacity for self-assessment so that they can become reflective and self-managing
- Assessment for learning should recognize the full range of achievements of all learners. (ARG, 2002, 'Assessment for Learning: 10 principles', available on the ARG website)

It is interesting that in the paper/pamphlet ARG (2006) *The Role of Teachers in the Assessment of Learning* (also downloadable on www.assessment-reform-group.org) we see a recognition of the negative effect on learning that a slavish adherence to external national tests at the end of each key stage has had on the quality of the taught curriculum. The ARG now looks back on 20 years of 'current summative assessment policies based on testing' claiming they are 'not justified by the value of the information gained' (2006: 13). They are also costly. The Office for Qualifications (OfQUAL) website is quite happy to inform you that 'delivering the national curriculum tests involves producing and distributing test papers equivalent to 237 million sheets of A4'! Just think of the cost of this and then consider the ARG's argument that they are not valid anyway and are restricting the learning on offer to 'practice for tests'. They want national testing replaced by moderated teacher judgements of pupil performance. They want less 'hard' data and a range of types of evidence of pupils' learning used. They acknowledge the detrimental effect the current testing regime has had on learning. This includes reducing pupil self-esteem, causing anxiety in pupils, and valuing test performance more than what is to be learnt. Most negatively, it has caused good teachers to restrict their teaching repertoire to cater for the national tests. Teachers have been forced to embrace Year 6 and Year 9 as revision years for national tests in the same way that Year 11 has become a revision year for GCSEs. We are in the grip of an assessment stranglehold where 'the tail wags the dog'.

On the 12th October 2008, Ed Balls, the schools secretary decided to abolish national testing at 14. This was reported in the *Guardian* on the day by Polly Curtis with the title:

'SATs for 14-year-olds are scrapped'

'The changes mean pupils will no longer have to sit externally marked tests at the age of 14, but ministers have insisted that primary school pupils will still have to undergo the most controversial tests at 11.

The schools secretary, Ed Balls, today informed Parliament of plans for sweeping changes to the national testing system, which sees 1.2 million pupils sit 9.5m papers every year.

The move cuts the testing burden on school in half.

The plans also include a new American-style "report card" for every school so that parents can access information about schools they might want to send their child to. Every school will receive a grade depending on their performance'.

Balls said: "If you ask, are we abolishing half the national testing system, yes, we are."

"These reforms will provide more regular and more comprehensive information to parents about their children's progress, support heads and teachers to make sure that every child can succeed, and strengthen their ability to hold all schools to account, as well as the public's ability to hold government to account."

He said that the changes followed an "ongoing debate" about the value of the tests but admitted this summer's crisis had been a factor in the timing. The government is urgently seeking a replacement for ETS, the company which failed to deliver this year's tests on time.

Balls denied it was a U-turn, insisting they were simply responding to mounting evidence that the tests are not useful for schools.

The changes announced today include:

- An end to national tests for 14-year-olds and the league tables based on those test results;
- A new school-by-school report card to give parents richer information than league tables;
- A review group will be established to oversee these reforms and they have been charged with looking at the impact of tests on 11-year-olds to tackle charges of teaching to the test.

Although first introduced in their current form in 1995 under the Conservative government, the tests have been a defining feature of Labour's education reforms.

It comes after a disastrous year when the delivery of the tests collapsed under the American firm, ETS, which had been brought in to modernise the system. The £156m contract with ETS was dissolved, and some schools are still awaiting results.

The testing system, has also been severely criticised by MPs in a select committee report, which said tests had "distorted" children's education.

A major inquiry into primary education by Cambridge University also found that SATs were feeding into a "pervasive anxiety" in children's life.

The move will be widely welcomed by secondary schools and teacher unions but others in primary schools will be dismayed.

It would seem that ETS, (the American company given the test of administering and marking the tests) and its subsequent failure to deliver results on time had more impact on deciding the future of end of key stage national testing than 13 years of commentary from practising teachers and eminent educationalists!

THE REALITY IN THE CLASSROOM: PRINCIPLES INTO PRACTICE

Good assessment practice in the classroom starts with a clear recognition of learning. Matt Cochrane in Chapter 3 on planning lessons has introduced the concept of *learning objectives* and also *learning outcomes*. A learning objective is simply a statement of what you want the pupils to learn. It might be an item of knowledge such as 'forces are measured in units called newtons'. You might want pupils to move past this simple 'fact' and go on to add more pieces of knowledge together and eventually form a concept that reflects understanding. For example, a recognition by the pupil that 'a force is that which tends to cause acceleration'. Key to this is an understanding that acceleration is a change in velocity.

These learning objectives are derived from the content of the course, module or programme of study that you are teaching – they are external to the pupil. Underpinning this are many more pieces of knowledge that can be acquired other than the fact that 'force is measured in newtons' but you have many lessons normally to build this conceptual pyramid – hopefully it will happen.

Alternatively, learning objectives may be the long-term incremental development of skills, attitudes, beliefs and values. These might be linked to how science works or they might be wider skills. As a result of the learning the pupils will be able to do certain things to demonstrate their learning. Quite simply they may be able to answer a simple written or oral question:

Question: What is force measured in?
Answer: Newtons.

So your learning outcome is,

Pupils will be able to 'name what force is measured in'.

It is internal to the pupil – a demonstration of success and an indicator of performance. This is a learning outcome, albeit a very simple one and I am safe in stating that good assessment practice starts with a clear recognition of the expected learning – what is on offer. You need to know with clarity in the classroom what you want the pupils to learn and what you expect them to demonstrate as a consequence of their interaction with you and the learning activities you will organize.

What this means is a reality that demands acuity and vision of purpose. Some years ago I read a line that I will always remember: 'The single biggest obstacle to effective teaching in schools is that some teachers are not clear about what they want pupils to learn when they enter the classroom.' They were right! You know the scenario.

Teacher: Today we are going to 'do' photosynthesis. Now what did we do last lesson? Was it the leaf?

This scenario is getting far less common as the teaching professions finds itself more and more populated by an informed and astute set of professionals that have really raised the bar in terms of standards, but as teachers we really must be clear about what learning we have on offer.

So good assessment practice starts with a clear recognition of learning. These objectives and outcomes should then be shared with the pupils. When you construct a sequence of lessons then share the learning on offer with the pupils, let them know what they are expected to learn. This might be knowledge and understanding or it could be skills – science specific or wider. The pupils should be able to answer questions that show they are aware of what they are doing and what they need to do in order to show success. In short, the assessment needs to be transparent and signposted.

Now what this, of course, demands is that you are clear about this and have planned your medium-term lesson sequence with integral assessment. What this also means is that you should not be in a position where last-second assessment tasks are being given out such as impromptu homework that conflicts with the school's homework policy. You have planned the lesson sequence using all the pieces in the planning jigsaw and your starting point are the learning objectives specified in the unit that you are asked to teach, and these are now shared with the pupils. You can use these objectives as learning targets and point to them as they progress through the lesson sequence.

As a teacher you have a wide range of tactics you can use to gather assessment evidence. You can collect evidence of assessment from written or oral class-work questions, observations of them working, discussions between you and them either individually or in a group, formal or informal tests, for example quizzes, you might set. You might give out homework. All of these strategies to collect assessment data should link and test the learning you have identified – that is, be valid. Formal tests can be returned to pupils with the mark scheme and you can let them see how their answers compare with the model answers. Individual pupils can then use the test as an audit of their learning. This atmosphere of transparency is sometimes overlooked by teachers and sometimes it is as if the means of success is kept by the teacher as a mystery. This type of practice focuses on assessment as a formative tool not as some kind of negative managerial tool to keep them in check. As a teacher you need to talk to pupils about their progress and use the evidence of what they have achieved to plan what happens next. If you are giving marks or grades then the pupils should understand what A, B, C or D means. They should know what constitutes satisfactory, very good or outstanding work. Likewise they should know why their work is not satisfactory. If you are going to write comments on their books then make them supportive and diagnostic. This means pointing out what they can and cannot do and giving suggestions as to how they are going to move on to use this effectively. Many teachers now keep diaries of the comments that they have made on pupils' work.

The Learn Project (2000) points out some important aspects of marking for teachers to think about and try to implement:

- Teachers should use grades and marks with caution because they are confusing and 'label' students
- Target mark important pieces of work so that you don't end up attempting to mark everything the child does
- Make sure your comments focus on the task pointing out gaps between a pupil's performance and the expected standard, and give ideas about how to close the gap if a gap is indeed evident
- Try to give feedback that encourages pupils to think about the task and not themselves

The last point is important. If you link assessment to ego then can you see that in any class there is only one 'winner'? I have seen schools employ class and year group league tables where grades and scores for tests are pinned up for all to see. You have got to ask yourself 'Is this wise?' Only one pupil comes top and for some children it can be humiliating. I often used to marvel at the poor child that worked incredibly hard over the years but continually came near to or at the bottom in these tests. How did he or she continue to motivate themselves? It was incredible that they marched on with a smile of resignation. On the other hand, some became disillusioned quickly and looked for other ways to boost their ego and created havoc at the teacher's expense as one way to do this!

Website

Watch the first 4 minutes of Paul in action in lesson 2. He gives back an assessment that he has marked, measured the learning and given some quite specific targeted feedback. He calls this 'next step marking' and really pushes the point that it tells each pupil what they are to learn to do better in the next round of tests. He asks them to make their own comment on the feedback. Think about the strategy. Does this fit in with assessment good practice?

SOME EXTREMELY PRACTICAL ADVICE

The first assessment job that all teachers new to a school must do is to get hold of all the historical data that they can about the individual pupils in the classes they are going to teach. Most schools have a wealth of past assessment information about their pupils. Some will be quantitative such as National Curriculum levels from the previous key stages, cognitive ability tests scores from Year 7 and some will be qualitative, for example, teacher diaries and notes, commentaries and so on. It is not practical to even begin to teach a group of children without any background knowledge.

The second assessment task for you is to familiarize yourself with the school's assessment policy and, in particular, the science department's assessment policy.

All schools will have a marking policy and any trainee or new teacher at any school needs to fall in with this. If they give A, B, C and so on then you need to do it and know why you are doing it. If grades are given for performance and effort then you must fall in with this practice. You may not agree with the system and the system may be flawed, but it is school policy. Likewise many schools include in the marking policy guidelines such as:

- Mark all exercise books once per week.
- Correct spelling of important scientific words.
- Standardize marking of end of topic tests.
- Homework and class work are marked using a common framework.
- Make comments as appropriate.
- Marks are appropriate for class work and homework.
- Tick work to show you have looked at it.
- Record in mark books all assessment data.
- Link performance to merits.

These guidelines are from one well-run school's science department and are given to new teachers as a booklet entitled 'Science Department – Assessment Policy'. The points are categorized as 'informal' assessment advice. They are typical of the type of guidelines you will meet in schools.

In all schools the formal summative assessment at the end of module tests is also compared with Year 7 cognitive ability tests (CATs) and used to target-set, recognize underachievement and act as a predictor of future performance. Schools describe intervention strategies based on quantitative and qualitative data. All the scores and levels from end of unit tests are usually stored in a whole-school student information management system (SIMS) but the informal formative assessment between you and an individual child will not be, so you need to record this – you need to get a 'mark book'. There are a number of ways to organize a log/record of assessment data. Some teachers use spreadsheets and databases to record a class's or individual pupil assessment profile, whereas others stick with a paper-based grid – all are valid and it does not really matter what you use as long as you have something that can be used to sit down with an individual pupil and reflect on learning. Can you see that if you have items such as a log of homework completion, comments on presentation and organization, end of unit tests scores and grades for class work and homework, then you can talk formatively about the pupil's progress. Most importantly, if you have a record of the individual's success and non-success linked to the learning objectives/outcomes of the lesson sequence, then their learning can be addressed in a diagnostic and potentially formative way.

Let us consider a unit of work that has a number of key aspects of learning that you want all the pupils to learn. Can you see that you could line them up in a sequence and even tick them off as the pupils acquired them? For your individual pupils you could create a table that might resemble Table 6.1.

Table 6.1 Formative Pupil learning record

Key learning item	Learning evident or not	Assessment Item
Read a thermometer accurately	Yes	Teacher observation 21 March 2008
List the different types of thermometers and link each to a use	Yes	Question 3, page 21 in textbook
Can explain the difference between heat and temperature	No	Mid-module test, question 4, page 2

Although this paperwork is pretty straightforward, after you have had the vision to recognize what is on offer, it still presents a fairly demanding, time-consuming task to do this for Year 8, Year 9, the two Year 7s you have and, of course, the Year 10 set one and Year 11 set five. As a secondary school teacher you will get anything up to 200 pupils passing through your gaze in any one week. How can you effectively do this? The answer is pupil self-assessment. You have really got to throw the onus, emphasis, whatever you want to call it for the recognition of the learning onto the pupil. There are many reasons for this but the most obvious is not to save your time; it is to empower the pupils, force them to recognize the learning on offer and reflect on their own learning. It is the only way to organize effective assessment practice. Put the outcomes, key learning items, whatever you want to call them, in 'kiddy speak' , make them accessible, share them with the pupils and let them do the spade work. They will come to you with the gaps for you to plug, and this practice personalizes their learning. It allows them the opportunity to drive the revision programme.

If you go online at QCA and trawl the sites of the Local Authority Science advisory teams (Dudley, Wigan, Sefton and Northumberland, to suggest a few) you can find a wealth of advice on pupil self-assessment frameworks. Often you will see a 'traffic light' system used where green is 'I am confident', amber means 'I'm not sure' and red means 'I'm lost!' A common alternative to the traffic light system is a 'smiley face' system – same purpose.

Recently I had a conversation with a head of department in a school with a large percentage of underachievers in the science department, who informed me that they had 'tried self-assessment but it didn't work and we've now given it up'. I find this odd, although I understand why it is happened. Pupils need to actively engage with this type of strategy and teachers need to empower and guide, and it is not a process that is quickly adopted when pupils have never really been active in their own assessment. To embrace such a strategy requires a long-term commitment from a staff pulling together with a common goal. Other schools with similar 'tough' profiles of pupils have made it work – the schools just need to invest in time for pupils to reflect on their learning and not just rush headlong through it.

Remember you do not have to assess everything, but you should try to assess the really important pieces of learning.

Point for reflection

Consider the framework of a typical school and the typical school week. Twenty five lessons of subject study for Years 7 to 11 in a week with five each day. Is this rapid fire timetable conducive to learning? Does it allow time built in for pupils to think about their learning? Think about how you might structure the school day to allow pupils time to think about what they had just learned. Find out if any 11–16 schools have experimented with leaving gaps in the timetable for pupils to reflect on the learning they have experienced in contact lessons with teachers.

WRITING A TEST

Certainly in your first year as a teacher you will have to put together a test. Most units of work have module tests written either by an experienced teacher or a commercial publisher but you will want to check on the learning of your pupils constantly. What should a good test consist of? Well it should be valid and test what you have actually taught, in other words, linked to the learning objectives/ outcomes. It should also be reliable – the questions should measure the learning in a number of different ways to allow the pupil to demonstrate the learning and make sure that they have the opportunity to express it in different ways. A test should be criteria-referenced, that is, if the pupil gets a question correct then they have passed the criteria, demonstrated the learning and are given credit. So if everybody gets 90 per cent plus then congratulate yourself and the pupils as they have demonstrated clearly the learning that you planned for them. The reality is not always like this. Many of the scientific concepts that you offer the pupils are conceptually and cognitively demanding – science is not easy. You might well find yourself attempting to teach concepts that have been identified as level 6 in the National Curriculum to pupils at level 3 in terms of recent performance.

There are many different types of questions you can use to build a test:

1. Multiple choice questions with a stem and options (usually four). These demand a correct response and have distracter responses. Pupils call these 'multiple guess'! If you make the distracters too 'wrong' then the pupils will guess the answers.
2. Matching pairs. This is the type of question where pupils are given a, b, c and d alternatives and they have to match up with 1, 2, 3 and 4. So A goes with 1 for example.

3. Multiple completion questions. These allow responses that cover several statements and allow the pupil to connect several ideas. This type of question gives the pupils multiple options like '1, 2 and 3 only are correct' or 'only 2 is correct'. Sometimes it is more intellectually demanding to interpret the question than it is to produce the science!

4. Short answer questions. These are questions that ask the pupil to do things like label a diagram, complete a graph, fill in missing words, simple calculations or give definitions. The key stage formal tests are full of these questions.

5. Structured questions. These are normally questions that are themed around a topic and give the pupil the opportunity to write short sentences on a question paper. They are often tiered by difficulty. Part E is more demanding than Part A.

6. Essay. This is a higher education favourite but not so common at Key Stage 3. It allows the pupil to expand on his or her understanding in a loose framework which demands good literacy skills.

7. Comprehension exercises. Pupils get a text to read then questions on the passage. This can test both literacy and the ability to extract information from text. You can also use it to test if the pupil can take information in one context and apply it in a different context.

As a teacher you should be aware of these forms of written questioning and plan to use a variety of the different types in tests. This will make your test more reliable and not biased towards or against a particular group (for example, gender or culture). You obviously need a well thought through mark scheme and, if graded or levelled, then have boundaries that reflect National Curriculum levels or in some way reflect the level of demand. Place your questions in a familiar context and reward harder questions with more marks.

Finally you need to recognize that pupils need time and advice to prepare for the formal tests that they are asked to sit at the end of key stages or at the end of units of work. Do not assume that they are familiar with the language of assessment. Many pupils do not know what 'describe' and 'explain' mean when they meet the words in a question. Also do not assume they are used to the multiple choice format or aware that in a particular examination they need to answer five questions in total, two from four in section A and three from six in section B!

QUESTIONING

The *Times Educational Supplement* (*TES*, 4 July 2003) carried an article that gave some amazing statistics about the extent of oral questioning in the classroom. It claimed that teachers ask on average two questions per minute. That is about 400 in a day and amounts to 70,000 in a year or approximately 2–3 million in a career of 40 years! It also claimed that questioning accounted for up to a third of teaching time, second only to teacher exposition and explanation. It went on to say that many of these questions are procedural; 'Have you got a pen?' 'Have you finished yet?' 'What are you doing under the desk?'

Why do we do it?

The *TES* article suggests we do it for a number of different reasons:

- Verbal questioning can help pupils to reflect on information and commit it to memory.
- Verbal questions can help to develop thinking skills, encourage discussion and stimulate new ideas.
- Verbal questions allow the teacher to determine how much a class understands and allows them to pitch the material at the right level.
- Verbal questions can help the teacher to manage the classroom, helping them to draw individuals into the lesson and keeping them interested and alert.

In short questions send a clear message that pupils are expected to be *active participants* in the learning process.

Verbal questions can be categorized as open or closed. A closed question is one in which the question seeks a single answer that is either right or wrong. You see this all the time in a classroom.

Teacher: What is the green pigment in plants?
Matthew: Chlorophyll.
Teacher: Well done, Mathew! You are right!
Teacher: Tony, do all plants have chlorophyll?
Tony: No.
Teacher: Well, Tony, all green plants have chlorophyll.

Can you see the potential pitfalls in this scenario? You decide on the right answer and the pupils have to guess your correct response. It also does not really allow them or you the chance to explore their understanding and knowledge. It might indicate that they have picked up something from last lesson though! The other issue is that you have to be aware of the phrasing of the question. Does it make sense? Is it ambiguous? What is the 'right' response? There are ways to avoid this scenario. For example:

- Discuss with a partner. This is where pupils when asked the question talk to their partner then build to a consensus answer.
- Group discussion – similar to above but larger base of discussion.
- Flash cards; traffic lights; true/false. Involves the whole class.
- Ten seconds to answer – ask the pupil and ask him or her to wait 10 seconds before responding. This ensures it is not the first thing that comes into the child's head that finds its way out of his or her mouth!

In addition you can be creative and novel with your question and answer routines. 'Beginning with a Letter' asks pupils to identify words that link with a scientific term and begin with a particular letter. 'Pass the Buck' asks pupils to write one sentence in answer to a question and then pass it on to another pupil for them to add the next sentence, and so on until it gets back to the original person. 'Tip of my Tongue' gives the pupil an unfinished sentence and asks them to predict what the missing word is. 'Fast Talker – Big Gob' asks them to say as many words as they can think of linked to a theme in 15 seconds. Can you see that with a little imagination, a presentation package and projector you can make questioning fun – it is not by accident that *Who Wants to be a Millionaire?* is one of the longest running and most popular television programmes in the UK. Children love quizzes and as a teacher you can use them diagnostically, formatively and for fun. For an interesting viewpoint on classroom questioning techniques and some suggestions to avoid the situation described in the teacher–pupil dialogue above you might read Nick Selley's 'Wrong answers welcome' article from *School Science Review* suggested in the reading list.

Alternatively you can think about making the closed question more open. An open question can lead to several possible answers and can even be so open that it requires the answerer to pour out all of the understanding they know about a certain subject. A completely wide open question might be 'What can you tell me about plant feeding?' Can you see that this is a question that can be used again with another pupil and can tease out of the pupil an assessment of the level of understanding? It might also be used to pull others into the question when used by a skilful teacher.

Many investigations start with a question, and the degree of 'openness' of the initial question may lead to very different routes, some restricted and some wide open. For example, 'What affects resistance?' can lead to a number of different pathways for pupils to follow, whereas 'How does length affect resistance?' is completely specific and closed. You need to be careful as the title or question can determine the variety of activities. Of course, it may be that you want a specific investigation done. I think the message is to think about the questions you are going to ask before you start the lesson and perhaps write them down on a sheet that you can refer to. Similarly with a modicum of creativity you can disguise your closed factual question with a variety of techniques.

My last point really concerns the management of oral question and answer sessions and hopefully will avoid management issues in the question and answer section of a lesson. You should rigidly stick to a routine when asking and seeking verbal questions. Maintain and drill the pupils into the 'hands up' routine – it will be chaotic if you do not. You can bring individual pupils into the lessons who are often reluctant to contribute. Have indicator pupils where you know if *they* can answer a question then the majority of the class will be able to. Most importantly, praise the pupils that contribute and please do not gloss over their contribution even if it is not what you expected. Remember it is very rare that there is not an essence of valid science bound up in a pupil question or a response to your question. As a teacher you should avoid getting into negatives like 'That wasn't the answer I was looking for' or 'No, you're not correct.' Instead tease out the misconception with remarks like 'I can see where that is coming from.' Wrong answers can be welcome!

THE REPORT TO PARENTS

> Certainly on the road to failure. He is hopeless and rather a clown in class, wasting other pupils' time. (John Lennon, Quarry Bank School, Liverpool)

> She must try to be less emotional in her dealings with others. (Diana Spencer, West Heath School)

It is a statutory requirement for schools to provide a written report to parents at least once a year. The school report is a vital element in the pupil, teacher, parent triangle which is a relationship that needs to be positive and productive if the pupil is to progress both in his or her science education and wider aspects of his or her personal and social skills. School reports are normally based on areas such as performance, attitude and effort. In recent years the school report has also included a National Curriculum level for each pupil in their subjects.

As a parent you want to know two things about your child:

1. Is my child sociable and getting on well with his or her peers and responding positively to persons in authority? This facet of emotional intelligence will be important to his or her economic well-being in the future.
2. Is my child performing in their learning at a level that shows satisfactory or better than satisfactory progress in relation to what has been achieved earlier on in primary school? All secondary schools will have past performance data and will use this as a target-setting tool to predict future performance. Informed parents will have this past performance data as well and will want to see learning moving on appropriately.

Many reports tackle these issues well. Many have a 'free prose' section where the teacher can write a comment such as 'a very pleasant young man who is always well behaved and polite' or 'needs to adopt a more mature attitude to his studies'. This second comment of course means that he is constantly messing about in lessons! In short this is a qualitative description of their relationships with staff and other pupils.

Learning is more difficult. Many schools now have a system that uses past performance indicators to set a minimum, baseline, gross target in a subject like science. More often than not these are not based on the end of Key Stage 2 formal assessments in Year 6 but, rather, on internal cognitive ability tests administered at the beginning of Year 7. From these an end of Key Stage 3 performance, in terms of the formal tests, is derived and a final grade for GCSE at the end of Key Stage 4 is predicted. Often pupils will get a predicted level or predicted grade and a 'progress grade' to indicate whether they are underachieving or, in some cases, actually doing better than was predicted. Schools talk about, and often put into place intervention strategies for underachievers. The problem with this picture is that it is eminently understandable for an educationalist but not for parents. If a report shows a target as level 5b for the end of Key Stage 3 in science then what does level 5b mean to a parent not conversant with what constitutes level 5 in the National Curriculum for science?

If the pupil is predicted level 5b then some parents (like myself) will ask the question, 'OK if you predict level 5b as a minimum then why isn't he or she doing better than this'? There is a danger of the 'pygmalion effect' where pupils achieve the minimum predicted grade because that is what the teachers expect – be careful of this. Nevertheless, can you see the difficulties with the school report?

Some schools try to make the learning more apparent. Statements such as 'Emma can describe the various types of thermometers but cannot explain the difference between heat and energy' are common in some schools' reporting systems. You have got to ask yourselves if parents want this detail.

The parents' evening has a similar theme. When you are a parent it sometimes feels as if all you hear is a succession of National Curriculum levels and targets against levels. As a teacher, of course, this is all necessary as part of the assessment profiling that you will do with the pupils and does give an insight into the progress against targets, but a procession of teachers giving out National Curriculum levels is not what a parents' evening should consist of.

You will have to gain experience of this liaison with parents and carers in your training period and it is vital you begin to exploit this triangle for the pupils' learning. Use the school's merit system as much as you can. Give the pupil a merit certificate with an explanation to the parent/carer of why this has been earned – then the pupil can take it home and show someone how well they have done in science. It is not uncommon for parents to give cash rewards for merits so even the tough case in your class will appreciate a positive to take home.

The Office for Standards in Education (2006) comments on the degree of parental dissatisfaction with school and parent communications as being problematic. My eldest son slipped out of set 1 in science and was relegated to set 2 on the basis of a Year 9 summative test. The only information I had was his own version of events; he told me he had been told he 'got level 5b and you needed level 6 to go into set 1 in Year 10' – there was no contact from the school whatsoever. This personal example is a common scenario. Important decisions that affect pupils' life chances happen daily in schools and parents often are not informed. Certainly if you only get an annual report the relationship between schools and yourself is patchy. Some schools now are using information technology to log many aspects of the pupil's relationship with teaching and learning and communicate this to parents. Many behavioural incidents are logged, as are the results of formative tests that the teacher might organize around the learning. Most teachers keep lists of assessment items such as homework completion, unfinished and below standard work as well as attendance and punctuality in their mark books. Many schools now have parental emails as well as phone numbers but still information back to parents is thin on the ground. I am conscious that anyone in any job can argue 'they haven't got the time' but for many teachers this has some validity – they do not have the time to pick up the phone or send a letter. Parents' evenings are held maybe once or at best twice a year and a teacher may see 30 parents in two hours. The system is not geared up to this type of open and frank exchange of views. In many private fee-paying schools it is different. If you are paying £8,000 a year or more for your child's education then if your child is to be relegated from set 1 to set 2 there will be communication!

Point for reflection

Some teachers spend time at the end of each day sending letters or phoning parents about both positive and negative events that involve their children. Discuss this practice with the pastoral team in your school and reflect on the advice they give. Get hold of a school report and evaluate it as a tool for informing the child's parents about the relationship between the child and the school.

What the research says

Paul Black and Christine Harrison (2001a; 2001b) over many years have initiated primary research into effective assessment practice and collated other research articles that allow us to access data that hints strongly at what works and what does not work in assessment practice. The work of the King's Medway Oxford Formative Assessment Project (KMOFAP), a project jointly established by King's College, London and 12 practising science teachers in six schools in Medway and Oxfordshire, offers insights into what works and what does not work in assessment practice. The findings are voiced largely through the voices of the 12 participating classroom teachers and give us some answers to the often thorny issue of classroom assessment practice.

The project methodology and conclusions are detailed in *School Science Review*, 83(302): 43–9 and *School Science Review*, 82(301): 55–61. Earlier findings, by Black and Wiliam and others, that hint at the principles underpinning effective assessment practice, that is, practice that drives learners upward and on in their learning, are referenced in each of the *School Science Review* articles. For these reasons I do not include them in the additional reading – you can spot them in the reference pages in *School Science Review*. It is worthwhile backtracking and reading these pieces of research and reflecting on their implications for practice. For example, R. Butler (1998) suggests that when marks are given for a piece of work then the comments are largely ignored! You might use them as a starting point for your reflection. The KMOFAP project puts the principles under a very close microscope, teachers in a classroom actually testing them out to see if they can be implanted in practice.

Good practice in terms of pupil and peer assessment, questioning technique and written feedback are commented on.

Further reading

Department for Education and Skills (DfES) (2002b) *Assessment in Science. Resource Pack for Tutors*. Ref DfES 0369/2002. London: DfES.
Lots of training materials for practising teachers that you can mull over. Interesting items with traffic lights, card games and group activities designed to make teachers think about their own assessment practice.

Department for Education and Skills (DfES) (2007) *Assessment for Learning: 8 Schools Project Report*. Ref 00067–2007BKT – EN. London: DfES. Available for download from www.standards.dfes.govuk or www.teachernet.gov.uk/publication.
Read how AfL works in a pilot group of schools.

Gardner, J. (ed.) (2006) *Assessment of Learning*. London: Sage.
Gardner edits a small number of chapters from influential players in defining what is considered good assessment practice.

National Curriculum: Task Group on Assessment and Testing (1987) *A Report*. London: DES.
Sets the assessment scene for the next two decades

National Curriculum: Task Group on Assessment and Testing (1988) *Three Supplementary Reports*. London: DES.
Both TGAT reports make interesting reading for a number of reasons. You can see how the group influenced the national assessment model with end of key stage formal assessment and performance levels linked to national attainment targets. Yet they also offer sound advice for what happens in the classroom.

Useful websites

www.ocr.org; also www.edexcel.org and www.aqa.org
The websites of the main awarding bodies in the UK. Consider the courses on offer and the routes through science 14–19 and 11–16.

www.ofqual.org.uk
New arm of the former QCA that has responsibility for testing, examinations and qualifications. The QCA has been split into two with one branch staying as the

QCA and taking responsibility for curriculum and learning issues, and OfQUAL taking charge of national assessment.

http://ngfl.northumberland.gov.uk/science/selfassessment
Some well put together self-assessment word frames for children to work with. Linked to the QCA exemplar scheme of work but shows examples of well thought through checklists/traffic light style self-assessment documents. Scheme is obsolescent but the ideas and material are useful.

www.assessment-reform-group,org
The Assessment Reform Group website. Group examines the role of assessment in education, reflects on recent developments and suggests options for a national assessment practice.

7 TEACHING DIFFERENT ABILITIES; TEACHING DIFFERENT PUPILS

Judith Thomas

This chapter examines:

- the principle of inclusion in science education, with particular reference to ability and pupils with English as an additional language (EAL)
- different ways that science teachers respond to different ability groups
- the role of the teaching assistant (TAs) in supporting the teaching of science
- the needs of the most able pupils
- the evidence relating to language and science learning.

Teaching science provides particular challenges in enabling all pupils to achieve to their full potential. In any educational/learning situation the key to individual success is motivation and the ability to succeed.

It is important to ensure the learning taking place is enjoyable and meaningful. What do we understand by the term 'learning'? It is essentially an observable, measurable change in behaviour that is the result of an experience. So when we teach we provide an experience for pupils, and as a result of that experience we are hoping that their behaviour will be in some way changed. This can apply to practical skills, theoretical understanding and the ability to solve problems. This change we can then measure with assessment and from this we can tell if learning has indeed taken place. Taking account of pupils' differences is the key to successful teaching. This ensures the teaching is appropriate, the learning experience is as expected and that pupils are progressing through their defined sequence of targets.

Learning cannot take place unless the pupil has motivation and the appropriate level of ability for the task in hand. Thus tailoring the lesson to the needs of individuals will ensure a much more productive lesson. The old saying 'Look after the pennies, the pounds will look after themselves' can be reinterpreted for your classroom: 'Look after the individuals and the lesson as a whole will run more smoothly'. Teaching styles are adapted to cater for individuals, who then engage in the learning process. With a feeling of success for pupils, their levels of motivation and enthusiasm will be raised further. The more confident individuals will begin to achieve to their full potential and be engaged in learning, thus taking less time off task to be disruptive.

WHAT DO WE MEAN BY INCLUSION?

Inclusion is the key to providing effective learning opportunities for all pupils. Inclusion is, and rightly should be, at the centre of the Every Child Matters agenda.
A personalised approach to supporting children means:

- Tailoring learning to the needs, interests and aspirations of each individual
- Tackling barriers to learning and allowing each child to achieve their potential.

Website

See 'Useful websites' (1) www.everychildmatters.gov.uk/etc/personalisedlearning for more information on the ECM agenda.

This should place the children's individual needs at the centre of the school ethos, so while it is essential to develop a whole-school approach to offer equal opportunity to all pupils, that does not necessarily mean offering or treating all pupils the same. It means getting to know pupils as individuals, taking account of different backgrounds and different needs, and responding appropriately. The key is tracking pupils' individual needs and working with them in setting appropriate targets. It is important to remember that *all* pupils are special in that their needs have to be met in order for them to achieve. Schools have a responsibility to provide a broad and balanced curriculum for all pupils. The National Curriculum statutory inclusion statement sets out three principles for developing an inclusive curriculum which provides all pupils with relevant and challenging learning.

HOW CAN SCHOOLS CHALLENGE ALL PUPILS?

Schools must:

- set suitable learning challenges
- respond to pupils' diverse learning needs
- overcome potential barriers to learning and assessment for individuals and groups of pupils. (QCA, 2008)

Set suitable learning challenges

This is concerned with setting appropriate learning objectives at a suitable level for the pupils in that particular class. The level of work must be appropriately matched to the levels at which pupils in the class are working. This may involve setting a range of differentiated tasks to enable all pupils to succeed to their own capability. The challenges for learning should also be meaningful, where possible relating to the pupil's own knowledge.

Respond to pupils' diverse learning needs

All pupils should be treated as individuals, and pupil ability and motivation are important for success. What do we mean by ability? According to Kyriacou (1998: 56) 'ability is closely linked to intelligence. Intelligence refers to a child's ability to learn and to meet cognitive and intellectual demands through their application of current knowledge, understanding and intellectual skills'.

Website

Lesson 2 of the video begins with the teacher giving back books with written feedback and then pupils are asked to set targets on how they will improve on an individual basis, building on pupils' own strengths and areas for development.

A pupil's ability at any one point in time must be a reflection of his or her prior knowledge or learning, and of his or her motivation, enthusiasm and general support from peers, home and school. Note that pupils who are low achievers for their year are not necessarily without ability. They may be disengaged from learning for a number of reasons. You, 'the teacher', have to get them back into the learning mindset.

At the other end of the spectrum the most able pupils often fail to achieve fully because they are not suitably challenged, and if they find work repetitive or boring this can lead to behaviour problems. Approaches to dealing with very able pupils can vary: some schools will accelerate pupils to the year above their age groups so they complete traditional school one year in advance of their peers. Academically these pupils thrive and progress through levels but sometimes maturity is lacking and can cause some disruptions. If you have younger gifted pupils it is important to integrate them into the lessons with care so that peers do not treat them differently.

Lessons for gifted pupils should not just mean more of the same; rather they should be provided with more challenging activities to apply their knowledge and skills. The introduction of the concept of a more personalized pattern of learning for all has helped the more able pupils. Project work with open-ended outcomes can take pupils to different levels. These could be in the form of individual programmes of study where pupils and teachers together set targets and aspirations to enable pupils to achieve the next level of learning. Supplementary materials provide pupils with challenges to apply their knowledge to different situations.

Pupils whose attainment falls below the average expectation for their age group may not be falling behind due to a lack of ability – there may be social and/or motivation issues. These pupils can be said to have mild learning difficulties for the purposes of your lesson planning.

They will remain in mainstream classrooms or laboratories catered for by the class teacher's differentiated planning. Pupils with more specific learning difficulties will hopefully be supported by learning support assistants (LSAs). These specific learning difficulties include reading, writing, spelling and number work.

Overcome potential barriers to learning and assessment for individuals and groups of pupils

These barriers may be encountered by pupils with special needs as mentioned above, but also by those who require special arrangements in the classroom in order for them to progress. These may be physical or emotional barriers. As mentioned earlier, pupil motivation is crucial. Language may be another barrier in the ability to read, understand and communicate in spoken and written English. This language barrier does not only apply to pupils who have English as an additional language.

Figure 7.1 attempts to show how, when the three principles are catered for, pupils in the middle triangle will be fully included in the teaching and learning activities in your lesson.

Website

See other inclusion materials published by QCA in 'Useful websites' (2).

DIFFERENTIATING THE NEEDS OF ALL PUPILS

Trainee teachers in school will quite often have similar targets set by their mentors as they progress from one placement to the next. These may be:

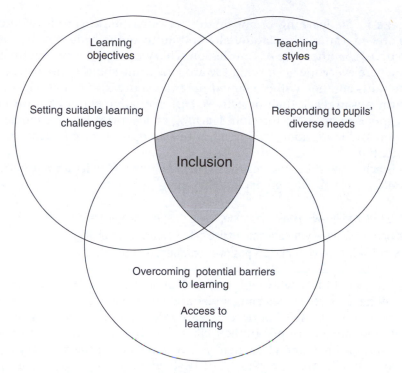

Figure 7.1 The three principles of inclusion

Include more differentiated approaches in your teaching.
Provide activities to stretch the more able pupils in your class.

These targets are closely linked to standards Q10 and Q19.

Q10 Have a knowledge and understanding of a range of teaching, learning and behaviour management strategies and know how to use and adapt them, including how to personalise learning and provide opportunities for all learners to achieve their potential.

Q19 Know how to make effective personalised provision for those they teach, including those for whom English is an additional language or who have special educational needs or disabilities, and how to take practical account of diversity and promote equality and inclusion in their teaching. (TDA, 2007c: 10)

Possibly these targets arise quite frequently because there is an assumption that when classes are set into ability groups then differentiation is not necessary. You will quickly discover how wrong this assumption is: one size does not fit all.

We need to realize that pupils are individuals and come with a range of interests, background knowledge and varying motivation in their readiness to engage in the learning opportunities on offer. Starting from where the pupils are, educationally, emotionally and motivationally, is very important to the success or otherwise of your lesson. This way teachers can set up classrooms where everyone is working towards the same subject knowledge base and life skills but they will be using different resources, stimulation, support and pathways to reach their objectives. Differentiation should be concerned with responding to these different learning styles, prior knowledge, ability, aspiration and motivation, giving all pupils an opportunity to achieve their full potential.

This is echoed within the aims for the new National Curriculum in 2008, that we should enable all young people to become:

- *successful learners* who enjoy learning, make progress and achieve
- *confident individuals* who are able to live safe, healthy and fulfilling lives
- *responsible citizens* who make a positive contribution to society. (QCA, 2008)

Pupils are individuals who will approach their learning in different ways. Some will have preferred learning styles and get their motivation for learning in a variety of ways. Teachers need to provide a range of teaching styles to motivate the range of pupils in their class. Children learn in different ways, as we mentioned in Chapter 5 when we covered some of the aspects of learning theory. Pupils are likely to learn best when a range of teaching and learning approaches are on offer. Ideally the teaching should be tailored to suit the needs of the range of individuals in your class. This is to ensure some of those barriers to learning are removed and that all pupils are given the opportunity to achieve.

Other barriers to learning also need to be removed in your planning stage, for example, the physical access to laboratories and equipment, or physical access to resources and teaching aids for sight- or hearing-impaired pupils. Barriers to literacy should be addressed by making sure all texts on offer are appropriate for the pupils who are accessing these materials so we do not exclude pupils from accessing science communication in written or spoken word.

Point for reflection

Reflect on how much your differentiation has improved since the start of your teaching career. Consider the strategies you have used to cater for certain groups and individuals. Can you see any change or improvement in pupils' attainment and/or behaviour in lessons where you have implemented effective differentiation?

Support and encouragement are key – all pupils need to feel they are valued and that they can ask questions in an environment where they feel comfortable to take risks and to have a go at giving their opinion. Remember that every time a child either asks a question of their own, or responds to one of yours, they are taking the risk (which can feel very substantial to them) that they will make themselves appear foolish, or that they will simply draw attention to themselves. At all times they need encouragement to aim to achieve to the best of their ability. Encourage pupils to develop a constructivist approach to learning as discussed in more detail in Chapter 5, because this helps pupils to build on their previous knowledge and to take responsibility for their own learning.

Support for pupils can be through structured frameworks or templates to aid learning. Scaffold frameworks in worksheets can give pupils support for each step in their learning. To fully engage with constructivist learning as suggested by Piaget, pupils need to be taught how to speak, listen and develop discussion. The Vygotsky social constructivist approach is important for them to learn to discuss and so develop their ideas and never be made to feel uncomfortable. A nice idea for investigation work is to suggest that 'there are no wrong answers in my science lessons, only ideas to be discussed and built upon'. A key to unlocking the adventure and wonder of science to all young people is in providing a purpose for their learning. It is important to make science relate to pupils' own lives in a way that will make them curious and eager to find out more.

STRATEGIES FOR DIFFERENTIATION

The key to the differentiated curriculum is the flexible use by teachers of a wide range of activities, resources and lesson organization. First it is important to think, who is this for, why do we need to differentiate and will this benefit the pupil(s) for this particular task?

How do we differentiate?

Within the National Curriculum, as teachers we are required to consider these three principles:

- differentiation by classroom organization – a way of helping pupils to access knowledge, increase understanding, develop concepts and practise skills
- differentiation by paired task – a way of helping pupils to self-assess, peer assess, target-set and practise skills to reach targets
- differentiation by outcome – a way of both accessing knowledge and experiences and assessing at the end of the teach-and-practice cycle.

The DCSF suggests the following categories of differentiation in their publications:

- *by task*: setting different tasks for pupils of different ability
- *by outcome*: setting open-ended tasks, allowing pupil response at different levels
- *by support*: giving more help (perhaps via an LSA) to certain pupils within the group.

Points for reflection

Points for reflection

Think about differentiating the following sets of learning objectives for a mixed-ability Year 7 class.
    Children should learn:

- that there are luminous and non-luminous objects
- that the Sun is a light source, but the Moon and Earth are seen by reflected light.

Children should learn:

- that different habitats have different features
- that different habitats support different organisms
- that the distribution of organisms in different habitats is affected by environmental factors, for example, light, nutrients or water availability.

Children should learn:

- that distillation can be used to separate a liquid from the solids which are dissolved in it
- that distillation is a process in which evaporation of a liquid is followed by condensation.

Think about:

- Which would be the most effective method?
- Which would be the most difficult for you in terms of resources?
- Which is the easiest to offer in lessons? Is this really the best to allow all pupils to achieve their full potential in your lesson?

WORKING WITH SUPPORT ASSISTANTS IN THE CLASSROOM AND THE LABORATORY

In school you will find there are other adults who may be in your classroom/laboratory. It is important that you find out who these people are and what they can realistically be expected to do in your class.

The roles of teaching assistants and learning support assistants have changed over the past few years. In November 2001 the Secretary of State for Education and Skills put forward the vision of the future that 'Classrooms will be rich in the number of trained adults available to support learning to new high standards. Pupils will benefit in the classroom through the help of teachers, teaching assistants and ICT technicians' (Morris, 2001).

Website

Certainly the number and range of support staff working in schools has increased over recent years. It can be seen that TAs are predominantly helping schools to run smoothly and efficiently, helping to raise educational standards, and providing support for teachers.

Evidence of this can be seen at www.tda.gov.uk/remodelling/national agreement/resources.aspx ('Useful websites' (3)).

Below is an extract from a case study of a school which has been identified as working more effectively with support staff.

Wyndham School in Newcastle has seen dramatic improvements in its results and in staff morale since it started making better use of its support staff. This is summed up by one of the school's parents: 'If the school had been the same as it was in 2001, I wouldn't have wanted my child to go there — now I wouldn't want them to go anywhere else.'

The school began remodeling its staff structure in 2001, following a poor Ofsted report and falling rolls. Results have improved steadily. In 2004, the Key Stage 2 results were above the national average in English, with a value added score among the highest in the country. More and more parents are now choosing to send their children to the school.

Support staff have been instrumental in the school's progress. They meet every fortnight with the head teacher to discuss what is happening in the school, looking at practical aspects, and examining any difficulties between teaching and non-teaching staff. This allows the school to be run much more effectively as any problems are ironed out and teachers can then concentrate on teaching.

Dame Pat Collarbone, Director of the National Remodelling Team, believes that 'Successful remodelling embeds a positive, ambitious and inclusive culture in schools that enables everyone to play a part in driving change forward. The contribution of support staff to Wyndham School's improvement is testament to this.' www.stat-athens.aueb.gr/-jpan/chapter8.pdf p.8.

The Office for Standards in Education (2002) have made comments that inspections have shown how well-trained teaching assistants are a key resource and are used very effectively in many primary schools. In schools that were judged to be good or very good teachers explain very carefully to classroom assistants and volunteer adults what they are expected to do. They also felt that the TAs provided invaluable support for pupils with language or speech barriers. There was evidence of the joint work between speech therapists, teachers and learning support assistants providing an excellent quality of support for pupils.

Point for reflection

Who are the support staff that you have observed in school?
What are their roles in school?
Who do they support?

The support staff that you see in your school may be employees of the school or the local authority or they may be volunteers (for example, parents, or volunteers from a local organization with specific roles to work with young people). Support staff can be titled classroom assistant, learning support assistant, special needs assistant, information communication support assistant, language assistant, bilingual support assistant, learning mentor, special schools assistant, to name a few. It is important for you to find out about the people you are working with, and to establish the expectations for these people in terms of work that they are able (and expected) to undertake.

Higher level teaching assistants (HLTAs) work in the school alongside the teacher, providing valuable support for teaching and learning activities. They can work across the curriculum or act as a specialist assistant for a specific subject or department. They can help to plan lessons and develop support materials and take the lead in lessons.

Website

The role of support staff in schools is shown in 'Useful websites' (4).

As you have seen, the term support staff covers a large range of people, and you are likely to be in contact with quite a number of them. The fine detail of their role will depend on their status and job title, but in the main they are there to provide support for pupils, teachers, the whole school and the curriculum.

The support for pupils in lessons can be the key to unlocking pupil motivation, understanding and ability to be included (particularly where bilingual support is needed). The support assistants can be supervising and assisting small groups within the main classroom or taking them to another location. They work with the pupils with special educational needs (SEN). They can help pupils to develop their social skills and can provide pastoral care – the support staff often being first point of contact for parents. In addition they may be first-aid qualified. One way they raise pupil confidence is by showing an interest in the pupils they work with who may otherwise be overshadowed in a large class.

Science departments will also have one or more technicians, and the school may also have technicians for ICT. These are the specialists who are there to support teachers in the preparation of resources and with technical know-how.

Support assistants are invaluable in spotting early signs of disruption that the class teacher may not have picked up on from the other side of the classroom. They can help to keep pupils on task – sometimes just the presence of another adult can bring children back to the matter in hand. The support in class can help with inclusion of pupils in a variety of ways. Support assistants can help in the preparation of classroom materials or delivery of specific parts of the lesson.

After the lesson the support staff can provide important feedback to the teacher in a number of ways. They can comment on specific pupil progress if they have been working with small groups of pupils or on a one-to-one basis. They can feed into assessment records of these pupils, thus helping to provide evaluation for the lesson as a whole or for the tasks within the lesson. They can also support teachers with some of the routine administration tasks.

For the whole school, where support staff are fully valued and built into the school structure, they can help to implement the behaviour policies within the school. They will model good practice, and they will be responsible for some of the liaison with parents. In addition they will have responsibility for liaison with outside agencies for the benefit and welfare of pupils in their charge.

Point for reflection

What do we need to do to ensure we are working effectively with TAs? Things you should consider:

- questions to ask the class teacher
- general issues to be aware of/consider
- practical things you can do to ensure an **effective working relationship** with the TA.

Point for reflection

The role of teaching assistants is in enabling pupils to access the learning on offer

The TAs can provide individual support for pupils within a lesson as they navigate through the science curriculum. Teaching assistants can be asked to work with small groups of gifted and able, pupils with English as an additional language, special needs, physical, motor skills, behavioural problems or pupils with lower abilities.

Key points for working with TAs

Where possible discuss your lesson plans in advance with TAs and let them help you plan the lesson. Do they feel comfortable to take the lead with small groups of gifted and able pupils or would they prefer to work with the less able pupils? If you are asking them to help with specific worksheets, remember to give them a master copy of the required answers in advance.

When you have the luxury of another adult, be sure to use him or her to best effect – make sure that his or her presence in your class enhances the teaching and learning taking place. Where TAs are subject-specific it may be that they would feel comfortable to team-teach with you, or deliver a part of the lesson while you work with individuals.

Communication is vital in involving a TA before the lesson and collecting evaluative comments after the lesson. Differentiation is the responsibility of the teacher but using a TA to best effect by making him or her a partner in the planning process will benefit the whole class.

The support provided to individuals needs careful monitoring: pupils who become too dependent on the TA will never become fully independent learners. The support should be staged so that pupils are given sufficient support to achieve but not so much that they can relax and let someone else do the work. The TA will get to know the pupil and be able to pick up on their level of understanding of a particular topic. Working with the teacher they can further develop resources for individuals. In some instances pupils reject their TA and feel they do not want to be singled out with an adult helper always with them. This can be defused if the TA works in the class with other groups and you the teacher work with the target pupil occasionally. Developing from this, careful thought should be put into pupil grouping as this can have a very disruptive effect on the class if not handled effectively. The importance of effective communication with TAs for lesson preparation, planning, delivery, assessment and evaluation cannot be overlooked. The effective working partnership of teachers and TAs really can enhance the teaching and thus the learning taking place in lessons, and have an overarching effect on whole-school ethos.

What the research says

What works well for the more able pupils keeping them motivated and challenged? www.nfer.ac.uk/research-areas/pims-data/summaries/lgt-what-works-for-gifted-and-talented-pupils-a-review-of-recent-research.cfm will help you to start thinking further about some key areas: why we need to identify the more able pupils and the problem of gaining a consensus in identifying these pupils. Differentiation is the key to all mixed-ability teaching, and enrichment is an important area for the more able in our classes. Enrichment will allow pupils to demonstrate their potential through creativity and imagination.

Can we praise too much? www.education-world.com/a_curr/curr302.shtml has an article by Ellen R. Delisio. Continual praise of pupils can become meaningless and psychologists have suggested that high self-esteem does not necessarily mean pupils will strive to perform better. The emphasis should be on *individual* needs, and building on pupil strengths by targeting and encouraging them in areas of personal interest and potential.

Further reading

Department for Education and Skills (DfES) (2005) *Higher Standards, Better Schools for All: More Choice for Parents and Pupils.* Norwich: HMSO.
This government White Paper includes information about the roles of professionals within the school workforce, and includes the following headings:

- The Challenge to Reform
- A School System Shaped by Parents
- Choice and Access for All, Personalised Learning
- Parents Driving Improvement
- Supporting Children and Parents
- School Discipline
- The School Workforce and School Leadership
- A New Role for Local Authorities
- Resource and Legislative Implications.

Drake, P., Jacklin, A., Robinson, C. and Therp, J. (2003) *Becoming a Teaching Assistant: A Guide for Teaching Assistants and Those Working with Them.* London: Sage.
More advice for working with other professionals in the classroom.

Maag, J. (2004) *Behaviour Management from Theoretical Implications to Practical Applications.* 2nd edn. Belmont, CA: Thomson & Wadsworth.
Tips for behaviour management

Marvin, C. (2003) *Access to Science: Curriculum Planning and Practical Activities for Pupils with Learning Difficulties.* London: David Fulton.
This book looks at the importance of science for pupils with learning difficulties, suggesting some practical planning approaches.

Watkinson, A. (2008) *The Essential Guide for Higher-Level Teaching Assistants.* London: David Fulton.

This book is a guide for HLTAs, guiding them through the teaching, learning and planning processes from their point of view. This gives a useful insight for the teacher on how to work most effectively with TAs to enhance pupil learning.

Useful websites

Live links to these websites can be found on the companion website www.sagepub.co.uk/secondary

(1) The Every Child Matters home page is at www.everychildmatters.gov.uk/aims/outcomes/
(2) Further inclusion materials can be found at www.nc.uk.net/nc_resources/html/inclusion.shtml
(3) This TDA site has case studies relating to remodelling – go the work force in schools: www.tda.gov.uk/remodelling/nationalagreement/resources.aspx
(4) This website shows a video describing the role of TAs in secondary schools: www.teachers.tv/video/3101

Further useful websites:

Inclusion guidance from QCA

Guidance on teaching pupils with learning difficulties:
www.nc.uk.net/ld/

Guidance on teaching the gifted and talented:
www.nc.uk.net/gt/

Disapplication of National Curriculum subjects at Key Stage 4:
www.qca.org.uk/14–19/6th-form-schools/s3–4-disapplication.htm

Respect for all: challenging racism and valuing diversity through the curriculum:
www.qca.org.uk/ages3–14/inclusion/301.html

8 TEACHING DIFFERENT AGES: KEY STAGE 3 TO POST-16

Judith Thomas

At the end of this chapter you will be able to:

- address some of the transition challenges of teaching across the key stages
- compare how schools approach the transition between the key stages
- guide pupils as to the range of post-16 and vocational science opportunities
- plan lessons to motivate pupils across the age range and key stages.

ACCOUNTING FOR AGE

What are the key differences when teaching pupils of different ages? Having had some experience over the years of working with students in science from Year 4 up to mature students I would argue that the group dynamics are very similar whatever the age range. Mature students still forget their homework or need chasing to hand in the coursework on time – does this ring any bells? When planning for any age range the mechanism for the planning cycle – teaching, learning, assessment and evaluation – is similar. This is the mechanistic part of teaching: the work which you need to do in order to plan and structure your lesson. However, there is a need to be flexible, to be creative and to dare to step out of the plan as the need arises to ensure that learning for all in your classroom is taking place.

Point for reflection

So what are the key differences between the different age ranges?

Key factors when teaching different age ranges include the level at which the subject will be delivered and the level of prior learning within subject areas. The level of communication and study skills (including how well pupils are able to work alone and interact with their peers) will be related to age and ability.

How can we bring imagination and enthusiasm into the classroom for all age ranges? When we reflect back to how pupils learn are we catering for their needs in the way we teach within the different key stages? Is there a danger of 'teaching to test'? This is how teachers are accountable – by the results produced. Can we be sure pupils have an understanding of science concepts, that common misconceptions have been challenged successfully and pupils are not just repeating facts from the lessons?

It is very important to remember that becoming a teacher is not completed with the recommendation for QTS – this is merely the beginning of a the learning process to become an expert teacher. Out in the classroom the unpredictable nature of teaching comes into play and the pupils arrive with a range of capability, ambition, motivation and attitude. The way teachers engage pupils in learning varies greatly. There is no magic formula to apply to make a good teacher or to measure what makes a good teacher – this cannot be put into a framework and measured.

Teaching is in some ways a science when we think of the preparation which must go into lessons, but it is also very much an art (Reeves, 2004) in the creativity and the diversity which must be applied to engage pupils.

Test results cannot always relay the full picture of an effective teacher. It is all the extra immeasurable things you will do that matter, which will show how you engage and motivate your pupils, whatever their age. This will be evident not necessarily in test scores but in the delight of seeing a pupil understand for the first time as 'the penny drops' and they achieve their goal. There will also be the times, again not measurable in test scores, when a demotivated pupil engages with your lesson and becomes involved in discussion because they want to be involved and learn more in your lesson.

The National Strategy sets out four key principles for secondary teachers to consider:

- *Expectations*: establishing high expectations and setting challenging targets.
- *Progression*: strengthening the transition from Key Stage 2 to Key Stage 3 and ensuring progression in teaching and learning across Key Stage 3.
- *Engagement*: promoting approaches with teaching and learning that engage and motivate pupils.
- *Transformation*: strengthening teaching and learning through professional development and practical support. (DfES, 2002a)

The progression of pupils is key as they move through their education. Learning really should be embedded as a lifelong process, and you as the teacher are there to facilitate and encourage those enquiring minds to develop, so they learn to question, to observe and to challenge. Pupils need appropriate targets and challenges in order to develop their learning during their education and throughout their life.

Points for reflection

When observing the different age ranges reflect on the group dynamics. Do pupils/young adults behave in the same way? For example, when they are split into smaller working groups, what do you observe?

When we ask pupils to work in groups can they automatically do this effectively or is this a skill which needs to be developed throughout?

Points for reflection

CHALLENGES FOR PUPILS

Transition is the change from one state to another, it can be encountered on a daily basis between lessons in secondary pupils as they change rooms and teachers, and can often result in disruption. Transition between tasks in a lesson was discussed in Chapter 4. Then there is the yearly change of rooms, of the teachers for different subjects, and curriculum changes between the key stages. All of these transition points are important; however, there are key transition points within a pupil's secondary school life. The move from Key Stage 2 to Key Stage 3 transition point is a crucial step, since for most pupils there is a change of school environment and the impact is huge. Equally unsettling for some pupils can be the transition from Key Stage 3 to Key Stage 4 because of the choices of subjects they have to make. Then moving further along the age range, the choice of post-16 and vocational courses is vast, and crucially these choices may have significant impact on any further opportunity to higher education.

So transition may for many mean a change of environment, a new range of subjects, and a new way of learning and assessment. The social aspect of school life is key in all of these areas of change – friendship groups can be a time of stress whatever age.

Point for reflection

Think about your first day at university or the first day on teaching practice. What were your emotions? Could you understand and remember all the things you were told? When you go into a primary

Point for reflection

school on an observational placement, find out what the school does to help their Year 6 pupils prepare for 'big school'. In your secondary school, what are the induction arrangements for new Year 7 pupils? Are there parallels with your own experience?

Change management is important for pupils of all ages, so detailed planning on the part of the school and the individual teacher is important. In addition to friendships other worries for pupils include the workload, the structure of the day and the expectations of the teachers; all of these can impact on a pupil's successful journey through the education system.

The aim is for schools to assist in ensuring that pupils' transition from one stage to the next is as 'seamless' and constructive as possible. This should be the aim for the transition steps throughout school life whatever the age of the learner.

A school may deliver lessons to help pupils to manage their relationships and friends. 'The way students deal with their emotions has implications for their social and emotional wellness both in school and out of school, so teaching students how to understand and deal with their own emotions is an important topic for teachers to address' (Erlauer, 2003: 16).

DEALING WITH THE CHALLENGES

The challenges are basically to know where our pupils are coming from and where we need to take them on the journey through science education, and to provide them with an awareness of all the possible routes and journeys we can enable them to partake. Erlauer (2003) talks at length about the 'Seven Brain-Compatible Fundamentals':

- emotional wellness and safe environment
- the body, movement, and the brain
- relevant content and student choices
- time, time, and more time
- enrichment for the brain
- assessment and feedback
- collaboration.

You will notice the links here with the Every Child Matters (ECM) agenda (see also Chapter 2) as Erlauer discusses pupil emotions and how they are closely linked to learning and memory capability. Can stress inhibit learning? I think we can all relate to times when stress may have clouded our judgement or learning capability. If we are asked to recall a memory from science in school most people will remember 'the practical that went wrong' and the fun that caused, or the gruesomeness of the rat dissection. Erlauer (2003) talks about memory being linked to strong emotion: associations help memory and learning.

The key to good learning must then be to create that positive classroom environment with the positive emotions to encourage learning. In science the use of models is an excellent example. Instead of describing the function of a red blood cell, turn the red blood cell into a delivery and collection van taking useful materials and collecting up and getting rid of waste materials. Or the white blood cell to fight infection can be turned into a soldier with a sword to fight the infection. Pupils will relate to these images, gaining understanding and remembering functions or concepts, again making the content relevant and meaningful to the age of pupil you are teaching. You can engage pupils with their prior knowledge to make learning more meaningful. Allowing pupils to take part in the learning process by helping them to make decisions about what to investigate or what they want to learn related to the central concepts.

Pupils learning to work together is an important life skill – interaction with their peers, the teacher and other adults is important in building that safe classroom environment. Humans are social by nature and, therefore, being involved in discussion and debate must be built into lessons for all ages to enhance the learning process. When pupils are interacting they can learn to listen, observe reactions and body language and challenge views or ideas that they disagree with or cannot fully comprehend.

Involve pupils in the assessment process and share the criteria on which their work will be marked whether these are criteria set by examination boards or in class where teacher and pupils can set criteria. Make use of peer- and self-assessment and ensure feedback is prompt and constructive, with targets set to achieve next steps. This should be a part of all types of assessment.

Once you have a picture of the social and emotional background of the pupils, the main questions for any secondary teacher to consider the first time they meet a class is 'What do these pupils already know and understand?' and 'What skills do these young people possess to enable them to progress in their learning?'

For those Year 7 pupils, one of the challenges facing you as a secondary teacher is to know what these pupils have covered in previous key stages, and in what depth. The results in the national tests may show they have the vocabulary to answer the questions but do they have the understanding to apply this knowledge in a range of contexts? Secondary schools often have to plan for pupils from a wide range of feeder schools which will all have covered the National Curriculum but in a range of ways and to different depths. Science in primary school may be taught by teachers who themselves have little confidence in science, while in other schools a science specialist is brought in to teach it, so the range and depth of teaching may vary significantly between schools.

ENCOURAGING PROGRESSION AND CONTINUITY

The key words continuity and progression have prevailed since the intro-duction of the National Curriculum which, it was said 'will also help children's progression within and between primary and secondary educa-tion and will secure the continuity and coherence which is all too often lacking in what they are taught' (DES, 1987: 49).

Continuity is a process in which all involved share the same views on aims and objectives, curriculum content, delivery, methods of assessment and recording (Keogh and Naylor, 2006). Pupils need to show progression through a specific set of targets and levels, so teachers carefully monitor pupil progress. It is sometimes forgotten in the pressure of performance and league tables that we are dealing with individuals who will develop and progress at different rates. It is important to prepare for pupils' tran-sition in order to enable progression, and to reflect on the prior learning and knowledge of pupils before planning schemes of work or lessons is crucial. It has often been felt by teachers in primary schools that their achievements were not recognized, that the secondary schools did not take into account the progress pupils had made previously. The National Strategy set out to make improvements in this area, for example, by encouraging cross-phase teaching and observing – primary teachers would visit secondary lessons, and secondary teachers would visit their primary feeder schools.

When pupils move from Key Stage 2 to Key Stage 3 they will suddenly have new teachers, new classmates, a different and usually much larger school building, a change of teaching style (and a range of styles) and a new struc-ture to the school day. These changes need to be managed, as has previously been mentioned, to keep pupil stress and worry levels to a minimum to ensure they are offered the best chances to settle in and achieve to their poten-tial in the new school.

This will also apply to the post-16 transitions where pupils move to new institutions. There will be higher expectations of pupils to take responsibility for their own learning and time management. Again the further education and sixth form colleges need to take these factors into consideration to ensure a positive learning environment is created for these students.

CHALLENGES FOR TEACHERS

Teachers will have many new faces to recognize and names to learn. The school and staff will need time to get to know the pupils as individuals. Staff will need to know the range of pupil ability and prior knowledge to allow time to get to know the capabilities, attitudes and learning styles for new classes. This can happen between any key stages and sometimes, in science, during the year if timetables for year groups are planned so the groups are to be taught by subject specialists.

Problems can arise in science where pupils receive different messages about the science they are being taught, and discontinuity between years can have an impact on pupils' progression and achievement. This is most noticeable in the leap from Key Stage 2 to Key Stage 3. This perceived dip could be attributed to lack of continuity for pupils in that the work they have already done can be disregarded and they start the topic over again. This can obviously lead to repetition, pupil boredom and possible disengagement with the learning process.

Transfer related activities

- Improving communication, in particular test results and pupil achievement.
- Summer schools for pupils at risk.
- Joint primary–secondary projects in the term(s) before transfer.
- Regular communication and interaction between the secondary and primary feeder schools, observation of teaching, shared teaching, offer of specialist teaching.

Secondary schools have to plan for pupils from a wide range of feeder schools. It is important the teachers from the secondary and primary schools communicate to look at the expectations of these pupils as they progress. The teachers can work together in the time prior to transfer to help pupils to manage their own learning.

Points for reflection

How can science teachers play a key role in preparing pupils for the move to Key Stage 3?

Devise some activities which youngsters will be able to carry over from Year 6 into Year 7. What are the implications for resources?

Transition can be organized at any level, from whole-school down to individual teacher impact. The exchange of information is key between school and between year groups. It is essential for teachers to record and monitor pupil progress and effort methodically so they can pass the information on to others. This can also include the exchange of materials and schemes of work so teachers can see exactly what these young people have already studied and to what depth. This may incorporate the use of bridging projects where teachers work together to deliver a topic in the primary school post-SATs and then the work is continued at the start of Year 7. This is a good way of sharing curriculum and teaching and learning styles, helping teachers and pupils adapt to the range of teaching and learning that takes place.

Examples of bridging projects:

- Year 6 pupils visit secondary school for taster sessions
- Year 7 teachers visit primary school to meet the pupils they will be teaching
- Topics in science are carried through from Year 6 to Year 7.

These projects are often facilitated by the local authority through funding.

It is also important that pupils are prepared for upheaval, for the changes they may encounter and the expectations of them as they progress, to further prepare pupils to think about their own learning pathways and their targets for learning.

Gray and Ruddock (2003) suggested that two out of every five pupils fail to make expected progress during the year after transfer. In part, this is because pupils have a less positive attitude towards school in Year 7 and some suggestion of less engagement in lessons, particularly among boys. They made further suggestions that progress was reduced in particular groups, for example, boys in English and girls in mental mathematics, in addition to a lower rate of progress in pupils with special needs or where English was not their first language and for pupils in receipt of free school meals.

It is essential that schools should make sure that pupil progression and curriculum continuity are in place as pupils move across the phases.

The Primary model within the Secondary sector

Making the leap between Key Stages 2 and 3 has been seen as an area for improvement for a number of years. Year 6 pupils are at the pinnacle of their primary years – the oldest in the school – and often have some responsibility as monitors or prefects. Once their secondary school has been confirmed, they will be moving to new schools to become the youngest members of a 'big' new school, probably without the responsibilities they have learned to use.

Ruth Sutton's (2001) research paper 'Primary to Secondary – overcoming the muddle in the middle' challenges common practice in many secondary schools where priorities are often set by the need to meet performance targets at GCSE and A level – the most experienced teachers are often timetabled to teach the older pupils and the top sets for GCSE. This might leave the most inexperienced or ineffective teachers to be timetabled to teach the new Year 7 intake. Sutton also found that some secondary teachers continue to believe that Year 7 pupils need a 'fresh start'. This is fine for behavioural and social issues but can be a disaster for pupil learning. During the summer break, children's retention of basic skills tends to erode. This is particularly true in mathematics and to a lesser extent in reading. Pupils will need enhanced reminders rather than re-teaching. This has meant some secondary teachers conclude that primary teachers have not taught the children very well and that now they will be taught 'properly'. Such attitudes only serve to erode professional respect and undermine trust in the previous teachers' assessments. This process occurs not only on transfer to secondary school but also between Key Stage 1 and Key Stage 2 and transfer to post-16 study.

Pupils in some secondary schools are now being taught using the 'primary' model: one teacher is responsible for delivering the core subjects and pupils only change teachers for certain subjects – for example PE, design and technology, modern foreign languages and, possibly, science. Schools and teachers are working together in many ways to smooth the transition for pupils as they progress throughout the education system.

It is important that you have a working knowledge of the science expectations in the key stages above and below the level you are teaching. This enables you to build on pupils' prior learning and to prepare them and guide them into higher levels of science education. You need a working knowledge of the post-16 options to be able to guide pupils to progress into higher-level science to meet their individual needs, having an awareness of the impact and development in the 14–19 agenda and the impact on science. These areas are still developing and changing, so keeping up to date is important. Try looking at the examination websites for AQA, OCR and Edexcel (see 'Useful websites'). Another area for further reading is the DCSF site, the 14–19 pages.

Three time elements dramatically affect when and how well students learn. Teachers can use the three time elements – time on task, time for understanding and consolidation, and the opportune learning time periods in a child's life in the classroom – to increase learning. Allow for thinking time, take account of pupils' ages, stages of development and interests. Find ways to enrich learning for all pupils, to make the lesson content relevant and interesting for them.

What the research says

Research has been carried out to consider why there is a perceived dip in pupil performance between primary and secondary. This has led to the development of a range of transition strategies – some cross-curricular within school and some science specific. These have had varying impact for pupils and this continues to be an area for development. This has been reviewed in Hargreaves (2002).

Further development continues as schools begin to develop the teaching of Year 7 through a primary model. Research into these areas will be developing.

Further reading

Hammond, P. (2007) *Creative Activities for Scientific Enquiry: Ages 7–11.* Leamington Spa: Scholastic.
This provides ideas to teach pupils about scientific enquiry skills through imaginative and creative science investigations. This will help you see the areas of science pupils may have covered at Key Stage 2.

Useful websites

Live links to these websites can be found on the companion website www.sagepub.co.uk/secondary

For the government's views on education in the 14–19 age range: www.dcsf.gov.uk/14–19.

Every Child Matters: www.everychildmatters.gov.uk/deliveringservices/commoncore/

The Standards site: www.standards.dfes.gov.uk/secondary/keystage3/

Transition document: www.teachernet.gov.uk/_doc/9591/Transition%20Report%20.pdf

Websites relating to 14–19 qualifications:

www.engineeringdiploma.com/pdf/14–19 DiplomaGatewayGuidance-webversion2.pdf

www.diplomainfo.org.uk for diploma examples of courses available in Lancashire

www.steps4me.co.uk/(X(f83a2d15-870d-4531-93e0-023e88c20203))/Subjects.aspx 14–19.

www.teachernet.gov.uk/teachingandlearning/14to19/

Examination boards:

AQA homepage: www.aqa.org.uk

OCR details on changes to the 14–19 curriculum: www.ocr.org.uk

Edexcel homepage: www.edexcel.org.uk/quals/hn/

Department for Children, Schools and Families: www.dfes.gov.uk/14-19/index.cfm?sid=1

9 SCIENCE TEACHING ISSUES: SCIENCE FOR ALL

Judith Thomas

This chapter discusses:

- the need for science for all – the importance to society of public understanding of science
- the need to plan lessons taking into account the needs of all pupils regardless of their ability, culture, religion, gender or motivation
- the importance of investigation/enquiry in the teaching of science
- the different types of enquiry that can be used in science lessons
- the importance of science and citizenship; how the investigations can and should be related to real life.

INTRODUCTION

Can you think back to your interview when you embarked on your teaching career – you applied to do a teaching course and were asked the inevitable question 'Why teach science?' So many times the responses to this question have been 'Because science is all around us and it is exciting' or 'It is important to have an understanding of science for everyday life.'

So why, then, when we ask our young people in school for their favourite subject do we so rarely hear science as a response? The pupils will go on to say 'Science is too hard' or 'It is boring – all we do is copy from books!'

Is the idea of 'science for all' a dream? It certainly should not be, and hopefully in this chapter you will begin to see why science is so important to our young people not only for the science knowledge, but also for the life process skills that can be gained through science study, thus enabling pupils to develop into adults who are able to take informed and responsible actions when engaging and reflecting upon different ideas, opinions and beliefs or values. They may be involved in investigating topical issues which could prove to have controversial findings where they need to make choices and convey this information to others.

The Wellcome Trust has produced materials and worked with schools for two main reasons: to ensure the scientists of the future are well informed, and 'to ensure that tomorrow's adults are scientifically literate enough to make informed decisions about the scientific and technological advances that will affect their own lives' (Wellcome Trust website, 2008; see 'Useful websites').

The new Key Stage 3 curriculum for science states the importance of science:

> The study of science fires pupils' curiosity about phenomena in the world around them and offers opportunities to find explanations. It engages learners at many levels, linking direct practical experience with scientific ideas. Experimentation and modelling are used to develop and evaluate explanations, encouraging critical and creative thought. Pupils learn how knowledge and understanding in science are rooted in evidence. They discover how scientific ideas contribute to techno-logical change – affecting industry, business and medicine and improving quality of life. They trace the development of science worldwide and recognise its cultural significance. They learn to question and discuss issues that may affect their own lives, the directions of societies and the future of the world. (QCA, 2008)

Within the wording here we can see the evidence of the input from research into public understanding and the development of the curriulum to make it relevant to pupils in their own lives in the skills and knowledge they will acquire.

PUBLIC UNDERSTANDING OF SCIENCE

The idea of science for all is not new; in 1985 the Royal Society declared, 'Science is for everybody'. The organization COPUS (Coalition on the Public Understanding of Science) and a journal entitled *Public Understanding of Science* were established in the early 1990s (Scanlon et al., 1999). These highlighted the importance of science education in society and had some influence over the compulsory education curricula. The thinking is that scientists and technolo-gists cannot operate without a knowledgeable supportive society (Scanlon et al., 1999). The curriculum content is important in providing courses that ful-fil certain criteria: the content should have a meaning in society and, for a majority of learners, should demonstrate usefulness. In addition, the curricu-lum should allow teachers to guide their learners to share in the wonder and excitement of science and to celebrate scientific achievement.

The purpose of school science education is twofold. First, there is a need for some young people to achieve science qualifications to enable them to progress along certain career pathways into the study of science at advanced levels, and into certain careers (for example, all primary teachers must now have an equivalent of GCSE science). Secondly, the purpose of science education, and, in our opinion, the more important purpose, should be to provide young people with a sound preparation for understanding science related to their own lives. The curriculum should provide an understanding of science relevant to individual needs, for example, health, diet, drugs awareness, fire hazard and electrical safety, in addition to providing opportunities for pupils to engage with social issues on a local, national or global scale. We hope to achieve this by developing an understanding of how the world in which we live can be sustained for the benefit of the present and future generations. Young people can engage with and debate environmental issues if they have some understanding of science processes.

The development of these science issues alongside the process skills involved with the study of science will further develop individual key skills. Thus enabling them to work in teams, to observe, to debate and evaluate phenomena. In addition they will be able to communicate findings verbally and in writing. They will in theory be better equipped to make informed decisions about science as it may impact on their lives. This being the case, we must ensure science teaching in schools is open to all pupils regardless of their gender, culture, ability or motivation. The public understanding of sustainable science is closely linked with the citizenship curriculum.

Point for reflection

Take a look at a newspaper for today – how many news items have links to science? Think how you could take one of these news items and incorporate it into your science teaching this week. Compare the approaches by different newspapers, and consider how accurately or well they report the issue.

Point for reflection

OPENING UP SCIENCE TO ALL PUPILS

Gender

Gender has been mentioned in Chapter 2 with a view to the Every Child Matters (ECM) agenda that all pupils should be offered the same opportunities. The view for planning science lessons is that we must positively plan to overcome any barriers due to gender. Lesson plans must show an awareness of stereotype that may cause bias in lessons. Look at the photography in textbooks, or examples that are used to illustrate a point. Rarely nowadays will you come across books with titles such as *Physics for Boys* but be aware of the traditional views of gender subjects and of the way we may respond differently to pupils – often subconsciously.

When planning for practical grouping in your laboratory be creative and experimental. Once you get to know the pupils do not just group them according to ability. Plan for groups that will enhance the learning and for the needs of the really timid pupils who do well with the theory but seem to be lacking in confidence in practical situations. In Chapter 5, the grouping of pupils in one of the sample video lessons was discussed by the teacher in his interview. Plan for mixed groups and pairs in some lessons: in others plan for single sex working groups.

Once divided into the practical group or 'team' give individuals within the team set roles. Give them a number, then for example with an acid and metals experiment the 'number ones' collect equipment (measuring cylinder, boiling tubes and rack, spatula) the 'number twos' collect and measure out the acid into each boiling tube, the 'number threes' collect and weigh out the metals and so on. Thus each member of the group is given a responsible job. Then everyone in the group has to make a results table, observe and record the findings. The group can discuss their findings and share these with another group in a 'snowballing'-type exercise leading to a whole-class plenary of findings from the day's practical investigation.

Planning your groups and the activity for individuals in a group will allow all pupils the opportunity to engage fully in the practical activity without feeling overshadowed by the more dominant characters always taking the lead, while not allowing pupils to just coast through lessons without really engaging.

Point for reflection

How can you prepare the pupils to work together as a team? Can you develop their speaking and listening skills during your science lesson?

Having observed challenge days run by SETPOINT at Liverpool Football Ground for mixed teams, all-girl teams and all-boy teams doing the same challenges on different days, it was easy to spot different behaviour patterns of pupils in the teams. These were pupils who had not met before teamed together from a range of schools. They quickly had to learn to work as a team. The pupils themselves divided the challenges. In the mixed teams mostly the boys made the go-carts, the girls made the shelter tent. In the mixed teaching groups the girls tended to opt for the smaller problem-solving challenges. With the girls or boys only teams, they were quite happy to do all the tasks with enthusiasm. Take care in science teaching to avoid gender bias. There are initiatives to tap into to encourage girls into science and engineering, for example, WISE (Women into Science, Engineering and Construction).

What does the research say?

Go to the WISE website, and follow the topical links on the page. For example, they have run a theme exploring myths in science education:

Myth: Trying to interest older girls in science runs the risk of turning off the boys.

Reality: Changing the science lesson to interest the girls also increases interest among the boys. (WISE website, 2008)

ENGLISH AS AN ADDITIONAL LANGUAGE/ LITERACY BARRIERS

Catering for pupils who have English as an additional language can be a real challenge when pupils are completely non-English speaking. The employment of teaching assistants who are able to speak the pupils' language is most beneficial. The TA can ensure the pupil understands what is going on in the lesson by helping to translate written and verbal instruction.

There is also an opportunity to 'buddy up' pupils with other pupils within the class who speak the same language and who have a better command of English.

Website

See Multiverse in 'Useful websites' at the end of this chapter.

Pupils with English as their second language will have reading and writing difficulties that will slow their progress in science. This applies equally to pupils with a low reading age who may be very adept at discussing the science verbally but are considerably disadvantaged when reading and writing becomes part of the lesson. Within the National Strategy training unit on science and literacy there are some useful suggestions to enhance your science lessons for pupils struggling with literacy. Some of the strategies suggested for pupils with difficulties apply also to pupils learning English as an additional language.

Science literacy can be confusing when we have everyday words with a new meaning in science; for example a cell can refer to a cell in the body or to a battery.

Website

Links to the video: in lesson 1 the development of thinking skills allowing pupils to develop their own ideas as a way of starting from their current understanding.

Point for reflection

Think of other everyday words that sound the same but mean something different in science. How would you ensure your pupils understood the science meaning in your lesson?

It is vital to introduce new vocabulary with care, ensuring all pupils in the class are visualizing the same meaning for this word. The starter activity described in video lesson 1 does exactly this by getting pupils to explain what the words mean to them. The teacher then teased out the use this word has in science. Make sure pupils are aware how to pronounce the word and write it down to learn the correct spelling.

When providing tasks where pupils have to read information from a text-book or worksheet it is important that you help all pupils to fully engage. Think carefully about what you want the pupils to get from the text: is it *meaningful* reading? Display the text on a projector, then overlay the text with a clear over-head transparency sheet and highlight the key areas that you want pupils to focus on. These may be key words, diagrams or questions. Break the task into some sort of structured framework; do not just say, 'Now, Year 7, read page nine and answer the questions.' Some of those pupils may not be fully able to read and access the information.

Point for reflection

How important is it to overcome the literacy barriers to enable effective science learning to take place? Find a worksheet, or a passage in a text-book, and adapt the language to make it more accessible to a younger age group.

PUPIL ABILITY

Planning for suitable lesson objectives appropriate for the range of ability is the key to a successful lesson. In planning and teaching the National Curriculum (NC), teachers are required to consider these three principles of differentiation.

- *Differentiation by classroom organization* is a way of helping pupils to access knowledge, increasing understanding, develop concepts and practice skills.
- *Differentiation by paired task* is a way of helping pupils to self-assess, peer assess, target-set and practise skills to reach targets.
- *Differentiation by outcome* is a way of both accessing knowledge and experiences and assessing at the end of the teaching and practice cycle.

The key to the differentiated curriculum is the flexible use by teachers of a wide range of activities and lesson organization. Pupils have a wide range of needs and preferred learning styles. You need to be aware of the ability and special requirements for all pupils.

Differentiation is contained in the National Curriculum statement of inclusion, and the first of these concerns setting suitable learning challenges (curriculum.qca.org.uk). Differention in the planning can be recognized in the graduated learning outcomes which may say 'All pupils will … /Most pupils will … /Some pupils will …'. One of the key dangers here is that some pupils may say 'Why should I do more work when you are only expecting some pupils to complete a fraction of the work you are expecting from me?' This can also be the case with differentiated worksheets or tasks if pupils feel they are being unfairly treated in the workload that is expected from them.

Where personalized learning and individual targets are set and shared with pupils, then the outcomes of the above differentiated outcomes may be different. If pupils are familiar with the use of peer and self-assessment and with the setting and sharing of targets they will take greater ownership for their own learning. Sharing targets with pupils enables them to see how they can progress through the levels to increase their grades. The use of a passport in some schools enables pupils and staff to monitor pupil progression throughout the year and in the next year or key stage. 'The personalised classroom does not entail having 30 separate teaching plans; it is about having one strong inclusive plan which allows as much room as possible for individual engagement, targeted support, a degree of choice and respect for the range of abilities and interests in the class' (DCSF, 2007).

Recent work suggests that:

- much differentiation should be done in medium-term planning sessions, looking six to eight weeks ahead, when specialists such as educational psychologists and speech and

language therapists can be timetabled to provide advice and work with the special educational needs co-ordinator (SENCO) and/or specialist teachers;
* sharing of differentiated plans, within and between schools, saves time.

Point for reflection

When you have observed lessons how many strategies for differentiation were you able to observe? Which was the most effective and preferred by pupils?

CULTURE/RELIGION

It is important that lessons are developed that will include all pupils in your class, and that examples given try to reflect the range of cultures and religion within your school and the UK. For example, when talking about diet look up the traditional meals for different cultures within the UK and from around the world. There are key links to citizenship that can be developed here: the diet and availability of food, investigations into local trade (can you buy locally produced goods?) and investigation into world trade and the farming industry (is it sustainable?). Are we overusing fertilizers and pesticides, and what is their impact on the environment? Link the science you are talking about to the local, national and international environment to connect pupil knowledge with background where possible. Look at how other countries use science and technology to build on pupils' prior knowledge and increase their general knowledge of their local environment and the wider impact we have on the world.

Point for reflection

Review the new National Curriculum and suggested links to citizenship. Is this really the role of a science teacher or would it be more beneficial for citizenship to be taught by an expert in citizenship?

PUPIL MOTIVATION: PEER PRESSURE

We have already read in previous chapters how people learn in different ways, and how initially people have to be motivated to begin to want to learn.

There are three key attitudes to lifelong learning: curiosity, confidence and scepticism (Massey, 1999: 58). Curiosity can be defined as a desire to know more about how things work and what they are made from. Building on this curiosity, people need to feel confident in their own ability to succeed – often measured in tests but also in the personal achievement of understanding a topic. Teachers and peers play a key role in confidence-building – too often able learners who lack confidence will become disaffected. Finally, there is a need for scepticism, an ability to differentiate meanings, not to take all ideas at face value but discover the alternative meanings.

IMPORTANCE OF INVESTIGATION/ENQUIRY IN THE TEACHING OF SCIENCE

Historically, science learning has been about hands-on practical work. It is seen as an enjoyable and effective form of learning. Hodson (1998) quotes Nerissian (1989) as saying: 'Hands-on science is at the heart of good learning.' However, in reality the practical science in many schools is often not enjoyable for pupils or teachers, and neither is it effective in improving learning. Dare we say practical work is often done just for the sake of doing practical work. Pupils follow a list of instructions, and investigations are carried out for examinable coursework. The objectives are to complete the investigation for the examination rather than thinking about why exactly pupils are carrying out investigations.

So what are the real benefits of doing practical work? If we leave aside the examination culture, practical work is important for the motivational aspect. If used well, pupil interest and curiosity in a topic can be raised. In all educational situations much depends on the learner and his or her desire to learn. It is important to strive to raise the curiosity of pupils, so they have a desire to want to know more and to try things in a different way.

In science we strive for the pupils to start asking 'what if?', to be actively involved in the learning process not just the 'hands on' but to have a 'minds on' approach (Wellington, 2000). If pupils are thinking, discussing and doing, then their minds will be actively involved. Their recall of information and understanding will be aided by the active approach: if they have had to work out and do for themselves their brains will have made those new neurone connections described by Greenfield (2004). This is the justification for the constructivist approach as discussed in Chapter 5.

When teaching science in schools many teachers will be asked at the start of a lesson 'Is it practical today?' Unfortunately pupils will often say that they are not allowed to do any practical work: 'We are bottom set and it is not safe!' Pupil behaviour is an important factor and will impact on the amount of practical in lessons.

Science is not and should not be just about learning the facts, it is about the process skills: learning to observe, measure, hypothesize, predict and evaluate the findings (Wellington, 2000). In addition, science is about communication, teamwork and self-discipline. It can be said the important part of science is what remains after the facts have been forgotten. When the science is put into a real-life context in a way which is very relevant to them, pupils will often see a purpose and engage more effectively with the learning.

Of course, facts will be forgotten, but there will be a comprehension and an ability to know how to investigate further as the need arises. This links back to the government ideal of public understanding of science: the 'informed citizens' (Gregory and Miller, 1998). Practical work in schools needs to be guided – pupils often fail to make connections between the 'recipes and instructions' they are following and the theory behind the practical. Practical activities can be daunting for the less confident individuals and a chance for doing nothing or having a bit of fun for others.

The management of practical lessons from a teacher's point of view is crucial for learning and for safety. If pupils are unclear about what is expected they will fail to engage with the work. In a class situation pupils are asked to work in groups so communication and teamwork is one of the first barriers.

There may be dominant figures that run the practical, giving others little or no chance to engage, because pupils all work at different rates. Would it be ideal for pupils to work individually? This, however, is not usually an option as resources are limited. Individual work is not ideal anyway, because the interaction between individuals is crucial in allowing pupils to 'bounce' ideas around which will enable them as individuals to begin to make sense of the information or process (Driver, 1994). There is the confidence aspect – some individuals are very wary of any practical within science. In practical work there are lots of things for pupils to take into consideration (how to set up the equipment, how and what to measure, the timing and sequences of procedures) in addition to being able to predict, hypothesize, measure, observe and, finally, evaluate the findings to link back to theory. All this can be very daunting.

Any practical work must promote interest and curiosity so pupils will engage fully with the task. The groups must be carefully planned and the outcomes from the lesson must be very clear to the pupils from the start. Calls for more authentic scientific practices in school are well documented (Brown et al., 1989), linking scientific approaches to the real world and showing how it influences so many consumers, engineers, judges and scientists, to name just a few.

INVESTIGATIONS AND ENQUIRY FOR SCIENCE LESSONS

Pupils will be able to pursue 'real' investigations with data collection to solve problems, for example the problem of reducing waste, recycling and sustainability. This type of problem-solving activity will help to develop a community for learners where the pupils will start to think about a serious matter (Brown, 2004). Waste management is potentially going to be a real problem in the future if we do not start to re-educate away from a throwaway culture to one of recycling and reduction of waste.

Here is an example of a learning activity we could develop and deliver over a substantial period of time: a problem will be set for the pupils aged 13/14 years leading to a long-term scientific investigation linking various areas of the National Curriculum and citizenship. The ideal time to start would be in the summer term after the national tests and it is something that can be further developed and continued with following year groups and with possibilities to include other year groups.

A problem could be set, with some background research and current reality presented by a guest speaker or an appropriate educational visit, in addition to book and internet research. The pupils can then begin to develop their own investigational ideas to investigate through practical activities. With the findings from these investigations, practical solutions and strategies can be further employed to solve the problem.

There are numerous examples of pupils bringing science in line with citizenship. Pupils are told that the council have decided to start charging the school by weight for all the rubbish that goes into the refuse lorry. The challenge for the pupils will be to investigate:

- what makes up the rubbish collected by the lorry
- how to reduce the amount of rubbish generated in the first place
- better ways to dispose of any waste.

The pupils will go away and begin to research into recycling (direct and indirect), waste management and initial reduction of waste. Visiting experts from the council, recycling and manufacturing industries will be invited to speak to the young people about what is already happening and what the problems are. Pupils will be given opportunities to ask questions and discuss with the experts (communications via email could be maintained with various outside agencies).

They will then begin to look at what rubbish the school produces, maybe survey to see if the packaging and so on could be removed so less waste is generated. The rubbish that is produced could be divided into:

- 'compostable' wastes (the pupils can investigate the conditions required for composting, which can be linked to carbon and nitrogen cycles, and/or they can set up different conditions to make a compost bin)
- metals (what are they, how can they be separated, what can we do with them?)
- plastics (different types, biodegradable or non-biodegradable, can the bottles be melted and remoulded, could they be shredded for another use or directly used for other things?)
- paper (can we recycle the paper, make our own paper, reuse it for pet bedding, or to make fuel pellets for open fires?)
- other toxic, or harmful waste.

The investigations would be developed with the guidance of the teacher, but each group would be working independently. From the findings it would be hoped that the pupils could develop some ideas to reduce the waste loads produced by the school and possibly develop some other community and environmental action at the same time – from setting up metal recycling collection points to collect money for the aluminium cans, to creation of composting bins, to separating the waste so it can be sent for recycling with the council. By helping to reduce the waste to landfill sites they are helping the environment. They can then present their conclusions and proposed actions to the rest of the school and begin to educate the wider community on the importance of waste management and recycling.

The whole package could help pupils to see how their science knowledge and practical skills can be applied in a very real situation, and that scientific practice is a complex and socially constructed activity (Hudson, 1998). They will see how the knowledge they have acquired through research and investigation can be used to make recommendations to help the school and the environment. The task would require them to work as teams, so communication is important. In addition, a methodical scientific approach would need to be developed so that they would reconstruct their ideas and understanding as they progressed through the research and as they collected results from the science investigations. This could be very much linked to National Curriculum citizenship and it is a real-life science investigation.

SCIENCE AND CITIZENSHIP

As stated on the National Curriculum website (see 'Useful websites'):

> Citizenship has a distinctive contribution to make to the aims of the National Curriculum. The citizenship programme of study provides opportunities to plan sequences of work, learning outcomes and teaching approaches that develop:
>
> **Successful learners** – Citizenship develops successful learners who are equipped to play a full part in public life and in the democratic process. Citizenship gives learners the ability to engage critically with challenging questions facing society today and to take action on political and social issues of concern.
>
> **Confident individuals** – A central purpose of citizenship is to develop understanding of the ways in which citizens can participate in decisions that shape the communities in which they live.
>
> **Responsible citizens** – Citizenship inspires pupils to think about their role in society and in the wider world, and about how their decisions and actions can make

a difference. Pupils engage with a wide range of political, social and ethical dilemmas that affect individuals, communities and the environment. (http://curriculum.qca.org.uk/key-stages-3-and-4/subjects/citizenship/keystage3/citizenship_and_the_national_curriculum_aims.aspx)

Practical work in science is important as long as it is seen to have a purpose, and by giving ownership to the pupils we help to engage more fully than if they were given strict instructions to follow. Citizenship and public understanding of science help to include pupils in debate and discussion, covering issues of science related to political, ethical and moral concern.

We must remember some of the issues we are looking at in science do not have any solutions as yet. There are issues that pupils will look at and discuss but as yet the government, politicians and research scientists do not have all the answers. Science enquiry is about developing thinking skills, being able to discuss and look at the different arguments put forward, not necessarily about finding the answers.

Here is a list of other examples of enquiry which could be developed and expanded along ambitious lines in the same way as the waste management project described above:

Acid rain.
Healthy diet.
What is organic food?
Hygiene, can we be kept too clean?
Biological washing powders.

DEVELOPING ENQUIRY

Think about:

- the relevance
- skills of observation and research
- discussion stimuli and importance in science learning.

The aim of science in school is to provide courses which will as far as possible carry out the almost impossible task of catering for pupils of all abilities and tastes – the disaffected pupils who we need to engage and inspire with interesting and exciting lessons; the pupils who want to pursue courses and careers involving science; the pupils who will use science in a practical context. This development is continued into the post-16 sector, as discussed in Chapter 8, to encourage more people to continue science to a higher level.

Every pupil is special in some way and these must all be included in the plan. Most of us have experienced those moments in our education when we have not felt at ease in our schooling, and we particularly need to consider those for whom this is an everyday occurrence.

What the research says

The take-up of science post-16 science is an important area of interest. The introduction of a wider range of post-16 science will, it is hoped, develop further interest in science beyond Key Stage 4. Key findings of the Royal Society research entitled 'Increasing uptake of science post-16' are that teachers make a difference which is dependent on their enthusiasm, involvement and subject content. There is a real need for strong specialist teaching, linked to strong teaching departments. Teachers need a wider experience to be able to attract more students post-16, but with a whole picture in mind. Further work could be done to look at what influences take-up of science and how can we make science more appealing.

This report of a conference held on Friday 10 March 2006 at the Royal Society, London, can be accessed at http://royalsociety.org/downloaddoc.asp?id=3352 (accessed September 2008).

Further reading

The government's Strategy for SEN produced by the Department for Education and Skills can be found in:

Department for Education and Skills (DfES) (2004c) *Removing Barriers to Achievement.* DfES publication 0117/2004. Nottingham: DfES. (Also available at the DfES website.)

Glass, S. (2007) *Prove it! Scientific Enquiry in Action.* Oxford: Heinemann.
This book helps to show how to carry out experiments and interpret the results.

www.healthlink.org.uk/PDFs/mkp_uptake.pdf
An example of research and how it is enhancing the research take-up through communication, networking and capacity development.

www.sciencecampaign.org.uk/
Here you can find information about CASE – a pressure group aiming to improve the scientific and engineering health of the UK. Our objective is to communicate to Parliament and the nation as a whole the economic and cultural importance of science and engineering, and the vital need for it's funding by government and industry. Some interesting discussion on suggestions for improving the take-up of science to level 3.

 *Useful websites*

Live links to these websites can be found on the companion website www.sagepub. co.uk/secondary

The National Science Foundation in the US lists some myths about girls and science on the Women into Science and Engineering (WISE) website: www.wisecampaign. org.uk/ (accessed July 2008)

Multiverse carries examples for helping pupils with EAL: www.multiverse.ac.uk/Browse2.aspx?anchorId=11941&selectedId=11941

Information about the citizenship content of the National Curriculum: http://curriculum.qca.org.uk/key-stages-3-and-4/subjects/citizenship/keystage3/citizenship_ and_the_national_curriculum_aims.aspx

For resources in this area, the Wellcome Trust homepage is at: www.wellcome.ac.uk/

10 CREATIVITY AND INNOVATION IN SCIENCE TEACHING AND LEARNING

Tony Liversidge

This chapter:

- discusses what creativity is and offers a rationale for why it is important
- outlines aspects of creative and innovative teaching and learning in science, including a creative curriculum framework, creative science classrooms and creative experimental work
- identifies some creative and innovative science activities and approaches, particularly:

  - using ICT
  - role play and drama
  - modelling
  - concept mapping
  - discussion
  - games.

An examination of the recent and current context of secondary science teaching indicates that it is likely you will be faced with an array of initiatives and innovations throughout your career. These may stem from such areas as government policies and local strategies or from school and department developmental plans and ideas. This has led to descriptions of initiative and innovation 'fatigue' occurring in science departments.

A key element of your response to this fatigue will be how positively you view it. On the one hand, you might view changes to the curriculum, the assessment demands and the greater administrative workload as causing an increasing pressure of work, which is having a negative affect on your ability to be creative and innovative. This is not an unreasonable point of view, and the government, other organizations such as the QCA and even school senior managers must take the blame for some of this.

On the other hand, you might view the changes in a more positive light and see this fluidity as an opportunity to add to, and develop, your own creative ideas. Providing new ways of doing things should be part of your teaching, particularly, in the view of Osborne and Freyberg (1985), to help your pupils to perceive the ideas of scientists as more intelligible, plausible and potentially useful to themselves than the ones that they presently hold. In my opinion, good recent opportunities for achieving this have been the potential for innovation at Key Stage 3 (KS3) through the National Strategy and the recent changes to the Key Stage 4 (KS4) national science curriculum. In addition, standing still is never an option for good science teachers and innovations and ideas should come from you, perhaps because of reflection on your lessons, or your teaching or the pupils' learning, or even some classroom-based research that you have undertaken, with the subsequent recognition that an aspect is in need of review and change. This is recognized in the standards for QTS, where, as part of your professional attributes, you need to demonstrate a creative and constructively critical approach towards innovation (TDA, 2007a).

The first part of this chapter discusses such creativity and innovation in science teaching by asking the questions 'What is creativity?' and 'Why is it important?', and you will be asked to reflect on your own creativity and how you might develop creativity in your pupils. It then goes on to identify some key elements of creative science teaching. The final part examines some innovative teaching and learning strategies, including investigations and innovative use of ICT, role play and concept mapping.

WHAT IS CREATIVITY AND WHY IS IT IMPORTANT?

What is creativity?

Being creative is an essential part of what makes us human and is possible in all areas of human activity. The history of science is one of continuous hypotheses and of re-evaluations of established ideas: of new insights or information, challenging and building on existing knowledge. The processes of scientific analysis and investigation can thus involve the highest levels of creativity and insight. This can be as true for the children that you teach as for experienced scientists.

Over the last few years, there has been an upsurge in interest in creativity and learning, but creativity can be notoriously difficult to define as the term has been used in different ways in different contexts. One of the most useful working definitions of creativity is given in the National Advisory Commitee in Creative and Cultural Education (NACCCE) report (1999: 50) *All Our Futures: Creativity, Culture and Education*, which states that creativity is 'imaginative activity fashioned so as to produce outcomes that are both original and of value.' Using this definition, the report recognizes four characteristics of creative processes. First, they always involve thinking or behaving imaginatively. Second, this imaginative activity is purposeful, that is, it is directed to achieving an objective. Third, these processes must generate something original. Fourth, the outcome must be of value in relation to the objective. Thus, if you were previously concerned that creative activity in your science lessons would involve a completely unstructured 'free-for-all' then the report should give you some reassurance!

Whatever your definition and thoughts about the associated characteristics of creative processes, your pupils will, at various times, either prompted or unsolicited, show creative characteristics. The QCA (2004) identifies five broad behaviours that pupils demonstrate when they are being creative:

1. Questioning and challenging.
2. Making connections and seeing relationships.
3. Envisaging what might be.
4. Exploring ideas, keeping options open.
5. Reflecting critically on ideas, actions and outcomes.

Additionally, Feasey (2005) gives some ideas from pupils on the characteristics of a creative person. A creative person is free thinking; daring; thinks of lots of ideas not just one; is always thinking of new things; reaches new heights; is encouraging and joyful and lets their imagination run wild.

Some regard these as characteristics that only certain pupils possess while others see all pupils as creative. In this latter context, Craft (in Craft et al., 2001) puts forward the notion of 'little c' creativity, which she contrasts with high creativity (the extraordinary creativity of the genius). She describes 'little c' creativity as a 'can do' attitude and as something that all of us can develop. Furthermore, if you equate Craft's 'can do' attitude to creative characteristics such as reflecting, questioning and exploring ideas and keeping options open, then I think that these are traits that you should be trying to develop in all your pupils.

Why is creativity important?

The *All Our Futures* report strongly argues that a national strategy for creative and cultural education is essential to help unlock potential and that creative practice in education will help you to teach the curriculum more imaginatively and develop creative skills in young people. Related to this there is a considerable body of evidence to show that engagement in creative activities can boost confidence and motivate young people to engage in learning by offering individuals the opportunity for self-expression and satisfaction.

Timperley and Robinson (2000) suggest that teachers may need to be helped to take a more creative approach to tackling the variety of demands placed on them. The reasoning behind this claim is that creativity mitigates the deadening effects of repetition and overload, and can serve as an outlet for teachers' personal and professional aspirations. Too much stress blunts teachers' creative powers and leads to conformity rather than innovation. Teachers then become entrenched in the mental rut of doing things in specific ways, which is inherently uncreative.

As Joubert (2001) creatively says, 'the only difference between a groove and a grave is the depth'!

However, you cannot be expected to be constantly innovative and creative. You may need to be convinced that the ability to be creative is within your reach and that with time and perseverance and commitment, the benefits to you and your pupils will justify the effort. Here you might be further persuaded by the fact that in studies such as those carried out by Woolnough (1994), having an inspirational and creative science teacher was not only the most influential factor determining a career choice in science, but also, for many who did not become scientists, a key determinant in their enjoyment and appreciation of science beyond school.

Points for reflection

- What does it mean to be innovative and creative in science?
- Does your school have a commitment to promoting creativity? How is this expressed or facilitated?
- Do you consider yourself creative in any part of your life? What is this creative part?
- Do you think that you are creative in your science teaching? What aspects do you consider creative?
- What are the skills, processes and abilities that pupils need to have in order to be creative in science?

CREATIVE AND INNOVATIVE TEACHING AND LEARNING

Fortunately, there are many creative science teachers and educationalists out there, and there is a wealth of ideas and suggestions available to you from a range of sources. As you might imagine, some of the suggestions cover broad themes such as classrooms, curriculum, teaching and learning and, in particular for science, experimental work. These are discussed in this section. More specific ideas about particular activities are given and discussed in the next section.

A creative science curriculum framework

Feasey (2006) reports that when teachers were asked the question, 'What do you think are the constraints for teaching and learning creatively in the classroom?' the majority of responses focused on:

- increase in paperwork linked to school inspection
- the high level of planning required
- feeling exhausted and unable to find the time and energy to be creative

- the amount of content in terms of curriculum coverage
- not enough time to allow pupils the opportunity to be creative in the classroom
- the concern that, if they taught creatively, it would jeopardize school results in national tests and school positions in performance tables.

Combine these constraints with the conflicting messages coming from the government and associated national bodies urging teachers to be more creative and innovative and you can see why there is a particular concern that science teaching is losing its vitality. However, she argues, we cannot let these responses excuse a lack of creativity in teaching and learning and, thus, a key question is how to maintain and improve standards in the established sense of achieving grades while at the same time developing a climate of creativity and innovation.

An important aspect is your school and departmental ethos. Your creativity and innovation and that of your pupils is more likely to be fostered in an environment where, for instance, pupils' scientific achievements and creativity are celebrated at every opportunity; where science work and artefacts are displayed in the department and around school; where visitors who have links to science, from industry, from universities, clinics and environmental agencies are invited into school and where pupils, staff, parents and visiting scientists are involved in science days, weeks, fairs, clubs and award schemes.

In relation to the science department, it is worth noting here that science staff need to be sure that the head of department (HOD) will actively sanction their creative practice. Affirmation must exceed 'have a go if you want' to include 'have a go with my full support'. Science teachers must see their head of department setting an example. They need to 'walk the talk'. This is also particularly true of your university tutors, school-based mentors and induction tutor(s) in the early years of your career.

Another aspect that Feasey (2006) identifies, is the importance of making more explicit links across different aspects of science, with other areas of the curriculum, including the arts, with external partners and with pupils' own experiences. This will involve you thinking about a range of possibilities and being more open to curriculum content, including undertaking more science outside the classroom with your pupils and perhaps more flexible timetabling, although I appreciate this latter aspect may be difficult for you to negotiate as a trainee or beginning science teacher.

A good example of cross-curricular work is reported in *Creative Space* (Cape UK, 2005), which sets out some of the lessons learned from a collaborative science project involving teachers, artists, scientific researchers and pupils which took place in primary and secondary schools in Leeds and Manchester in 2003–04. The project findings highlight the usefulness of teaching strategies that cost nothing in financial terms. For example, these included the importance of pupil–teacher and pupil–pupil group dialogue and conversation; the usefulness of drawing and three-dimensional (3D) modelling as an aid to understanding; the value of allowing time for play and experimentation; the need to give pupils more responsibility for asking and answering questions and the motivating effect of having to explain and demonstrate ideas to other people. Is there any reason that you can think of why many of these cannot be some of the 'usual' ingredients in the making of a science lesson?

Creative classrooms and laboratories

Another way in which you can make a significant contribution to the development of your pupils' creativity in science is through your attention to the environment in the classrooms and laboratories in which you teach. In order to help you think about this environment, Feasey (2005) has helpfully categorized three dimensions of the creative classroom, namely, the *physical environment*, the *social and emotional environment* and the *thinking environment*.

In a physical environment which provides the stimulus for working creatively, she notes that resources are well organized, so that pupils know where they are and when given access are responsible for choosing, using and returning them. It might be worth you asking yourself the question as to whether this is the case in your laboratories! In addition, science displays that support thinking and working creatively would contain pupils' ideas; would offer questions and problems to challenge; would encourage them to try activities out, handle materials and make observations; would allow pupils to register their responses and ideas, and would be fluid and change to provide different areas of interest. Again, you might like to think whether this is true of the displays in your laboratory.

A social and emotional environment where creativity flourishes is one where pupils feel safe to express their ideas. Such an environment encourages pupils to listen to one another, respect other pupils' ideas, support and help each other, be independent, take risks and learn from mistakes. In my experience, it takes time, a good knowledge of the pupils in your class and some working 'ground rules' to create this environment. You should expect that initially, pupils might not be prepared to listen to one another and might be hesitant about putting forward their ideas or taking risks for fear of put-downs and ridicule from their peers.

In a creative thinking environment, pupils are expected to think for themselves, listen to the ideas (thinking) of others, are allowed to think differently, problem-solve, take risks in thinking and should be prepared to make mistakes. In such an environment, pupils are required to participate and you should have high expectations in relation to their contributions. For example, you could ask them to identify what they are doing in terms of the processes of science as lessons proceed and *why* they are doing it, thus valuing process as well as product. So, as pupils collect data, it is worth alerting them to the fact that they doing just that. As they suggest explanations for phenomena, it is worth informing them that they are theorizing. In this way, Monk (2006) suggests, you are keeping a conversation going with pupils, helping, for instance, to strengthen the teaching of 'how science works'.

It is certainly the case that the government has recognized the importance of teaching such thinking skills through the curriculum (DfES, 2005b). Perhaps a good example of this in science education is CASE – Cognitive Acceleration through Science Education (Adey et al., 1995) – which is an approach to science teaching with the intention of raising pupils' intellectual performance. The authors argue that the use by teachers of the 'thinking science' method that they have developed, based on the ideas of Piaget and Vygotsky, encourages pupils to reflect on their own thinking (metacognition) and to develop their reasoning power in solving problems.

In science, the programme is designed as a series of lessons, which are delivered at regular intervals to Years 7 and 8. A typical CASE lesson has five 'pillars' or components:

- the concrete preparation stage where the pupils are familiarized with a problem through a context with a regular or predictable pattern
- cognitive conflict in the form of unexpected results which the pupil has to try to explain
- metacognition, where pupils think, share their ideas and talk about their thinking
- construction, where the pupils make their own sense of the problem context
- bridging their reasoning to other contexts so that it can be generalized and available for future thinking.

The CASE team also points out that it is the training for teachers in the use of this method and the subsequent change in their practice through using it that is a significant factor in pupils' success. Thus, they say that there is no reason why the method could not be employed in other subject areas. You might like to read more about Adey and Shayer's research and their findings in relation to the gains in cognitive development and the improvement in GCSE grades of the pupils they studied in Shayer, (1996) and (2000) – see the further reading section at the end of this chapter.

Creative and innovative teaching and learning

Fautley and Savage (2007) identify four key elements of creative learning, namely, enjoyment, motivation, experiential learning and divergent thinking. These elements can be simply translated as a notion that creative learning by problem-solving and exploring a range of possibilities, thereby helping pupils to develop their imagination, can be motivating and fun.

For this to happen in your classroom and beyond, the sort of conditions described in the previous section need to be present where emotions are engaged (through the memorable sights, sounds and smells of science!) and motivation is high. If the learning in your laboratory is fun and you give your pupils the chance to be creative, Oliver (2006) says, then this will not only make the experience of learning memorable but can also facilitate higher-order thinking, thus enabling the difficult concepts to be tackled because pupils have not 'dulled their emotional response'.

Website

Have a look at lesson 3 on the website. In this extract, you will see the pupils listening to music as they enter the lesson. Paul is encouraging them to develop an emotional response to a volcanic eruption.

In my opinion, the teacher having his or her own sense of fun can also enhance learning in fun ways. This does not mean that you have to try to be a stand-up comedian (although a collection of terrible science jokes might help, as I have found!), but my experience is that if you teach enthusiastically and with a smile on your face then this will 'rub off' on your pupils. In fact, I think that the greatest compliment that one of my pupils ever paid me was when he said 'Hey, sir, we don't do much work with you, we always have a laugh!' (this might be my epitaph …). So, I asked him to open his science folder and to have a quick look through the work we had covered since the start of year. As he did so, I could see the smile broadening on his face as he realized the extent of the work he had actually done, but that he had not seen it as 'work' because he had actually enjoyed what he had been learning (and I suppose the way I had been teaching).

Furthermore, you should try to demonstrate creativity in your teaching by being an inspiration, knowing your subject well, but showing your pupils that you are continuing to learn about science yourself and that they cannot expect you to have all the answers. Here, stimulating their curiosity, setting them real-life challenges and giving them access to different kinds of materials and expertise, including using ICT to research and find things out for themselves, is a creative strategy.

Sometimes a creative moment can happen unexpectedly in your classroom. However, in teaching for creativity, what you do is plan to engage your pupils and hope for the unexpected to happen. Mesure (2005) argues that for an activity to engage pupils it should have some of the following ingredients: glamour, risk, a sense of control or interactivity, personalities, characters, stories, emotions, expression and relationships. It is amazing how often a newspaper, magazine, comic, television programme or film will provide such material that can be subsequently integrated into your lessons. A simple way to do this is to take the trouble to preserve 'useful' information like this, either electronically or in folders/scrapbooks for future retrieval when you are in search of inspiration.

Experimental work also offers your pupils (and sometimes you) the opportunity for the unexpected. Ireson and Twidle (2006) argue that there is an important prerequisite for all experimental work – that your pupils should not have the answer prior to carrying out the experiment – otherwise, they ask, is it actually an experiment for them? Unfortunately, beginning teachers commonly (and experienced teachers occasionally!) make the mistake of giving away too much information too soon. How much interest would striptease dancers arouse if they threw all their clothes off at once? In this respect, I can never forgive my chemistry teacher who used to regularly tell the class the results of our experiments before we actually did them! I do appreciate that there is some element of 'confirming theory' in this approach, but to me it spoiled a lot of the fun. For me, while acknowledging the needs of holistic learners requiring an overview of lessons to help them slot the individual activity 'pieces' into the 'big picture', a lesson should gradually reveal rather than expose outright – as this provides the unexpected element for pupils. Within this framework, well thought-out questions can be used to challenge, elicit ideas and opinions, encourage participation and motivate interest.

Website

Have a look again at lesson 2 on the website. To what extent (if any) are the answers given in advance? Could more have been done to inject a bit of mystery and discovery into the lesson?

In addition, there is often the temptation after doing experimental work (including investigations) for the teacher to tell pupils that their ideas and findings were 'interesting' but then give them 'the real answer'. However, this can promote science as simply a set of facts and can minimize the importance of science as a way of working. Does this lead to pupils 'fiddling' the results of the experiment to fit your expectation or the previously known result and then regurgitating the conclusion given by you for homework? A more creative strategy might be for you to draw out the similarities and differences between your pupils' ideas and that of current scientific views (Edmonds, 2004).

Experiments should allow pupils to predict, collect data, analyse it in the light of their predictions and draw conclusions. For Ireson and Twidle (2006), *investigations* go one step further than this – as often the teacher does not know the answer and pupils can work to their own plan. There are many different types of activities that come under the heading of 'investigations'. These can range from those that are quite closed and teacher-directed, to those that are much more open and pupil-centred.

In considering this range, Watson et al. (1999) note that *fair testing*-type investigations have dominated schemes of work in schools. Sometimes these are carried out in a closed, teacher-led manner. Science teachers often cite time constraints as one of the main reasons for this. Unfortunately, an over-abundance of this type of investigation can seriously stifle pupils' enjoyment and creativity. Nowhere is this perhaps more evident than in the 'turn-off' of Years 10 and 11 pupils, where investigations used for GCSE assessment can be so 'contrived' as to be far away from the original curriculum intentions of allowing pupils to work in ways akin to those used by 'real' scientists.

In order to broaden your investigative horizons, Watson et al. (1999) have put forward other categories of investigation and examples. My suggestion to you is that these potentially offer creative alternatives to fair testing-types. These are:

Classifying and identifying – 'What is the chemical?' 'How can we group these invertebrates?'
Pattern-seeking – 'Is pupil fitness related to their exercise habits?' 'What conditions do woodlice prefer?'
Exploring – What happens when different liquids are added together?' 'How do plants get their water?'
Investigating models – 'Why do elephants throw water over themselves?' 'How can we model the cooling of a hot body when it is insulated by layers of material?'
Making things or developing systems – 'Can you design a pressure pad switch for a burglar alarm?' 'Devise a way to determine the water content of an apple.'

This is not the only categorization of investigations in the literature. For instance, you might also want to look at Wellington (2000) who suggests two schemata for types of investigational work done in science lessons; one a typology of investigations and a second being a framework of their dimensions. See the further reading section at the end of this chapter for the reference.

In addition to thinking about a range of types of investigation, Jones et al. (1992) have indicated that even though they are more time-consuming, open-ended approaches provide significant benefits for pupils' learning. Pupils (particularly able ones), place a high level of importance on 'owning' investigations. This might involve problems or observations that are brought to your science classroom by your pupils rather than you, because then they will be more motivated and inclined to seek the answers. As an alternative you could think of some innovative start points of your own, developing scenarios that draw pupils into a 'real-life' investigation (such as crime scenes, survival situations and solving domestic, school and industrial problems – see the website accompanying this book for some further ideas).

You need to take the risk of allowing pupils to formulate their own hypotheses and then carry out experiments to investigate these. One strategy that I found useful was to allow pupils to do this by planning their own method and then I would collect these for scrutiny. Often I would find that a number of pupils had chosen a similar method and this gave me the opportunity to put them into the same group to do the experiment and thus not only be economical on resources, but also foster group discussion.

Another issue in investigative work is that very little, if any time is allocated to repeating and refining experiments in the light of findings – pupils do not see science investigations as iterative processes. Exposing pupils to a cyclical investigative process provides an opportunity for them to be creative and for this reason it is taken as a baseline for activity within the CREST

Awards programme (West, 2007). (See the 'Useful websites' section at the end of this chapter for the British Association website and information about CREST awards.)

Creative science teaching also involves giving your pupils time to make sense of what you have taught. As Ross et al. (2000) state, 'we mustn't allow ourselves to say the syllabus is too crowded for such luxuries' (p. 50). Here, active learning techniques are useful, such as active listening (to the teacher), active reading (for example, directed activities related to text – DARTs), writing (for example, creative writing, note-taking), talking (explaining) and doing (practising skills). Active learning will help your pupils to *reformulate* their ideas and practise their skills to make them a part of their understanding and the way that they do things. One of the most satisfying aspects of such teaching is that moment when you see a pupil's 'lights go on' – what Sutton (1992) wonderfully describes as the 'Aha!' effect.

Another creative teaching and learning strategy that you should use is to allow your pupils to work together in groups so that they can share, discuss and develop their ideas. There are a number of theoretical perspectives in the literature that are relevant to group learning and group creativity. For instance, the domain of social constructivism (based on the work of Vygotsky) which propounds that an individual finds out things first by their interaction with others, and then they become part of the intellectual functioning of the individual. Pupils can be helped a cross a 'zone of proximal development' which represents the difference between what they can achieve alone and that which they can achieve with support from the teacher or their fellow pupils.

When deciding on group work, you need to make choices about the composition of groups based on assessment of their abilities related to the particular task that you want them to do. Working in a group means that, not only can physical tasks be distributed among members of a group, but also cognitive tasks can too. This allows pupils to work on separate aspects of the creative process, but work on them together. It means that you do not just simply have group work as a pragmatic substitute for individual work, but that you have thought about how the members of the group can contribute their abilities to successful learning within the task. For example, your pupils could work in groups to produce and give a presentation on a particular topic, which is then challenged by their peers for its authenticity, reliability and accuracy. Some pupils would be the researchers, some would produce the presentation, some would give the presentation and others could challenge the different groups. Such a strategy allows activities to become more discursive, more open and more investigational. In fact, Monk (2006), says the presentations might creatively be set up as attendance at a 'mock' conference.

Before leaving this discussion of creative teaching and learning, I want to mention assessment and in particular, the most common form of assessment in most classrooms – question and answer (Q&A). While teaching to the test can be a barrier to the development of creativity, you cannot ignore the issue of assessment. The problem is not the need for assessment, but the nature of it. By using summative forms of assessment for test and examination purposes, the education system gives them high status and potentially downgrades the importance of formative assessment. Yet, formative assessment is particularly important in supporting your creative teaching and your pupils' learning, and has been shown to promote higher standards of achievement.

A key aspect in directing pupils towards creative processes is questioning. There is evidence (Bloom, quoted in Fautley and Savage, 2007) that most of the questions in lessons are low-level knowledge questions (often described as 'factual recall'). What might be helpful in developing questioning skills is to use a list of question 'stems', particularly for developing pupils' analytical, synthesis, evaluation and creating skills (see table 10.1).

Table 10.1 Question stems

Type of question	Question stem
Analysis	How might it have been different if . . . ? What happens in the bit when you . . . ? Can you explain what went on when . . . ? Compare . . . with . . . ? Can you distinguish between . . . and . . . ?
Synthesis	What would happen if you changed that bit where . . . ? How could you do . . . differently?
Evaluation	What was successful about . . . ? What changes might you make . . . ? Can you justify . . . ? How do you feel about . . . ? Can you suggest . . . ?
Creating	Are you able to devise . . . ? What would . . . look like if . . . ? How would . . . be made up? Can you produce . . . ? Imagine what would happen if . . . ? If . . . then what about . . . ?

The types of question in Table 10.1 can be linked to questions designed to develop pupils' metacognitive skills. Metacognition refers to pupils reflecting on their own thought processes. Developing metacognition as part of teaching for creativity involves discussing with pupils the thought processes they are going through and reflecting on how they arrived at the decisions they have made, not just on what those decisions were.

Questions designed to foster metacognition are reflexive and get pupils to think creatively about how they arrived at their answers. Such questions might be:

What evidence do you have for … ?
Why do you think this is right?

Why are you doing it like this?
How do you know your measurement is accurate?
Would someone else doing this come up with the same answers?
Can you make any generalizations?
Is this what you expected?
How would you go about explaining this to someone else?
What did you have to do to solve this problem?
Can you give an example of where you have seen something like this elsewhere?
(Fautley and Savage, 2007)

In conclusion, it is important to remember that you cannot just read about creativity in books such as this and then instantly make it happen in your classroom. You need time to gain a range of teaching experiences and develop your confidence by sharing and exploring your ideas with other teachers and then trying them out. In this way, you will learn how to adapt your teaching styles and strategies to not only develop the creative abilities of your pupils, but yours as well, giving a way of teaching that is motivating for you, and which values you as a creative individual. I believe that all science teachers are capable of doing this despite the external curriculum and assessment pressures.

Points for reflection

- How does the science department environment in your school reflect and stimulate creativity?
- How do you encourage pupils to be active in your lessons and have the opportunity to put forward their ideas?
- How do you keep track of your pupils' creative progress?
- What would risk-taking look like in your science teaching?
- How can you structure lesson content in a way that your pupils will really feel as though they are discovering something new as if for the first time?
- Who asks the questions in your science laboratory?

CREATIVE AND INNOVATIVE ACTIVITIES

In this final part of the chapter, I single out some science lesson activities that I feel offer the potential to develop both your creativity and innovation and that of your pupils. These include activities using ICT, role play and drama, games, modelling, concept mapping and discussion.

Using ICT creatively

The challenge of creative use

Morris and Wardle (2006) note that as a science teacher you will be aware of how pupils are growing up with ICT as a central part of their lives and with high expectations of its use in school. There is a wide range of possibilities and as the technology develops, the limits of use will only be the limits of your expertise, enthusiasm or creativity. However, always remember that in your planning you should be thinking about whether the use of ICT is appropriate and thus if it will give benefit to teaching and learning by supporting pupils and enhancing and extending tasks. These two points feature in the National Strategy guidance (DfES, 2004a) and it is crucial that you keep them in mind when reflecting on your use of ICT. In relation to appropriate use, my little 'aide-mémoire' that makes me stop and think when I am planning is that I do not need to word process notes to the milkman! With regard to benefit for teaching and learning, as well as your own evaluation, you could always ask pupils, as part of their reflection on the lesson, to articulate how ICT has contributed to their learning.

In our work with ITT students over the past decade or so, we have seen a major increase in their ICT capability. However, in a number of cases, this capability is often only transferred into limited classroom usage – particularly early in training where there seems to be an overemphais on teacher talk using presentation packages such as PowerPoint. I think this is because they see such use as teacher controlled and led, and therefore 'safer'. Whilst PowerPoint does provide a good visual impact, it can be used mechanistically, and fail to engage pupils. The prepared slides can be very constraining by providing a script, and encouraging questions that can only have one correct answer, the one that is to be revealed on the next slide. Any unexpected response to the question, although correct, may be seen as inferior, because it does not match. The danger is that there is little scope for discussion or creative, original ideas, hence the comments from teachers such as:

> If you are interacting as you are going along, you are much more in tune with the way that the children are thinking. When pupils ask questions, you have to respond straight away. It is much harder to respond if you are relying on something that you have already prepared, because you cannot change it there and then.

> I only ever use slide presentations to supplement what I am doing on the board. That way, I am dictating the pace of the lesson rather than the PowerPoint. I tend to use slides only for the key elements, and always write on the board a lot as well.

> You cannot divert off to something else because you are very reliant on the slides that you have prepared. I am not a huge fan.

Your challenge is to be more creative and use presentational software to manage the interaction with the pupils alongside the screen images. Perhaps this could include embedding hyperlinks to provide 'thinking and discussion interludes', and then even turning over the production and delivery of presentations to your pupils!

Limited ICT usage is not confined to early-stage science teachers however. Hennessy and Osborne (2003) put forward reasons such as lack of time and lack of confidence, expertise and training, which can potentially lead to exposure of weaknesses to pupils. Ross et al. (2000) add teachers' worries about time-wasting (for example, pupils worrying about presentation rather than content when preparing work; pupils playing games while pretending to work); management (helping a lot of pupils with their problems); or not enough Personal Computers (PCs) or equipment, and computer crashes. In relation to the latter, try to free yourself from technical problems so that you are free to concentrate on the science. Have a technician on stand-by if you have such a 'luxury'; thoroughly check that the programme/CD-ROM/DVD/USB stick works beforehand or always have a 'Plan B'!

Notwithstanding these issues, ICT can provide an important environment for promoting creativity. Although it is not an inevitable consequence of an ICT-rich curriculum, an open and enquiring atmosphere, where a variety of resources are available, is exactly the environment where creativity can thrive. For example, ICT can provide enjoyment and thus be motivating, perhaps allowing pupils to work more independently. This can allow you to take on more of the role of facilitator, but remember, even in such situations, it is still important to plan the kinds of interventions that you will make and the kind of questions that you will ask to challenge pupils (Boohan, 2002b).

Using ICT, you can increase the pace of the lesson by allowing quick switches between different displays, model scientific phenomena, explore patterns and relationships, test hypotheses, and sift, sort and analyse large sets of data quickly and easily. It can also offer good opportunities for collaborative working, stimulate discussion and change a pupil's attitude to taking risks and worries about being wrong, because of the way that it provides quick and simple feedback.

Modes of use

Clearly, the ICT resources and facilities at your disposal will influence your use. Wellington (2000) lists five modes of ICT use (A to E) that are determined by resource availability, which you should bear in mind when planning.

Mode A involves using one PC linked by data projector (DP) to a screen or interactive whiteboard (IWB). More and more laboratories and classrooms in schools are being equipped with these. They can save time that you might otherwise have spent writing on a conventional board. You can display the lesson objectives, brief notes or key facts about the topic, show the new vocabulary that is needed, or give a brief recap of previous work. This kind of use is illustrated in the following comments from teachers.

I always use the screen to project the lesson's objectives, and then return to the page at the end of the lesson.

If I have a lot of notes I might put them on a slide and have them ready to display. The projector is useful especially if you cannot turn your back on a class whilst you are writing on a board.

Rather than spending a lot of time writing on the board, I make sure that the notes are already up there on the display. It saves teaching time.

However, you can use them more creatively to work through some aspects of a CD-ROM or DVD, showing snippets and pausing for questions or going to websites and using interactive games and quizzes that you can find there. You might also think about checking out video sites such as YouTube where you will find a number of interesting experiments and science-related clips – but beware the bizarre!

A major extension of the use of data projectors is to project the image onto an IWB. It can take time to become conversant with the full range of interactive facilities, and before you use an IWB, you are certain to need some time to explore on your own. Many inbuilt features of the IWB can add interest to your lessons. For instance, there is an on-screen timer that you can use to set short-term targets within the lesson, there are cover and reveal facilities that can be used to predict and check results, and there is the possibility of recording and storing sequences of IWB use and playing these back quickly and easily.

Another strength of the IWB is that it provides a quality image, with far more scope for dynamic presentation and interaction than was available previously. Pupils can demonstrate their ideas visually using the board, and this may be very helpful for pupils who have difficulty using language to communicate them.

Modes B and C in Wellington's classification involve using PCs situated in your laboratory or classroom or in an easily accessible nearby room or 'open area' in the science department. This arrangement probably gives the greatest possibility for flexible and creative use in your science lessons. You might use one PC for a task that is part of a circus or to demonstrate/explain to groups while the rest of the class are engaged in other tasks. Groups could work on different tasks, some of which need computers and some of which do not. You could differentiate by using computers for extension or remedial work or even, in perhaps the most flexible use, allow pupils to use the computer to access information as and when they need it. This will help to develop your pupils as creative and autonomous learners because they themselves will decide when to use the computer, what they need to access and for how long, and evaluate whether the computer has helped in what they are trying to find out.

When you plan to use a whole suite of computers (which may be in the science department or elsewhere in school) you are using Mode D. You might need such a suite when the whole class is engaged in individual or group work, for instance when they are doing research projects. Difficulties can arise here if you only rarely use the suite because your pupils will tend to see the lesson as separate from their normal science lessons, and you will have to work hard to convince the pupils that the science that they are studying is the focus of the lesson rather than the computer. Here, you might want to have a look at Cox's (2000) 10 golden rules to follow when planning and using ICT in science teaching, which is in the further reading section at the end of the chapter.

Wellington's final mode (Mode E) is the use of PCs out of lesson time, for example, independent pupil use at home or in the library. When you are thinking about using this mode you will need to consider access and equal opportunity issues so that pupils are not disadvantaged or prevented from doing the work fully and properly. However, it does offer scope for extended learning and collaboration, for instance when asking pupils to retrieve information from the Internet. Using this resource, your pupils can carry out research by going to sites (such as news sites) for up-to-date information on current issues and they will have opportunities to exchange information about science within the school, the local authority, the country and the world.

Bear in mind that you will need to think about the number of sites that you want the pupils to access and work on – better to limit these to avoid too much flicking backwards and forwards due to information overload. You will also need to think about the length of task and the complexity of the information on the websites. If the task is too long and the information is too difficult to understand, pupils will switch off. You will also need to be aware of wholesale 'cut and paste' and the dangers of presentation over substance, particularly in project work!

A wide range of resources

The availability of ICT resources has increased enormously over the past decade. There is now such a vast array that teachers are in danger of wasting time looking for the most effective materials as well as trying to come to grips with a plethora of different hardware and software. Rather than being put off by this, you can get help and up-to-date ICT information from more experienced colleagues, textual and electronic sources and conferences such as the ASE Annual Conference, BETT and the Education Show. You might also decide to focus at first on certain key pieces of hardware and software that are potentially going to be of most use to you as a science teacher. My suggestions would be word-processing (WP), desktop publishing (DTP), spreadsheets (SS) and data loggers (DL) and their software.

It is not my intention to give a detailed description and analysis of these. There is plenty of information elsewhere (see, for instance, some of the references in the further reading at the end of this chapter), but a brief overview will perhaps give you some pointers as to their creative use.

Word processing and DTP software enables you and your pupils to present information in a professional way with the accompanying ease of addition, amendment and deletion. This type of software also facilitates expressive modes of writing, because of the formatting options available. One way of helping pupils to do this is to change the audience for their writing from you as their teacher to others, using genres such as:

- a diary
- an article for a magazine or a report for a newspaper
- a letter to another pupil (a peer friend or older/younger pupil), or an adult (for example, their parents or a public figure)
- a lesson summary for a friend who missed the lesson or a parent explaining what they did
- a story, for example science fiction
- a play
- a piece for a textbook
- a recipe
- a poem
- a cartoon strip
- a brochure
- alternatively, written by a time-traveller from the sixteenth century!

(With acknowledgement to Bullman, 1985; Wellington and Osborne, 2001.)

Pupils could also write up their experiments more creatively rather than using the traditional apparatus, methods, results and conclusion formula. For example, they could draw their method as a diagrammatic flow chart; write a story of what happened (their results) and then give a bullet-point summary of their ideas of why this happened as a result of discussion with their partner or group. Key concepts could be included in a concept map. Their work could be presented as a folded mini-booklet with a page for each of the elements.

Spreadsheets come into their own when modelling scientific phenomena and exploring what would happen if the values of certain variables are altered, or if a formula is changed. You can also use them in conjunction with a data logger where pupils can manipulate data and display it graphically so that interpretation and analysis can take place much more readily because the time-consuming graph-constructing task by your pupils is not necessary. For instance, you could present the graphical results obtained from an experiment where a data logger has been used and ask pupils to tell the 'story' behind the graph. To help them you could have various statements that they need to drag and drop to the correct points on the graph.

Data-logging software is also helpful in making measurements, calculating changes, gradients and areas. It can enable you to go further with your teaching because your pupils can make immediate observations of the data, ask questions about it, make comparisons to, and links with, other data and look for trends. A good illustration of this is given by Frost (1998a), who says that instead of solely investigating the question 'Does a wool jumper keep you warmer?', your pupils can also quickly collect further data that will allow them to ask 'How much warmer does a wool jumper keep you?' and 'Would a cotton sweatshirt be as good?'

Before I leave this discussion of the use of ICT, I want to mention another piece of equipment that is at an early stage of introduction, that is, the personal response device. This is a small, hand-held device, which enables pupils to select one of up to four possible answers to a question on the computer screen. Personal response devices are quite expensive pieces of equipment, because a class set is needed for them to be effective. However, the main advantage of the device is that it enables those pupils in your class who are reluctant to voice their answers, or who are unable to explain their thinking, to take part as much as their more eager or articulate peers. It is also particularly useful in a large group, where it can be difficult for you to make every pupil feel involved.

When a vote has taken place, the class results are shown on the screen, so it is clear how many pupils voted for each of the four answers. This enables pupils to get immediate feedback and to compare their answers with answers given by others. It also, importantly, provides you with information about the full class, and as such is a very useful assessment tool.

The device can also be used for self-assessment in a variation on the 'traffic lights' system. In this version, pupils press button A if they have fully understood the topic, B if they have partially understood, and C if they have not understood at all. A more reflective use is to present pupils with a question, and all have to give an immediate, intuitive response. You then give the class about five minutes to discuss the question in groups and then ask for a revised response. The software then allows you to compare the percentages of intuitive and revised answers.

Points for reflection

- Do your pupils have access to suitable ICT facilities? If this needs to be improved, what can be done?
- In what ways do you incorporate ICT into your science teaching?
- Think of a pupil or group of pupils that you teach whom you feel need more support to be creative in their use of ICT in science. How can you help them to develop their flair and potential?

Role play and drama

Role play can help pupils to understand scientific phenomena by being *actively* involved and having to think things through in order to participate. Parkinson (2002) discusses two types. The first type includes activities where phenomena are modelled, for example particles or electrons. These are usually quite short-lived and are probably the best type to attempt with a new class until they become more open and less self-conscious.

The second type, involves activities where the pupils take the role of a person and discuss or debate. These can take up to a whole lesson or even longer. This type needs more preparation than the first, but when these are successful, they are a good way of getting pupils to construct arguments by appreciating other points of view. Parkinson (1994) notes that for success, you should produce briefing sheets that include reminders about the relevant science, details of the role and pointers to appropriate reference material so that your pupils can prepare properly. They might be encouraged to bring in 'props' to elaborate their role. You might also need to think about whether your laboratory is suitable or whether to arrange to hold the lesson in another room.

Dramatic activity arguably gives pupils even more licence to be creative, by allowing them to think about depicting science through activities such as tableaux, mime, dance, movement and plays, but similar principles to role play still apply. These are:

- Select different pupils to take lead roles each time you do a role play or dramatic activity.
- Always involve all pupils in some way, even though they may not have leading roles – for instance, as audience, extras, observers or note-takers.
- Step back and let the activity run and only intervene as 'the teacher' if a situation gets out of hand, otherwise try to contribute 'in role'.
- Follow-up work such as discussion of how pupils felt in role, what they have learned and what the key issues were is essential.
- Use the role play as a stimulus for further work, for example a newspaper article on a role-play council meeting to decide on where to site an incinerator.

You might want to have a look at the article by McSharry and Jones (2000) in *School Science Review* for some further ideas and examples (see the further reading section at the end of the chapter).

Modelling

Parkinson (2002) notes that different types of models are used in science and can help pupils' learning, particularly in connection with things that they cannot see, by relating to something that they are familiar with. Scientific models are the result of creative acts of the imagination and it is through models that people try to make sense of the world and making it more real by finding out the 'why' of things. Models can be powerful learning tools and can explore the very fast or the very slow and, as such, offer opportunities to experience phenomena that it is not possible to experience in the school science laboratory. However, it is important to realize that models can also be misleading through simplification or that they may have features that do not correspond to the phenomenon or object being modelled (Boohan, 2002a).

In order to use models creatively, you need to adopt the pedagogy of repeatedly demonstrating the process of modelling in action. This will help your pupils to form mental models that are very close to the original, that is, closely matching vital elements of those models. Assimilation of this approach will also lead to your pupils being able to 'metacognitively model' the process of modelling itself. Able pupils can do this more easily.

Examples of a wide range of models and how they can be used in science can be found in Gilbert (1993) – see the further reading section at the end of this chapter.

Concept mapping

Wellington (2000) describes a science concept map as a special kind of metacognitive tool. Its purpose, he says, is to relate science words or phrases to one another in a scientifically valid form. If you cannot find words to describe the scientific relationship between two ideas then it is not valid to make the link. If the map does not have these relationships, then it is in danger of simply being a 'topic web'.

The value of concept mapping for teaching and learning has been discussed extensively (see, for example, Adamczyk et al., 1994) and there is research evidence (for example, Horton, 1992) that, with regular use, concept mapping is an activity that helps pupils to make significant improvements in their learning of science. One of the reasons for this is that concept mapping is not an activity that is undertaken by pupils on their own (Wellington and Osborne, 2001). When you get pupils to complete concept maps in groups, the discussion, sharing and questioning of ideas and interpretation that goes on gives you and your pupils much more insight into their understanding. If you have ever tried concept mapping you will know that one thing that accompanies the activity is the general buzz of the discussions with the occasional argumentative outburst!

You can use a number of approaches such as:

- 'free range' maps (where only the main topic heading is given and pupils are given a completely free choice in what they include – these are most useful for experienced 'concept mappers' and/or your able pupils)
- 'object only' maps (where the key words – known as prime descriptors – are given and pupils are required to fill in the links between them – the propositions)
- 'proposition only' maps (where the propositions are given and pupils have to fill in the prime descriptors, which may or may not be provided)
- 'picture maps' (where prime descriptors and propositions are written inside different shapes, which can then be cut out and matched to a pre-prepared template or where photographs and pictures are used instead of prime descriptors – these are particularly useful when working with less able pupils)
- 'scrambled' maps (which as the name suggests need to be unscrambled so that they make scientific sense)
- 'fallacious' maps (where your pupils have to spot the incorrect prime descriptors or propositions and insert correct ones).

For further detail about these types see Adamczyk et al. (1994), Wellington (2000) and Wellington and Osborne (2001), and the concept mapping activities on the website accompanying this book.

Furthermore, Oversby (2002) states that concept mapping is an excellent formative assessment tool. The reason for this is that the discussion, sharing and questioning of ideas in the initial formulation of the map (say at the beginning of teaching a topic), together with the possible review and amendment (either during or at the end of a topic) gives you much more insight into pupils' initial and developing understanding of the science concepts being taught than many forms of summative, test-type assessment.

Not only this, but concept mapping can be a very creative and fun activity in my experience, particularly where its production has included novel and unusual links, adding colour, symbols, diagrams and photographs. You can even obtain specialized software to enable you and your pupils to draw concept maps, for example, Inspiration and Mind Genius (see www.techready.co.uk in the 'Useful websites' section at the end of the chapter for information about purchase of these).

Finally, before leaving this discussion of concept mapping I want to briefly mention 'concept cartoons'. These have been devised by Keogh and Naylor, (2000), and are simple drawings of a number of individuals expressing their views about the science involved in a number of everyday situations. They can be used for a variety of creative pupil activities, including as a stimulus for discussion, as a start point for an investigation or as a start point for pupils producing their own cartoons.

Discussion

Parkinson (1994) reminds us that as science teachers we may feel that we spend a lot of time trying to stop pupils from talking, never mind using activities that promote this. Thus, your major worry about discussion might be how to maintain control – whether your pupils will talk about the topic or just gossip; whether it will be too noisy; what you should do while they are discussing; what you should do about pupils who are misbehaving and what you should do about quarrelling.

Despite these worries, Wellington and Osborne (2001) argue that as well as being a 'hands-on' experience, learning science must be a 'minds-on' activity that requires pupils to practise the discourse of science using scientific vocabulary in its correct scientific sense. They liken the learning of science to learning a foreign language and say that no one would dream of teaching a foreign language without giving pupils the opportunity to talk and use it – so why does science teaching give so few opportunities to do this?

The key point here is that you are trying to initiate talk which is *purposeful* and which allows your pupils to test their understandings and be creative and innovative through talking about and explaining to others what they know. This includes what Bullman (1985) describes as 'active listening', where pupils are expected to respond appropriately to what is being said and 'active talking' which increases pupil participation in their own learning and helps to prevent boredom and frustration.

In order to achieve purposeful talk, you will need to work hard to develop the social environment described earlier in this chapter where pupils feel encouraged to contribute and these contributions are respected and valued by their peers and the teacher. Solomon (2002) notes that this is particularly important in experimental work, where pupils need to talk over their results to receive confirmation of their accuracy from others. She also adds that the single most important criterion for ensuring that pupils have a free discussion to interpret their experimental results is that the teacher should have no hidden agenda that 'the right answer' should be reached. Thus, the concepts and theories talked about might not be what the teacher expects. This will take a certain amount of confidence for you to 'let go of the reins' in this way.

Obviously, classes can vary enormously and you may have to work with your pupils on how to discuss and debate. There are particular skills in making your own points, listening to what others have to say and then arguing about who is correct. You have to be able to make your case systematically and provide evidence to support your points or dispute those of your 'opponent'. Thus, you might need to include a developmental sequence involving initially more teacher-led (but beware of teacher-dominated) discussions; the physical arrangement of the pupils; tighter formulation of the parameters of the discussion (for example, timing; who speaks; when they speak and for how long) and where you choose group composition.

To develop small-group discussion, you could ask one member of the group to read a short passage while others in the group prepare questions for discussion. In addition, you could have previously prepared these so that they can be used if necessary to keep the discussion flowing. Give pupils roles, for example, presenting, feedback or making notes, and rotate the roles for the next discussion. Resources pitched at the right level for the group should be readily available. Perhaps you might use some question prompts such as 'Some people think that it is a good/not a good idea because … ', 'Having looked at the arguments for and against I think … ' to help pupils to structure their reasoning and decision-making. You will also need to make clear to the group what a desirable outcome is, for example what you want the pupils to do resulting from their discussion (Levinson, 2007).

Games

A wide range and variety have been used in the science classroom and it is impossible to try to cover them all here. There are the old 'favourites' such as hangman, odd-one-out, noughts and crosses and charades. Others have been adapted from board games such as Trivial Pursuit, Pictionary and Dingbats, and game shows such as *Give us a Clue, Mastermind, Who Wants to be a Millionaire?* and *Family Fortunes.*

Some of my favourites include:

- Bingo – where pupils cross off words on their bingo card that are the answers to the questions being asked.
- Beat the clock – where they have one minute to answer the questions and complete the equation.
- Circular questions – where one pupil has a card with a question on one side and an answer to another pupil's question on the other.
- Crack the code – where you scramble an experimental sequence and pupils have to put the steps in the right order, thereby giving a code number.
- Gone in 10 seconds – where you use the timing facility in PowerPoint to make questions on slides disappear after 10 seconds.
- Loopy links – where they have to make a link between two unusual things, for example why is a proton like a slice of bread?
- Play your pH right – where you put household bottles and containers in a row and pupils have to say whether the pH of the substance is higher or lower than (or if you are being cruel – the same as) the substance before it.
- Relevant/irrelevant – where they sort statements into those that are relevant to the topic and those that are not.
- Splat – where pupils compete in pairs to be the first to hit the word on the board that is the correct answer to your question

A further list of ideas can be found on the website accompanying this book.

Points for reflection

1. Thinking about your last teaching practice or last term's teaching have you engaged in any of the following 'creative' activities?

   - Shared one of your ideas with a colleague in the science department?
   - Shared one of your ideas with a colleague in another department in the school?
   - Shared one of your ideas with a colleague in another school?
   - Asked for advice from a colleague in the science department?
   - Asked for advice from a colleague in another department?
   - Involved an LSA in some aspect of your planning?
   - Contacted an outside agency in connection with a possible collaborative activity?
   - Observed a colleague teach?
   - Shared a laugh and a joke in the staffroom?
   - Jointly planned a lesson?

Points for reflection

- Team taught a lesson?
- Praised or thanked a colleague for help?
- Looked at resources with colleagues?
- Rewritten a lesson and shared it with a colleague?
- Used a new idea in more than 25 per cent of your lessons?
- Used a new idea in more than 50 per cent of your lessons?

2. How many of the 'wow' experiments at KS4 do you not do because of:

- health and safety worries?
- lack of time?
- lack of resources?

3. Can you think of any creative solutions to the dilemma in question 2?
4. Think about a KS3 and a KS4 module that you have taught. Reflecting on the activities and ideas discussed in the chapter, make some notes on how you could make your teaching of these modules more creative and innovative.

What the research says

How do we ensure creativity in the classroom is working to encourage pupils to think and develop social skills? Creative teaching is not about delivering the facts. According to the 'teachingexpertise' web page entitled 'Learning and Thinking' (www.teaching expertise.com/articles/creativity-school-714, accessed October 2008):

The new 'survival requirements' are:

- confidence that we know how to learn;
- being able to deal positively with change (practically and emotionally);
- flexibility and creativity in the ways we think.

Creativity in the classroom is key to pupils' development in this fast-paced, ever-changing technological environment. There must be consideration for all pupils' learning styles and personality. Not everyone will feel comfortable at first to get involved; they fear failure. Pupils need to feel safe to enable them to take risks, so provide them with thinking time and develop their confidence. How can teachers develop these skills to become effective creative classroom practitioners?

How can the success of the creative approach be measured?

Further reading

Parkinson, J. (1994), *The Effective Teaching of Secondary Science*. Harlow: Longman. For more information on the stages of group work and how to manage them.

Shayer, M. (1996) *The Long-term Effects of Cognitive Acceleration on Pupils' School Achievement.* London: King's College Department for Education and Professional Studies.
Shayer, M. (2000) GCSE 1999: *Added Value from Schools Adopting the CASE Intervention.* London: King's College Department for Education and Professional Studies.
Both these references offer more information about thinking skills and in particular CASE.

Investigations

Watson, R., Goldsworthy, A. and Wood-Robinson, V. (1999), 'What's not fair with investigations?', *School Science Review*, 80(292): 101–6.
Gives a classification of types of investigative work.

Wellington, J. (2000), *Teaching and Learning Secondary Science. Contemporary Issues and practical approaches.* London: Routledge.
Look at Chapter 8 'Investigations in science' for his frameworks of investigations.

Using ICT

Cox, M. (2000) 'Information and communications technologies: their role and value for science education', in M. Monk and J. Osborne (eds), *Good Practice in Science Teaching. What Research Has to Say.* Buckingham: Open University Press.
10 golden rules to follow when planning and using ICT in science teaching.

Morris, P. and Wardle, J. (2006) 'Teaching science with ICT', in V. Wood-Robinson (ed.), *ASE Guide to Secondary Science Education.* Hatfield: ASE.
Further examples of use of ICT.

Frost, R. (1998b) *The IT in Secondary Science Book.* London: IT in Science.
A multitude of ideas for using ICT.

Wellington, J. (2000) *Teaching and Learning Secondary Science. Contemporary Issues and Practical Approaches.* London: Routledge.
Look at chapter 10 'Using ICT in teaching and learning science' for areas of activity in science linked to specific items of ICT and ideas for ICT use.

Role play

McSharry, G. and Jones, S. (2002) 'Role play, a science teaching and learning', *School Science Review*, 82(298): 73–82.
Examples of role play.

Parkinson, J. (2002) *Reflective Teaching of Science 11–18.* London: Continuum.
Parkinson offers help on the sequence of events when using role play to debate an issue.

Modelling

Gilbert, J.K. (ed.) (1993) *Models and Modelling in Science Education*. Hatfield: ASE.

Grevatt, A., Gilbert, J.K. and Newberry, M. (2007) 'Challenging able science learners through models and modelling', in K. Taber (ed.), *Science Education for Gifted Learners*. Abingdon: Routledge.
Information about models in science and their use in your teaching.

Useful websites

Live links to these websites can be found on the companion website www.sagepub.co.uk/secondary

www.creative-partnerships.com
The Creative Partnerships website which gives further information about this organization's activities.

www.the-ba.net
The British Association for information on science clubs and CREST awards.

www.ngfl-cymru.org.uk/vtc-home.htm
The Welsh national grid for learning with links to a range of science teaching resources.

http://tre.ngfl.gov.uk/
The Teacher Resource exchange site of the NgFL.

www.bettshow.com/
BETT is the world's largest educational technology event. On the site is 'Education Watch' keeping you up to date with news from the world of educational ICT.

www.teachernet.gov.uk/supportpack/index.aspx
A TeacherNet website which has lesson plans, multimedia resources, video case studies and ICT support materials.

www.teachernet.gov.uk/teachingandlearning/subjects/science/
This area of TeacherNet points to guidance, ideas and resources for science teachers.

http://partners.becta.org.uk/page_documents/research/wtrs_science.pdf
A review of research into the use of ICT in science teaching available on the Becta website.

www-saps.plantsci.cam.ac.uk
The Science and Plants for Schools website with a range of ideas on practical investigations involving plants.

www.schoolscience.co.uk/
School Science website of the ASE which has a wide range of teaching resources.

www.upd8.org.uk/
The upd8 site of the ASE with many activities related to science in the news.

www.techready.co.uk/Assistive-Technology/Concept-Mapping
Information about the purchase of concept-mapping software.

http://weblearn.sheffcol.ac.uk/links/Science/
Links to over 750 science websites.

http://madsci.org/
The Mad Science laboratory that never sleeps!

11 SCIENCE OUTSIDE THE CLASSROOM

Tony Liversidge

This chapter:

- offers a rationale for science learning outside the classroom and laboratory
- discusses the pros and cons of taking pupils out
- identifies the key aspects of organizing successful experiences, highlighting health and safety and curriculum integration
- outlines a range of opportunities for learning within the school environment and external to the school.

A RATIONALE FOR TAKING PUPILS OUTSIDE THE CLASSROOM

With so much involved in the planning and running of school visits and trips, including what some teachers see as risk assessment overload and excessive form-filling, coupled with the current 'blame culture' and potential litigation in the event of an accident, it is easy to wonder why they still take place at all.

So, you may be thinking to yourself why not just let children get these experiences with their families. After all, they spend about two-thirds of their waking lives outside school. Let their parents have the responsibility. You just would not bother. If you were like this, then you would be contributing to the current real concern (see for example Rickinson et al., 2004) that pupils are being distanced from outside-classroom learning.

However, you might be open to a little persuasion. If you were to ask me about what I remember about science at school, and what particularly turned me on to science, I would wax lyrical about my favourite science teachers like Mr Dixon, Mr Booth, Mrs Macarthy or Mr Newbould. I would reminisce about certain events in lessons such as the exploding oxygen mixture and the legacy of the black stains on the ceiling above Mr Dixon's teaching bench. However, also high on my list of memorable experiences would be my lower sixth biology field trip to Preston Montford Field Studies Centre – and not just for the fieldwork – but I won't go into that now!

In addition, as a secondary science teacher, some of my fondest memories are of taking fourth, fifth and sixth form (Years 10, 11 and 12) pupils on biology field trips and outward-bound courses. We even managed to get some science into our ski trips! Closer by we studied the school grounds and playing fields, local fields and woods, and I am positive that pupils enjoyed these experiences, because they talked about them, sometimes for quite a long time afterwards. It is for these reasons that I am a great supporter of taking pupils outside the classroom to give them experiences that are simply not possible otherwise.

These personal reasons might make you think twice, but might not be enough to persuade you to stick your neck out. So, are there any others? To start, Ofsted (2000) have reminded us that the curriculum consists of all the planned activities within and beyond the timetabled day, including extra-curricular activities which enrich and support learning.

Pupils themselves value out-of-school experiences in helping them learn science. In a recent study by Cerini et al. (2003) pupils rated 'going on a science trip or excursion' as the most enjoyable, and the fifth most useful and effective strategy for learning science out of eleven strategies given. If you ask science teachers, they will also agree that when given these opportunities, most pupils' best behaviour, qualities and engagement come to light.

Slingsby (2006: 51) states that the purpose of teaching science to children at school is 'to introduce them to thinking like a scientist, to using scientific knowledge and understanding to help them live their lives and to coping with new knowledge as it comes to light throughout the rest of their lives.' (p 51) To do so without ever leaving the classroom or laboratory, he argues, is to miss a vital ingredient.

Braund and Reiss (2006) contend that laboratory-based school science teaching needs to be complemented by out-of-school science learning that draws on the actual world (for example, through field trips), the presented world (for example, in zoos, gardens and museums) and the virtual worlds available via ICT. Thus, if you want your pupils to make sense of the world around them then working on science outside the classroom is vital.

Finally, if you have not been convinced by the above arguments then the government might persuade you! In an attempt to halt the decline in numbers of school trips over the past decade, the government published *Learning Outside the Classroom* in November 2006. This manifesto (DfES, 2006: 1) states that 'every young person should experience the world beyond the classroom as an essential part of learning and personal development' (p1). Besides indicating the many and varied educational benefits, the manifesto seeks pledges from individuals and organizations who are prepared to actively champion learning outside the classroom and make public the actions they intend to take.

Thus, to quote Peacock and Dunne (2006: 87): 'The question perhaps is not, what do we gain by going outside the classroom? But, what science are children missing by not having these experiences?'

THE PROS AND CONS OF TAKING PUPILS OUTSIDE THE CLASSROOM

The cons

As indicated at the start of this chapter, many science teachers feel pressured by a variety of factors into thinking that trips are either not possible or so difficult as not to be worth the effort. I do not want to dwell on the negatives, because as you will see from the next section I feel that the pros greatly outweigh the cons, but it seems to me to be only appropriate to briefly mention those that have been put forward. An analysis of these cons shows that they can essentially be grouped under four headings, namely learning, planning, financial and personal.

First, a criticism of learning in out-of-school settings such as science centres is that it is rarely substantial, that misconceptions are easily initiated and that the engagement and enjoyment are more important than the educational gains. Thus, for science visits organized to entertain and motivate pupils it might be difficult to reconcile the learning of science concepts. However, argue Braund and Reiss (2006), this is the same problem that you will face in almost every lesson in school. The solution that you will probably aim for is to try to achieve a balance, where pupils are motivated to learn because they are enjoying what they are doing.

Secondly, that the time you spend planning the trip is not repaid by the benefits that accrue. You will need to plan thoroughly, including full risk assessment, taking into account hazards such as those associated with the venue and travel. You will need to complete the required documentation and gain authorization. Then, if the trip is sanctioned, you will need to brief pupils and accompanying staff (and sometimes parents). You may also have to placate other staff whose lessons will be missed! However, if the trip or visit is a success, in my opinion your efforts in planning will be repaid many times over.

The third consideration is cost. You will need to think about how expensive it is for pupils, how expensive it is for your school or science department (for example, in terms of insurance or extra equipment) and whether the activity warrants it. Here, if you meet a financial or other organizational 'dead end' in school do not forget to explore other avenues for support – SETPOINT might be a good start. Every area of the UK has a SETPOINT that is tasked to support STEM (Science, Technology, Engineering and Mathematics) activities in its region. Many SETPOINTS organize and deliver activities themselves, and are happy to discuss possibilities with schools. They can also put you in contact with businesses via their database of contacts that might also be able to offer help and funds (see the 'Useful websites' section at the end of the chapter).

The final consideration is the effect on you personally. Absolutely no visit or trip is worth organizing if it is going to cause you so much worry and stress that you become ill. Thus, if your first thought is that the out-of-classroom activity will give an extra opportunity for pupils to misbehave, perhaps you should speak to other members of staff who have run successful trips for their advice and reassurance. You might also need to be strategic in terms of the times when visits and trips might take place, the types that you organize and the number of pupils that you take (perhaps think 'local' and 'small' at first), until you build confidence and expertise.

The pros

The introduction to this chapter should have made you aware of some of the reasons that have been put forward in favour of work outside the classroom, particularly because it can provide such unique experiences. In order to strengthen the argument, let me add some more, starting with those in the government's *Learning Outside the Classroom Manifesto* (DfES, 2006). The points they make are that learning outside the classroom will:

- improve academic achievement
- provide a bridge to higher-order learning
- develop skills and independence in a widening range of environments
- make learning more engaging and relevant to young people
- develop active citizens and stewards of the environment
- nurture creativity
- provide opportunities for informal learning through play
- reduce behaviour problems and improve attendance
- stimulate, inspire and improve motivation
- develop the ability to deal with uncertainty
- provide challenge and opportunity to take acceptable levels of risk
- improve young people's attitudes to learning.

In addition, Braund and Reiss (2006) describe five ways in which out-of-classroom contexts can add *specifically* to the learning of science. These are:

1. *Improved development and integration of concepts* – when science is taught in new and exciting ways, pupils are more enthused and this stimulates a desire to find out more. Such direct and relevant experiences provide a powerful knowledge and skills base that deepens and enriches learning.

2. *Extended and authentic practical work* – can demonstrate or replicate the sort of work that scientists undertake, or that which is relevant to solving real-life problems. Examples are fieldwork, theme parks, hands-on museums and visits to industrial or commercial premises. In addition, the latter can enable pupils and teachers to interact with a range

of science professionals, with a two-way updating of current developments. They can foster school–business links and these can provide better information about how commerce uses science and about science-based careers within business.

3. *Access to rare material and 'big science'* – museums, botanic gardens and zoos act as a repository of typical or rare specimens and artefacts. The stories associated with specimens help to raise questions about the ways in which scientific knowledge has been generated and the social enterprises that people have engaged in. 'Big' science is the sort of science that requires large or sophisticated equipment, for example, visits to radio telescopes, particle accelerators, space centres and genome campuses.

4. *Attitudes to school science* – stimulating further learning and developing a more positive attitude towards science. Furthermore, some pupils will shine in these environments unlike in school. Hill (2007) notes that out-of-classroom experiences can provide a powerful route to the Every Child Matters outcomes, in particular, enjoying and achieving, staying safe and being healthy.

5. *Social outcomes* – providing for collaborative work and increased responsibility for learning. Work can be more extensive and thorough and provides more autonomy for learners, as it is not bounded by the school day and lesson times. Fieldwork is a good example of this as it can also provide an opportunity for a residential experience with associated collaboration and socialization.

Peacock and Dunne (2006) have also provided a well-written rationale of the benefits of science education outside the classroom. They argue that experience of the physical, social, environmental and ecological aspects of the real world, provides an expanded science curriculum embedded in meaningful and purposeful contexts. It also enables your pupils to practice manipulative and investigative skills and can help you to identify their misconceptions and clarify them 'on the spot'. Such experiences can also be novel, exciting and stimulating, and can offer opportunities for you to build closer relationships with your pupils. I certainly feel that this has been the case for me through my experiences.

If the above has convinced you that taking pupils outside the classroom to study science is worthwhile, then the next section will offer you brief guidance on how to do this successfully.

Point for reflection

Bearing in mind your particular school and circumstances and reflecting on the discussion in the previous section, select one of your classes and make a list of the pros and cons for taking them out on a visit. If the pros outweigh the cons is this enough to persuade you to organize a visit? If not, what might you need to do in order to reassess the situation?

SUCCESSFUL EXPERIENCES

Organization

In spite of teachers' concerns, every year there are many days spent on out-of-school visits and the majority of these take place without any problems. Even where incidents and injury do occur, in most cases these are simply accidental. However, the value of thorough planning and attention to detail cannot be overstated. I do not intend to go into detail here about how to plan a trip, but I do feel that it is appropriate to mention certain important elements.

First, a key aspect is your *duty of care*. Essentially your teaching contract will set out your professional duties and cover the main requirements of your duty of care to safeguard pupils. Case law has developed so that the standard of professional care expected is that of a competent professional, acting in accordance with the views of a reputable body of opinion within the profession. This amounts to a requirement that you will act as a reasonable person in the circumstances of a class teacher. A breach of a duty of care can amount to negligence. In the 'compensation culture' that now exists, teachers feel that they will be held responsible for whatever happens to pupils in their care. It is perhaps easy to forget that pupils can be responsible for their actions and that accidents do occur. Finding a teacher (or their employer) negligent in the event of an accident will be influenced by whether or not it might reasonably have been foreseen. This is why you need to carry out a thorough *risk assessment* (RA) and why you need to follow government, local authority and school guidelines and procedures as part of your planning.

Risk assessment can be quite daunting for those meeting it for the first time, but as a science teacher, you will be no stranger to it. Many of your lessons, particularly those involving practical work, will have associated risk assessment criteria, although probably these will not be as extensive as the risk assessment you will need to undertake if you are going to take pupils on a visit or trip.

Safety professionals identify five steps in making a risk assessment:

1. *Identify hazards.* A hazard is something that has the potential to cause harm, but it is not a risk unless there is some form of human intervention (for example, an icy playground can be a hazard, but if nobody goes on it, it is not a risk).
2. *Decide who could be potentially harmed and how.*
3. *Decide how any risks could be removed, reduced or managed.*
4. *Record findings and actions.*
5. *Review the assessment and revise it if necessary.*

So, for instance, if a group of your pupils is going to do a beach study, you (if you are the party leader) must first assess the potential hazards. These might be rocks, pools, waves, vegetation, materials on the beach, and so on. Then you need to consider what the risks might be, which will vary according to the number of pupils, their age, experience, ability and any special needs that they, and accompanying adults, might have. Risks might be that pupils might fall into a deep rock pool; slip on the rocks; get hit with falling rocks (if working near cliffs); get swept away by a freak wave; get cut off by the incoming tide; have an allergic reaction to contact with vegetation; cut themselves on debris. Then you will think about reducing these risks, for example, 'no-go' areas; wearing gloves and other protective clothing; timing of the work bearing in mind tide times and so on. You will need to make sure that any accompanying adults have CRB (Criminal Records Bureau) clearance, particularly if the trip involves an overnight stay.

Using some form of transport will bring another set of risks. Travelling by coach is a safe option, but you should always consider what action to take in the event of an emergency.

You will need to record all this information using an appropriate form(s) and then submit it to the member of senior management in charge of visits and trips in school. This is because they are responsible for ensuring that leaders of school visits and trips, accompanying staff and other adults have the necessary qualifications, experience or training and that any visit complies with relevant regulations.

A further important point that I should make here is that your risk assessment will need to be continually reviewed and updated according to the conditions at the time of the activity. Thus, river sampling might be very pleasant on a warm summer afternoon when water levels are fairly low, but becomes a very risky exercise in mid-winter when the air and water temperatures are very cold and the river is full of fast-flowing water.

If all this sounds a bit much, do not be afraid to seek guidance if you are in doubt about any aspect. A lot of help is available from official guidelines such as *Health and Safety of Pupils on Educational Visits* (DfEE, 1998) and *Safety in Science Education* (DfEE, 1996). Nichols (1999) has also written a comprehensive guide on fieldwork for the Institute of Biology (IOB) (see the further reading section, Nichols, 1999, at the end of the chapter). Other organizations such as the Field Studies Council, the Royal Horticultural Society, the Youth Hostelling Association and the Woodland Trust offer advice and support (and sometimes funding for particular types of project) (see the 'Useful websites' at the end of this chapter). Also, do not forget to utilize the expertise of any specialist staff that are often available at many visit centres. They can provide planning support and can help you to design a 'tailor-made' programme for your pupils.

 (To get you thinking you might like to have a look at the scenarios on the accompanying website and decide what you would do in the circumstances described!)

Curriculum integration

In addition to the paramount importance of health and safety, another important factor in successful out-of-school experiences is how well they are integrated into the curriculum. Braund and Reiss (2006) argue that when it is thought through and carried out successfully, out-of-school learning can complement and extend work in school laboratories and classrooms. However, if we get it wrong, not only may we in the future continue to lose many of our best students from studying science, but the very worth of science may be increasingly questioned by those in power who sanction the use of large amounts of money on school science.

This sounds quite serious and although I would not go as far as to say that getting it wrong will cause the worth of science to be brought into question, I would agree with their point about the need to think carefully about how science work done outside laboratories and classrooms can complement that done inside them. I would also agree with them when they say that one way to achieve the goal of enhancing school trips is to focus on working with teachers to extend their pedagogies to make more productive use of the type of learning that informal settings can afford. If you want to read more about their ideas read their book, *Learning Science Outside the Classroom*, referenced at the end of the chapter (see the further reading section at the end of the chapter).

At this point, it might be helpful to outline the model of integration between school and museum learning developed by Griffin (2004). The model consists of a set of three useful guiding principles that can apply to any setting and which you can use to focus your thinking. These are integrate school and setting learning, provide conditions for self-directed learning, and facilitate learning strategies and activities appropriate to the formality–informality of the setting.

Integrate school and setting learning

Try not to view the visit or trip as a 'one-off' as this helps to play down the 'trip mentality'. It should be part of the work of the current topic being studied (rather than at some time before or after, which is perhaps more convenient from a logistical rather than educational point of view) and should be prepared for beforehand and followed up afterwards. In this connection, it would seem that recent developments to the science National Curriculum are also in line with a more context-based approach. This means that science outside the classroom including links with industry should form an important element of the curriculum.

Further, when considering links with industry, you would do well to heed the useful advice offered by Ross et al. (2000), namely: identifying your needs and those of the pupils; establishing initial contact with the organization in plenty of time; maintaining one point of contact; ensuring mutual familiarity with both environments (this will necessitate a preliminary visit on the part of one or the other); evaluating the exercise in terms of the original needs; giving feedback to both parties and, if the liaison works, maintaining a long-term link.

Perhaps the activities can also be cross-curricular, offering the opportunity to work collaboratively on a project with colleagues from other departments in school. Whatever the work, you must be very clear about the objectives of your visit and focus pupil activities on achieving these. You must also prepare the pupils so that they know the objectives, that is, why they are making the visit, and not just prepare them in terms of practicalities and logistics.

In connection with preparation, many organizations, for instance museums, offer preparatory workshops through in-service training (INSET) and open evenings for teachers, and are also very willing to discuss specific requirements in order to help you design a particular programme for your pupils. You may even think about a *series* of visits, so that pupils are less likely to view these as 'add-ons'. Peacock and Dunne (2006) argue that serial work helps your pupils to take part in longitudinal studies (common in the field of science – less common in school science), which can be very stimulating and challenging for all pupils, particularly the most able, where they can have a controlling say in the ongoing management and direction of the work. Even if it is not possible for a particular group of pupils to visit a site more than once, it is still possible to build up data banks by collating the findings from year-on-year visits and these can provide more realistic and extensive information for pupils to access.

Provide conditions for self-directed learning

For example, try to avoid the constricting 'gap-filling' worksheet by giving your pupils an element of choice in what they do, perhaps through a project that they have been working on in school. The Ideas and Evidence section of the science NC gives plenty of pointers, for instance, how scientists work today and in the past, social and environmental questions and ethical issues.

Facilitate learning strategies and activities appropriate to the formality–informality of the setting

Think carefully about how much writing or how much collaborative group work you want your pupils to do while at the visit site. There might be opportunities for presentations and performances by experts or hands-on workshops. In the follow-up, think about how pupils will record their work, for example, extended writing (such as projects and investigations), photographic displays, videos, collections, maps, cartoon strips, posters or oral presentations as a worthwhile and tangible reminder of their experience.

Point for reflection

Look through your school's syllabus at the modules/topics that you will be teaching over the next term or year. Identify one of your KS3 classes and one of your KS4 classes (and a post-16 class if you have any) and think about the possible integration of a visit or trip into an appropriate module for each class. What trip or visit would this be and how would you integrate it into the curriculum, that is, how would you prepare the pupils? What would they do while on the visit and how would you follow up afterwards?

A RANGE OF OPPORTUNITIES

A wide range of possibilities exists for out-of-classroom science with your pupils. In fact, the number of possibilities is probably only bounded by your own, your colleagues' and your pupils' creativity and imagination, but I want to highlight some here to start you thinking.

In school

Potentially, the easiest place to carry out science work outside the classroom is your school itself. This can be a rich learning resource on the doorstep, by offering opportunities for both formal and informal learning. Quite clearly, because schools have a wide range of buildings and grounds, with greater or lesser problems with upkeep and vandalism, you might need to be quite creative in thinking what might be done.

You might start with a survey of the school grounds that involves pupils as a useful way of collecting data to help with decision-making. Pupils could also complete a questionnaire asking for their views and ideas – they are usually quite frank and can be very forthcoming on how things can be improved!

Some projects will be easy to carry out, requiring little, if any, extra equipment and materials. Existing school buildings can provide a useful resource for learning about energy use, waste and recycling (including composting and litter) for example. Buildings and other walls can be used to study materials, pollution and habitats. Modest expense might be needed to set up and monitor a weather centre, or develop some habitat areas within the school grounds, for instance bird tables, bird boxes in trees, flower beds, vegetable plots, meadow areas, bulb planting and hedgehog boxes (you will find a good list of suggestions in Kelsey, 1995).

The creation of a pond, a bog or herb garden, a maze or even activity trails and areas would involve more time and expense. For ideas on the latter, see Borrows, (1984) and Forster (1989). Keep in mind that funding might be available in school, particularly if the proposed activities are linked to the school development plan!

Another good way of harnessing your pupils' enthusiasm for science and offering them an opportunity for breadth and extension is to set up a science club. However, the best way to organize such clubs is to have a clear programme and ground rules (with input on content and rules from pupils). Perhaps, as Parkinson (2002) suggests, you could have a circus of activities that pupils work round over a period of time. You could get them working on activities related to national organizations such as Salters' Chemistry Club, BAYS (British Association of Young Scientists) or CREST run by the BA (see 'Useful websites' at the end of the chapter).

Outside school

A wide range of possibilities

The locality around your school can offer a number of science-based opportunities for your pupils, perhaps some that are even within walking distance. These can include the study of streetscapes, building and demolition sites, city farms, parks, gardens, shopping malls, supermarkets, hospitals and local businesses such as opticians, dentists, physiotherapists and clinics.

Further away there may be visits to urban places that contrast with your pupils' own environment, or other environments such as: woods; quarries; farms; nature reserves; becks; streams; rivers; canals; lakes; the sea and seashore; ports and harbours; manufacturing companies; power stations; wind farms; sewage works; observatories; sites of special scientific interest; National Trust and industrial heritage sites; mines; caves; cemeteries; zoos; botanic gardens; museums and interactive science centres (ISCs). Many of these will have websites that will aid your planning and could provide resources that you might use.

In relation to ISCs, I love Wellington's (1998) description that they are like elephants, hard to define, but we all know one when we see one! He describes two types of exhibit that exist within ISCs – the experiential and the pedagogic. The first category gives the opportunity for pupils to experience (and perhaps interact with) some everyday phenomenon such as whirlwinds, optical illusions and water vortices. The second category sets out to teach something such as the position of organs or bones in the body, the operation of an engine or the separation of dyes by chromatography. It will be part of your planning to think about the balance between the two during your visit.

Some of the places mentioned above will also enable you to develop links with the world of commerce and technology. Ross et al. (2000) state that effective links between education and industry are a crucial bridge between the world of work and the world of education – they 'add value and improve business competitiveness by raising the aspirations and skills of the individuals involved' (p 167). They also note that 'if a pupil can see and understand the reasons for learning a particular subject then the learning process becomes more effective' (Ross et al.,: 169). This seems to me to be a great way of avoiding the perennial question, 'Why do we have to do this?'

Harrison (1998) notes a number of industry-related curriculum activities, such as scientists in schools, teachers and pupil placements, support and contexts for science activities, loan of equipment and provision of expert advice and services. In addition, a plethora of resources has been produced by organizations and companies for use by science teachers. You will need to think about how best to use these, particularly in relation to any bias that might be there from the producer. Thus, you need to ask questions such as 'what are the bits that are most credible?' and 'what important information has been left out?'

A number of the sites mentioned above offer potential for fieldwork. Remember fieldwork can be done in suitable areas close to school and data can be collected in a day or less. However, they can be much more extensive and involve taking part in expeditions, summer camps and visiting outdoor, field study and environmental centres in the UK and abroad. This could involve staying away for a few days or more, which can be a powerful way of developing key life skills such as communication and team-working and building confidence and self-esteem.

Dallas (1980) offers some ideas on fieldwork. In terms of use, think about the concepts that can be established more easily by actually being there and seeing at first hand rather than via second-hand classroom methods. Questions like 'what is there?', 'why is it there?', 'why is it where it is?', 'how many of them are there?', 'what is helping or hindering it?' and 'how is it recycled?' can be useful in helping pupils to think about the places they are studying.

Finally, do not forget to bear in mind opportunities to attend lecture demonstrations, conferences and local science society events as well as entering science competitions and fostering school–higher education links and visits.

Other outside sources

Wellington (2000) gives an interesting perspective in relation to science outside the classroom in his consideration of 'out-of-school science sources' and their role in informal learning (as opposed to the more formal learning via the curriculum in school – although he acknowledges that the division is not always clear-cut). Such sources might range from everyday experiences such as slipping on ice, to watching television or accessing a DVD.

He reports on the work of Lucas (1983) who produced a review of sources of informal learning and distinguished between intentional and unintentional sources and between accidental and deliberate encounters with learning sources. Thus, a visit to an interactive science centre is likely to be a deliberate encounter with an intentional source. That is, learning via experiencing scientific phenomena at first hand and reading explanations of what is happening. However, a visit to somewhere like Alton Towers might be a deliberate encounter, but with an unintentional source of learning, say perhaps learning about friction whilst watching a rollercoaster. On the other hand, learning about escape velocity from web browsing about space might be an accidental encounter from an intentional source whereas learning about AIDS from watching *EastEnders* may still be accidental but with an unintentional source.

This chapter has been primarily concerned with the teacher planning a deliberate encounter with an intentional source, but to take your thinking further, you might be interested in reading Wellington's account of using other sources, including using material from newspapers (see the further reading section at the end of the chapter).

Point for reflection

Point for reflection

Based on the nature of your school and grounds as well as its location and bearing in mind the suggestions in this chapter and in the further reading:

- note down the ways in which you could possibly use your school buildings and grounds for science outside the classroom;
- make a list of the external locations, both within the locality and within your region that are possible venues for you to take your pupils on a visit or trip.

What the research says

Tilling (2004) carried out a study to answer the following questions: what is the need to study out of the classroom in science? If all your needs can be accessed electronically why go out of school – you can run a virtual field trip!

The article describes how the Field Studies Council provides many courses for teachers and pupils because they believe that out-of-classroom or residential visits are an intrinsic part of education and personal development. So much so, that they provide training so that teachers can have the confidence and knowledge to provide safe effective fieldwork for their students.

There is something that cannot be measured in the experience gained through fieldwork where real investigation is carried out on real data, and this is key to providing a broad and balanced curriculum.

How, then, in the climate of risk and recent poor publicity can teachers justify the time and cost involved in taking pupils out of school? The Office for Standards in Education have reported that outdoor education has many aspects of good practice giving a depth to the curriculum. In addition to curriculum benefits, pupils can acquire life skills to equip them for future employment.

www.publications.parliament.uk/pa/cm200405/cmselect/cmenvaud/84/84we37 .htm (accessed September 2008).

Further reading

Braund, M. and Reiss, M. (eds) (2004) *Learning Science Outside the Classroom*. London: RoutledgeFalmer.
Lots of information and ideas about making learning outside the classroom productive.

Borrows, P. (1984) 'The Pimlico Chemistry Trail', *School Science Review*, 66(235): 221–33.

Forster, S. (1989) 'Streetwise physics', *School Science Review*, 71(254): 15–22. Information on activity trails and areas.

Department of Education and Science (DES) (1990) The Outdoor Classroom *Building Bulletin 71*. London: DES.

Department for Education and Employment (DfEE) (1996) *Safety in Science Education*. London: HMSO.

Department for Education and Employment (DfEE) (1998) *Health and Safety of Pupils on Educational Visits*. London: DfEE.

Department for Education and Skills (DfES) (2006) *Learning Outside the Classroom Manifesto*. Nottingham: DfES.

Nichols, D. (1999) *Safety in Biological Fieldwork*. London: IOB. Detailed information, guidance, checklists and exemplar planning materials.

Kelsey, M. (1995) *Developing the School Site as a Resource for Science Teaching*. Kingston upon Thames: Croner Publications. A list of suggestions for work on the school site.

Wellington, J. (2000) *Teaching and Learning Secondary Science. Contemporary issues and practical approaches*. London: Routledge. Information about a range of sources for science outside the classroom.

 Useful websites

Live links to these websites can be found on the companion website www.sagepub.co.uk/secondary

www.the-ba.net
The British Association for information on science clubs and CREST awards

www.fieldworklib.org/
A website devoted to science fieldwork – the Fieldwork Knowledge Library developed by the Institute of Education and the British Ecological Society.

http://www.field-studies-council.org/documents/research/ITE%20report.pdf
Initial Teacher Education and the Outdoor Classroom booklet

www.field-studies-council.org
Field Studies Council

www.rhs.org.uk
Royal Horticultural Society

www.yha.org.uk
Youth Hostelling Association

www.woodland-trust.org.uk
Woodland Trust

All the above five organizations can provide information and advice on various types of visits and trips.

www.kew.org/
Royal Botanic Gardens

www.mlayorkshire.org.uk
Creative Minds Science Club tool kit

www.nhm.ac.uk/
National History Museum

www.planet-science.com
Information about science clubs

www.resources.schoolscience.co.uk/Salters/chemclub34.html
Information about Salters Chemistry Club

www.scizmic.net
The science discovery clubs network

www.setnet.org.uk/ www.nebpn.org
SETPOINT (business) contacts for out of school activities

www.sciencemuseum.org.uk/
Science Museum in London

www.24hourmuseum.org.uk/trlout/TRA11863.html
24-hour museum – listings of UK museums and interactive science centres (and their websites)

12 REFLECTIVE PRACTICE AND PROFESSIONAL DEVELOPMENT

Tony Liversidge

This chapter:

- discusses the stages of reflective practice
- examines how to evaluate your lessons on teaching practice
- offers comments on how experienced teachers evaluate their lessons
- gives a rationale for researching practice, describes what classroom-based research is and outlines the possible stages in such a research project
- describes how to gain a teaching post, including formulating an application and being successful at interview
- identifies aspects of professional development, such as keeping a professional portfolio, your Career Entry and Development Profile and the induction year
- discusses the need for a continued commitment to professional development throughout your career
- summarizes the support for professional development that is available to you from local advisory services and professional science associations
- reviews the processes for the Career Entry and Development Profile, and the induction year
- outlines possible opportunities for involvement in further higher-level study.

Teacher training has been considered by some as a means of providing teachers with a tool kit of skills. Osborne and Freyberg (1985) argue that these skills are neither simple, nor directly teachable and that it is more useful to regard teaching as an activity that relies on a continuing component of experimentation throughout a teacher's career. This is not an easy task, but you can set about this by keeping a key principle in mind – that you need to continually think about what you are doing, why you are doing it and how to do it effectively as well as systematically evaluating what you have done, particularly in terms of what pupils have learnt. This is what is meant by *reflective practice* and it is the reflective science teacher who will improve their practice and successfully develop their career.

REFLECTIVE PRACTICE

Reflective science teachers

You will be aware that the QTS Standards include a requirement that you should 'reflect on and improve your practice, and take responsibility for identifying and meeting your professional needs' (TDA, 2007a: 8) and thus that a significant part of your teaching course includes the expectation that you will reflect on and evaluate your teaching. Wright (2008) argues that developing the habit of reflecting on your work is perhaps the most significant driver of your training because this will improve pupil leaning and will improve your own practice. In fact, you probably feel that your tutors and mentors expect you to evaluate 'anything that moves'! However, the reason that tutors do push you on this aspect is so that you will develop these good habits – you do not want to be the teacher who the old adage describes as having ten times one year's experience rather than the converse!

Notions of the *reflective teacher practitioner* have much in common with those of Schön (1983) who developed ideas about the role of reflection in professional practice. Applied to teaching, in making the many decisions that you have to make during a science lesson, you are *reflecting in action* whereas you are *reflecting on action* when you think about what went on and try to plan for a more effective situation next time if appropriate. These types of reflection are often incorporated into a well-used model known as the PTAE cycle – **P**lan, **T**each, **A**ssess and **E**valuate as shown in Figure 12.1.

The cycle works in a clockwise direction, starting with planning. Your reflection on, and evaluation of, your previous science lesson with a class will inform the planning of the next lesson (or lessons). Chapter 3 you recall was all about planning lessons. The next stage is to teach the lesson (Chapter 4) and you will probably find that you are in fact evaluating all the time while teaching. This is the reflection in action (sometimes called 'thinking on your feet') that enables you to make the many decisions that have to be made about how the lesson needs to proceed. Next, the assessment that goes on during the lesson is helpful in telling you how much the pupils have learnt (Chapter 6). You can then evaluate the lesson, which should help you to plan the next lesson that you teach and so on. In this way, the best science teachers never feel that they can stop thinking about what they are teaching and what their pupils are learning – this is the 'experimentation' described earlier by Osborne and Freyberg.

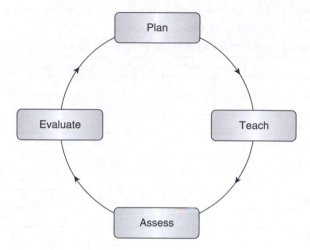

Figure 12.1   The PTAE cycle

Lesson evaluation

Lesson evaluation by beginning teachers
In relation to the evaluation stage of the cycle and reflection on practice, Parkinson (2002) has identified three stages that you will go through. These are: 'impressionistic' (one or two instances stick in your mind and colour your interpretation of the whole lesson); 'beginning to focus' (you look at pupil achievement and perhaps focus on one or two specific issues) and 'reflective practitioner' (you look at a range of evidence and are able to make sound judgements about how to improve).

During training, you will be expected to produce detailed written lesson evaluations, which document these reflective stages. To facilitate this, I recommend that you set up a template that gives a series of prompts or questions to provide a focus. Figure 12.2 is a completed example of how to do this.

Stage 1, *impressionistic reflection,* takes place soon after the lesson has ended, often as a quick personal reflection on what went well or what went less well. The first part of the pro forma in Figure 12.2 facilitates this. The danger here, however, is the potential subjectivity of your evaluation, which may be affected by one or two key incidents. In my experience, many beginning science teachers allow what might be relatively minor negative lesson events (usually related to behaviour or classroom management issues) to cloud their whole evaluation and they will regard the lesson as being quite poor when in fact the majority of the lesson has been good.

The lesson evaluation in Figure 12.2 was produced by a trainee teacher on their final (or 'synoptic') school-based experience. The lesson was with a mixed-ability

Lesson Evaluation

Quick lesson rating – my performance *(To be completed at the end of every lesson)*

Criteria	Very good	Good	Satisfactory	Unsatisfactory
Knowledge		√		
Resources		√		
Lesson objectives			√	
Behaviour Management			√	
Risk assessment		√		
Differentiation				√
Feedback to pupils			√	
Assessment			√	
Variety and pace			√	
Level appropriate?			√	
Visuals – high quality?		√		

General comments (related to the quick overview)

I had practised the practical beforehand and was able to guide pupils in their observations. Some groups took much longer than others did – why? Worksheet was well prepared, but not challenging enough for most able in class – they finished quickly and were a bit disruptive towards end of lesson.

Were the learning outcomes achieved? How do you know?

Possibly – some good answers to questions in plenary, but I will need to mark worksheets to get a more detailed view.

Detailed Evaluation

Things that went well	Why they went well
1. RA thoroughly prepared 2. Most pupils engaged during practical 3. Some good contributions to plenary	1. Enabled me to give clear practical guidance 2. Clear instructions and me monitoring groups during practical 3. Pupils enjoyed practical and this made them think

Things that were less successful	How can I avoid this/ improve upon this in the future?
1. Worksheet 2. Some groups took longer to start and therefore finish 3. Time for plenary	1. A more challenging question at the end for more able 2. Give a warning to these groups that they may be changed if they don't work better 3. Make sure I leave more time for plenary – get pupils started on experiment quicker

What learning has taken place this lesson?

Learning	Evidence
All pupils practised the skill of accurately measuring temperatures. Some pupils understood why temps. had to be taken at 30s intervals	Observations and conversations with pupils during practical
	Correctly drawn graphs
All pupils were able to draw the graph, but some needed quite a lot of help	Via Q&A in plenary. (I will also need to mark their worksheets to check this)
Most pupils were able to identify which container was best	

Targets arising from this lesson
1. Get pupils started on practical work sooner so that enough time is left for a full plenary at the end of the lesson
2. Think about structuring worksheet(s) for this class with more challenging 'thinking' questions at the end
3. Using 'indicator' pupils of different abilities to answer questions in the plenary

Figure 12.2 Science lesson evaluation pro forma

Year 7 class, who were doing an experiment to settle the argument between their science teachers about which type of container kept their coffee hottest during break (a ceramic cup, a polystyrene cup, a cardboard cup or an insulated cup with no lid). In their quick rating and overview, the teacher has identified that the more able pupils in the class were not challenged by the questions on the worksheet as they were simply required to write down what they did, what results they got, draw a graph and then say which cup was best – fairly factual stuff.

Lessons potentially consist of complicated sequences of events and it can be difficult to identify key aspects and even more difficult to analyse them and understand why they happened. This is where discussion with a more experienced colleague (a tutor, mentor or other teaching colleague) who has observed your lesson can help with a more *focused reflection* (stage 2).

In their book, Battersby and Gordon (2006) note that student teachers learnt more from situations that have been taxing and from 'failing' experiences than from those lessons which seem to lack 'key' incidents. In my experience, there is some truth in this as such aspects are readily put forward in discussion in our university sessions. However, it is important to not just focus on the 'negative' experiences as key elements of your learning, but that you and any observer of your lesson also need to identify the things that went well and *why*. By doing this, you are more likely to be able to incorporate such strategies, procedures and resources into future lessons. You will make mistakes – everyone does – but the important thing is to learn from them and not make the same one twice!

Thus, a useful model to adopt here is the *feedback sandwich* as it can help you to develop a positive attitude to receiving advice, and a positive attitude to change. Specifically, you should demonstrate during training that, you can 'act upon advice and feedback and be open to coaching and mentoring' and 'have a creative and constructively critical approach towards innovation, being prepared to adapt their practice whose benefits and improvements are identified' (TDA, 2007a: 8).

Using this model, you start by discussing the things that you and they think were successful, and why. Early on in your teaching experience, this might be about your performance, for instance, your science subject knowledge, pitching at the right level and managing the classroom and the pupils' behaviour, but over time should move on to be more concerned with the pupils' learning experiences. You will be looking, for instance, at whether the pupils have been engaged and interested in what you have asked them to do; how enthusiastically and accurately they answer your questions and what questions they ask you; what the quality of their written work is and how well they complete any assessment tasks.

The next part of the discussion considers the things that that you both think went less well and why, formulating targets relating to how to improve and not make any of the same mistakes again. Finally, the discussion should be finished off with a summary of the discussion and whether any of the successful aspects could be applied to other classes/situations/topics. This, as Parkinson (2002) notes, avoids you getting into situations where you have put into practice something that you have been told in a previous discussion, only to be told that you are still doing things incorrectly (sometimes an issue when you are having observations and discussions with more than one colleague).

Wright (2006) gives examples of some questions that can guide you or your observer. These include:

- Is the content of the lesson scientifically accurate?
- Do teachers' plans provide for progress of all groups of pupils and those who need individual support?
- Do teachers share the objectives of each lesson with the pupils so that they have a clear idea of what they are expected to learn?
- Are the different activities planned and organized for effective learning with appropriate consideration being given to health and safety?
- Are pupils given enough opportunity and time to think through, explain and explore their own science ideas using enquiry, investigation, research and discussion?
- Is marking regular and consistent?

Parkinson's third stage, *reflective practitioner*, occurs when you undertake further focused self-reflection, for instance when you are planning for the next lesson(s) with the same class. However, it is important to remember that you cannot possibly evaluate everything that goes on in your lessons and so you should focus on two or three aspects – maybe things that have gone particularly well or badly. However, the fundamental question that should underlie all of your lesson evaluations is 'Did the pupils achieve the learning objectives of the lesson?' Here, Wright (2008) offers three questions to help you make this judgement: What were they meant to learn? Did they learn it? How do I know? Your answers to these questions will help you to set development targets. As you can see, the second part of the pro forma provides a framework for you to do this.

In the evaluation in Figure 12.2, you can read that the teacher felt that the practical went well as most pupils were engaged. As the teacher notes, this is probably because he/she had practised the experiment beforehand, done a thorough risk assessment, had given the pupils clear instructions and monitored the class while they were carrying it out. I think that another element here is that the practical was set in a 'real life' context – to settle an argument between their teachers!

Where the lesson could have been improved, was in relation to pace and getting the pupils working on the practical more quickly to leave time for a more thorough plenary at the end. Also, certain groups needed to be monitored more carefully at the start to get them going quicker – the teacher has decided to have a word with these groups to try to get an improvement.

In addition, another area for development is in relation to challenge for the most able pupils. A target for the lesson is to think about having more 'thinking' questions at the end. Such questions might include, 'why do you think this cup kept the coffee hottest?' or 'what could you do to provide more conclusive evidence?'

Finally, the third target is in relation to using 'indicator' pupils in their plenary. This is a strategy whereby you would identify certain pupils in your class as 'typical' of a level of ability and, rather than trying to ask all pupils a question, you would choose one of your 'indicators'. Whom you choose would depend on the difficulty of the question. Clearly, this would also need to be a fluid situation, otherwise the pupils would soon get wise and leave the answering to the identified pupils!

(For comparison, you should have a look at some other examples of lesson evaluation templates and completed evaluations on the accompanying website.)

In addition to lesson observations, Wright (2006) notes that scrutiny of pupils' work and talking to them about their attitudes to science and the effectiveness of teaching and learning can provide a lot of valuable information. Further reflection on action involving thinking about conversations, observations of other teachers' lessons, meetings, professional development activities, university sessions and assignments, reading and research – in fact just about everything – can provide a source of information and evidence which can help to frame your thoughts.

Through adopting such a staged strategy of reflection and evaluation, you will accumulate a lot of information related to your professional progress and development. This will be found in your teaching file(s) or perhaps in a reflective diary, but most commonly on training courses, you will be required to also collate, organize and critically analyse key aspects of this material in a *professional portfolio.* Such an analysis might provide a description of an experience with a commentary that asks why it happened and the use of reading and theory to help support with ideas from the literature. This is an excellent way of providing evidence that you have met any required teaching standards.

Website

Try this approach on one of the lessons on the website

Lesson evaluation by experienced teachers

Once you have completed your training, you are unlikely to write out detailed formal evaluations of your lessons in the type of format described above. What you are expected to do, however, is to continue to use professional reflection to informally evaluate your lessons, to review your performance and to take responsibility for improving your teaching. The effort that you put into lesson evaluations, and the support that you receive, should help you to develop the necessary skills so that you can continue to improve your teaching, both with and without the continued support of colleagues. The evidence that you gather and its critical analysis will also help to develop your professional portfolio.

The following examples of evaluation come from interviews with experienced teachers, with brief commentary on them.

> A successful lesson for me is when I know the pupils are going out of the classroom and they have achieved the objectives that we set at the beginning of the lesson. I aim to measure whether they have achieved them or not through my assessment in the lesson. I find that the plenary is really useful for that – asking the questions at the end, and giving them the opportunity to reflect.

This teacher is making the links between lesson objectives, pupil learning and assessment of that learning. However, perhaps it is not always possible to assess what all pupils have learned during your lesson, particularly through a Q&A plenary at the end and further assessment might be necessary for example through homework or in the next lesson(s). The point about giving them an opportunity to reflect is an interesting one – how this is done is key (that is, does the teacher allow pupils time for group discussion and for *them* to raise any questions?).

> I evaluate my lessons almost straight away rather than going away to think about it. It tends to be a mental note as I am going through: that didn't work, don't do that again; that works really well; or those elements of the lesson didn't fit together very well.

> I go away and analyse later. I analyse what has happened and I go through what I taught, and then I make lots of mental notes.

> At home, I will make notes in my planner or write on the back of my planning forms directly for the next day or maybe for the next year when the topic comes round again. The notes will trigger straight away – I'm not going to do it like last time or what I did last year really worked.

These teachers are talking about the different evaluative strategies that they use from the informal mental note that they do straight after the lesson, through mental notes done some time later to making written notes on planning forms. I must say that I would advocate you using the latter method, because if you are anything like me you will possibly forget some of your mental notes! If you have written these down in your planner or on your lesson plans then, unless you lose your plans, they will still be there for you to reference no matter how much further in the future you come to look at them.

> If something doesn't work perfectly I say to myself, well, that didn't work, but it is not the end of the world. It's not because I'm a bad teacher; it's just that today it didn't work, and tomorrow I'll try a different approach.

> If I change anything through evaluating the lesson it tends to be the difficulty of the task. If I pitch the lesson too high or too low, then I note it down. If the work is too easy, the pupils get bored, and then that is when you can start having behavioural problems in the lesson. Sometimes I change the task completely or the length of time that I spend expecting the pupils to do things.

> I think that evaluation is something that gets easier as you go along, because you get over-critical of yourself initially and then as you go along you get a bit easier on yourself. But you also have more options and know when something doesn't work, and you are not scared to try something different.

Comments like these indicate the benefit of having the experience to realize that we live in the real world and sometimes activities do not go as well as we have planned. In these instances, you reflect and think how to develop them for next time – the level of task, the time allowed or even omitting the task completely. Good science teachers are constantly doing this, but they also leave well alone – 'if it ain't broke, don't fix it!'

Points for reflection

Remind yourself about the three stages of reflection described by Parkinson (2002) and then look at the science lesson evaluation pro forma in Figure 12.2. Does this pro forma provide a structure to support his stages? If not, how could you redesign it to do this?

Compare the pro forma with any that you have been given on your training course (or those on the website). What are the key similarities and differences? Do any of these pro formas allow you to answer Wright's (2008) three key questions from page 209 (What were they meant to learn? Did they learn it? How do I know?)

How would you adapt the evaluation pro formas that you use in your initial training for use in:

- your first year of teaching
- your early years of teaching
- later in your career?

REFLECTIVE PRACTICE AND CLASSROOM-BASED RESEARCH

Why do teachers need to research classroom practice?

In the introduction to this chapter, I suggested that as a reflective science teacher, you should continually improve your practice and thus success-fully develop your career. This reflection will help you to make choices and decisions, but an interesting question posed by Millar (2002) is to ask to what extent these decisions are influenced by knowledge that has arisen from science education research. To answer this question, he argues that if evidence from research is collected and applied systematically to inform the decisions, this will lead to better outcomes for learners. You will recall that I indicated in the previous section that part of reflection on action involves this very same use of research evidence to inform practice.

However, there are some issues to consider here. As Gilbert (2002) notes, research in science education does not provide 'timeless truths' because the context of practice is continually changing. Ratcliffe et al. (2002) state that more discussion with practitioners in professional set-tings about the variety and purpose of education research methods may assist teacher evaluation of research evidence. Moreover, Hopkins (2002) argues that research findings should not be regarded as 'panaceas to be followed slavishly'.

An even more severe indictment is given by White (2002) who notes that science education is not exempt from the general criticism that research has not had sufficient influence on practice. He states that there might be a number of reasons for this, but concludes that problem areas are lack of time to plan, lack of equipment, large classes, a mandated syllabus and a rigid examination system. In addition, the autonomy of teachers in deciding what goes on in their own classrooms and their isolation in this respect as well as the fact that they have not been traditionally rewarded for their research contributions means that custom dictates that the majority do not have much inclination to engage in research studies. Even if they do manage to investigate an aspect of their work, they can find it difficult to have time to share their findings with others.

The solution to this, contends White, is for teaching to become a research-based profession through the greater involvement of practitioners in research. This view is supported by Taber (2007), who describes a strong model of teacher professionalism where classroom teachers are expected to actively evaluate their own work and to seek to improve it using evidence. To some extent, he says, researching your own professional work is 'part of the job' for today's teacher. Thus, this requires you to have both the conceptual frameworks for thinking about teaching and learning that can provide the basis for evaluating your teaching *and* procedural knowledge to undertake small-scale classroom enquiry.

In other words, Taber is advocating that you undertake research in your own and your colleagues' classrooms in order to examine and develop your teaching and create a more dynamic learning environment. However, in order for this to become a reality, White (2002) argues that significant changes to the existing situation such as changes to teachers' conditions of work to give them time to experiment and share their findings with others, needs to occur.

Although lack of time continues to be a perennial issue for science teachers, there has been a recent impetus to engage teachers as sole researchers or in teams as part of their professional development. This is evident in the fact that beginning teachers on undergraduate and postgraduate courses as well as those undertaking higher-level professional study and development are now expected to engage in research projects, assignments and dissertations as essential elements of this work.

If you are a science graduate, you may have become familiar with research methods in science as part of your undergraduate science course, but unless you have engaged in some educational research, you will have far less familiarity with the methods associated with this type of study, which are quite different and typically do not include controlled experiments and manipulation of variables. Thus, the next part of the chapter gives an overview of what a classroom-based research project into teachers' practice is and how you could set about undertaking it.

What is classroom-based research?

Hopkins (2002) refers to classroom research as an act undertaken by teachers to enhance their own, or a colleague's teaching, to test the assumptions of educational theory in practice, or as a means of evaluating and implementing whole-school priorities. He suggests six principles for such research, which are particularly relevant for any teacher. They are as follows:

1. The teacher's primary job is to teach and any research method should not interfere with, or disrupt, the teaching commitment.
2. The method of data collection should not be too demanding on the teacher's time (and furthermore, that the teacher needs to be certain about the data collection technique before using it).
3. The research methodology employed must be rigorous enough to allow any changes developed and implemented as a result of the findings of the project to be based on reliable data.
4. The research focus undertaken by the teacher should be one to which he or she is committed.
5. Teacher-researchers need to pay close attention to the ethical procedures surrounding their work.

Classroom research should adopt a 'classroom exceeding' perspective – it should be disseminated so that it contributes to building an improvement in practice across the members of a school community.

With these principles in mind, the next part of the chapter outlines the stages of a typical research approach, but before embarking on your project – a word of warning – familiarize yourself with any course or project requirements first. Thus, you need to ask questions such as: What type of research project is actually expected? How and when is it to be presented? What are the expectations of tutors or supervisors? How can I best use their advice to guide me to a relevant and well-written project? Who else might be able to help me? Can I work collaboratively on the project?

Stages of classroom-based research

Robson (2007) sets out the 'project milestones' of a typical research study in a very simple and accessible way. These are very useful in helping to give thought about the overall design of your research and thus helping you to come up with a project that does what you intend it to do.

First, and perhaps quite obviously, you need to decide on a *focus or topic for your project* and then *formulate the questions to which you are seeking the answers* (your research questions). You will then need to settle on *the ways in which you will get the answers* to your questions by deciding on the approach to your research. These are the styles or strategies that you will use which can range from 'tightly controlled experimental design collecting quantitative (numerical) data, to ethnographic approaches relying on participant observation and producing largely qualitative (non-numerical, usually verbal) data' (Robson, 2007). You will also need to make decisions about your research methods, such as questionnaires, observation, documentary analysis, etc.

The next milestone is to *seek the answers*, where you will gather data either first hand (primary data) or from existing information, for example documentary analysis (secondary data). Then you will need to make sense of the data by doing some kind of analysis and interpretation. Finally, you will *tell others what you have found* by writing a report and this will include recommendations for action.

Selecting a focus

Selecting a focus for your research can be easy, particularly if it is given to you, you only have a short list to select from, or you have a burning desire or need to study a certain topic area. On the other hand, it can be notoriously difficult, as many of the undergraduate and postgraduate science students that I have worked with have found, because the possible areas of science education that might be addressed for classroom study are so diverse. Thus, their choices have included looking at pupil peer and self-assessment; using concept mapping as an assessment tool; role play in science; the use of models in science; misconceptions related to key science topics; the value of science homework; the use of ICT in teaching science; why girls do not study physics post-16; creative science activities and pupil motivation; the pros and cons of taking science out of the classroom and so on. So you can see, there is a lot of scope!

Whatever the focus, Robson (2007) advises that any topic should fulfil three main criteria. First, and in my opinion most importantly, is that it should be *of interest to you* in order to maintain you through the lows and 'sticky patches'. Another advantage here is to choose an issue that is important to your pupils, the science department or your school. To some extent, you can then incorporate your research into the normal course of your school activities, people are more likely to be interested in what you are doing and you may get more support for doing it, including sharing ideas and working collaboratively where the project allows. This would be particularly relevant if you were on school-based experience and here your mentor may be an important person with whom to negotiate a focus.

In addition, Taber (2007) also notes that having a genuine interest in the topic of focus becomes increasingly important as the level of the project increases, say from undergraduate to master's or doctoral level study, because of the increasing amount of time that will need to be invested in order to produce an acceptable report.

The second criterion is that it should be *feasible for you to deliver something worthwhile on the topic given the available time and resources*. Hopkins (2002) gives some sound advice here. First, he says, do not tackle issues that you cannot do anything about. For instance, it may be difficult to change the banding or streaming system in your school in the short or medium term. Secondly, if you have not undertaken any research studies before, only take on small-scale and limited issues to prevent discouragement if things do not go to plan. However, he notes that whatever the scale of the project, it is important to make connections between your research, teaching and learning and your school's aims or developmental priorities.

The third of Robson's criteria is that it should *meet any course requirements*. Thus if you are studying on an undergraduate or postgraduate training course or, say, doing a higher degree, you should follow formal and informal guidance and advice about what is expected by writing up as required; by not exceeding any word counts and by meeting deadlines and so on. You will be 'throwing' marks away if you do not follow this guidance and one of my sources of frustration is that some students still fail to do this, despite all the help offered. So, my advice here is to make maximum 'use' of your supervising tutor by attending tutorials and regularly liaising with them, particularly in relation to starting off on the right track, but also to help them to guide your study and writing along the way.

Once you have decided on a broad research area, you need to focus this on a particular aspect. Having a working title will help. I like the two-part approach where the first part is a 'catchy' question (as an attention grabber) and the second part gives a little more detail about the focus. For instance you could have 'Board or bored? A case study of the use of the interactive white board in the teaching of the periodic table to Year 10 pupils' or 'Just a lot of messing about? The uses of role play in teaching about particles' and so on.

From topic to research questions

The next step, which is to formulate your research question(s), is more difficult and ideally, you should try to make these as unambiguous as possible. These are the what/who/where/when and why questions such as 'What is currently happening?', 'Why is it a problem?' and 'How can I go about doing something about it?' A good idea is to try to generate a list of these questions and then select certain ones to pursue and find the answers to – this will depend on the nature and size of your project. For example, if you were undertaking the interactive whiteboard (IWB) study, you might want to know the answers to questions such as 'How do teachers use the IWB?', 'What resources do they use?', 'How do they make the use of the IWB interactive?' and 'Which pupils are most engaged/least engaged?'

However, it is important to note that you may only be able to tentatively formulate your questions at this stage. It is more likely that you will be able to refine them after you have looked at some of the work done in the field that you are investigating. Thus, this is what you need to do next.

Reviewing the literature

Whatever focus you choose it is unlikely that there will not already be a body of existing relevant research and it is important for you to find out what is already known about your topic in order to help you conceptualize and think about your focus. This is commonly referred to as the literature review.

Ideally, you would search out and evaluate all relevant prior research. Depending on the topic focus, this might be a massive task and one that is unrealistic for your purpose (although extensive literature reviews are expected at master's and certainly doctoral levels), but reading and considering some of the most relevant studies will be invaluable. Do not forget your tutor or supervisor as a useful source of information. Your topic might link into their research interest areas and thus they might be able to give you a 'kick start' in relation to useful starting references.

Searching for sources can be very absorbing (hours can drift by in a library or pursuing a trail online!) but also very time-consuming and, notwithstanding a bit of serendipity, it is best to have a 'plan of attack'. Undertaking a key word search should be part of your plan in looking through library catalogues and the Internet. Within a search resource, using the 'help' key will give you guidance on how to search with 'or' (to combine key words to give more 'hits'), 'and' (to link two key words and reduce hits) and 'not' (to reduce items of a particular type) being useful parameters. Whichever search strategy you use, there is one cardinal rule: *when you come across relevant sources, make sure that you keep a full bibliographic reference for each of them*. This will potentially save you hours of frustration trying to find the reference again – take it from someone who has been there.

While uncovering sources, or when you have accumulated a number of them, the next task is to read them. Taber (2007) suggests a useful method of critically reading relevant research studies and getting an overview of what they are about by using a summary sheet to make notes in relation to certain key headings. Those he offers are:

- study (who did the study and when)
- focus (what the study was about)
- aim/purpose/rationale/research questions (what the study was trying to find out)
- methodology (what type of research it is)
- sample (size, nature); data collection techniques used
- ethical issues
- analytical processes (how the data was analysed)
- findings – type of knowledge claims made (what the authors are claiming to have found) and how does this inform education (how this applies)?

As part of this process, he suggests that you should be asking yourself a series of overarching questions such as: 'How do they know?', 'How confident can

I be that the claims are justified by the evidence?', 'What kind of evidence would be needed to support such a claim?', 'Do these findings have a limited application?' and 'How could I find out if these findings apply to my own professional context?'

(Taber gives an example of a completed analysis sheet on page 13 of his book – see the further reading section at the end of this chapter.)

Once you have read and analysed your sources, the next hurdle is writing a coherent review. The danger here for novice researchers is that this is not simply a case of trying to include as many as you can in what amounts to a descriptive list. First, it is vital that you should bear in mind that sometimes one or a couple of studies might be really central to your project and these can form the 'backbone' of your review. Even if this is not the case, it is usually best to limit yourself (especially in small-scale projects) to including a few key pieces of work and give detail of why they are relevant to your own study. Secondly, and perhaps most importantly, you should heed the words of Taber (2007: 57) who advises that when a literature review is done well it is 'a synthesis of findings that sets out how the researcher understands the current state of the field'. (p. 57)

Methodology

Selecting a methodology for your research will guide your plan, which in turn will frame what data you collect and how you analyse it. On the face of it, this might sound relatively simple, and indeed, Taber (2007) offers a useful analogy here in terms of strategy and tactics. Effective research, he notes, has an overall coherent strategy (methodology), which outlines the way that the research aims are achieved. This strategy will then translate into a set of tactics (methods or techniques) that build towards the overall aim. In other words, your methodology is the strategy that you employ, and your methods are the tactics that you use, for answering your research questions.

However, you will find by reading the literature on research methodology further, that there is a whole world of discussion about the principles underpinning this choice. This discussion usually involves consideration of philosophical stances on research, which are often described as *research paradigms*. You may have come across these with various labels such as 'qualitative' and 'quantitative' or 'fixed' and 'flexible' or 'positivistic' and 'interpretivist'. Using these labels, writers have attempted to present a way of modelling the complex phenomenon of research, including the field of educational research. Further examination of such models is, however, beyond the scope of the current discussion. My advice is that if you are interested in this particular aspect of research, you should look at Taber (and other texts such as Robson and Hopkins – see the further reading section at the end of the chapter) for further information. These texts also give details about a range of methodological strategies such as experiments, surveys, case study, ethnography and grounded theory, which I do not intend to cover here. However, at this point, it might be useful to just give a little more information about a methodology known as *action research*.

Berg (2001) notes that this approach has often been used over the past 20 to 30 years to investigate the classroom. An action research approach is one that emphasizes the involvement of the researcher in a situation, with a view to improving it (Robson, 2007). There are many variants of action research, but it is typically seen as a cyclical process involving investigating a particular issue by planning a change; finding out what happens after the change; reflecting on this; planning further action and so on.

Robson also notes a number of advantages of action research for you as a teacher–researcher. First, the effect of your presence as the researcher on the situation is integral to the method. Secondly, it provides a means of addressing and resolving practical problems. Thirdly, it can contribute to a cycle of development and change and finally that it can contribute to your professional and personal development.

Thus, this could be an approach that you consider suitable for your research project. If so, the texts above will provide further details.

Methods of collecting data

Three things that all researchers should consider when planning their methods are *reliability*, *validity* and *ethics*. *Reliability* relates to repetition and you can argue that your data is reliable if you get the same results when a measurement is repeated under the same conditions. However, in the classroom it is virtually impossible to do this! For example if you reuse some kind of test and see whether you get the same answers from your pupils, then logically the conditions are not the same because the time will be different and they may have changed in some way in the mean time. This raises a possible dilemma, as in small-scale pieces of research you would normally use one main method of data collection. Thus, in this sort of case, and in order to reassure readers of your work about its reliability you might, on the one hand, need to give a very detailed description of how the test was carried out. On the other, you might decide to use *triangulation* and employ another method of getting information from your pupils, for instance by interviewing them or get data from different individuals. This enables you to give a better answer to the question 'Why should I believe you?' but of course extends the scale of your project. These are the kinds of decisions that are often part of the research process.

A second major concern with the data you collect is *validity*. Validity refers to whether something measures what it is supposed to measure. A measure can be reliable and not valid, but it cannot be valid if it is not reliable. If you are using a very structured, experimental design, there are often mathematical methods of assessing various types of validity. However, when you are using more flexible designs and qualitative methods your reader has to be convinced that you are telling the 'whole truth' and not that you have 'cherry picked' certain data to include because it fits with what you think is happening, rather than being a fair and unbiased account of the situation.

The third key element for your consideration is *ethics*. Information about ethical aspects forms a central part of the literature on research and there are many sources of advice (such as BERA, see 'Useful websites' at the end of this chapter). As a starting point, you might find the following, which are Anderson's (1998) standards for ethical research, helpful in guiding your thinking:

- that risk to participants is minimized by research procedures that do not expose them to such risks (the principle of *do no harm*)
- that the benefits of the research outweigh the anticipated risks to participants
- that the rights and welfare of participants are adequately protected
- that the research is periodically reviewed
- that informed consent is obtained and appropriately documented.

Underpinning this principle and the preceding considerations are the areas of *informed consent*, *confidentiality* and *anonymity* for you to consider. With regard to *consent*, it is part of your duty of care as a teacher not to allow your pupils to be part of an inappropriate project. You may also need to seek permission from senior managers in the school, parents or, when individual pupils are involved, the pupils themselves. As Taber (2007: 133) writes, 'research participants can only meaningfully give consent if they know what they are being asked to approve. Generally the researcher needs to explain *why* they are doing the research and *what* they will ask the participants to do'. (original emphasis) Thus, participants should be free to say no or stop participating whenever they want. There is also an added dimension here if you as a teacher wish to undertake research on one of your classes. In this case, you need to try to consider any disruption to the normality of the classroom as independently as possible, especially whether your pupils would feel under greater 'pressure' to participate because you are their teacher.

Probably the best way to do this is for you to use a consent form with the following information on it:

- an explanation of the purpose of the research and the procedures that will be used
- a description of any reasonably foreseeable risks to the subjects
- a description of any benefits, including incentives to participate
- an offer to answer any questions concerning the procedures
- a statement that participation is voluntary and that the subject is free to withdraw from the study at any time.

The form needs to be signed by, or on behalf of, the participants. This makes things clear and would provide some measure of proof that consent is given.

In respect of *confidentiality*, you should assure participants that any data gathered would only be used for the purposes of the research and only shared with any members of the research team. In addition, you should try to assure *anonymity*, so that anyone reading your report will not know the real names and locations of the people concerned. Here, 'made up' names are often used for pupils, teachers and schools or they are given a letter (pupil A, teacher B, school C and so on). However, you may sometimes encounter a difficulty with anonymity, particularly in detailed studies of a small number of cases. Here, it is also often appropriate for you to offer to let participants see any writing about their part in the research, giving them the power to ask for removal or amendment of any element.

A wide range of data collection methods is used in classroom-based research. These include observation, field notes, audio or video recording, diaries, interviews, questionnaires and using documents. It is beyond the scope of this section of the book to give details about research methods and so for more information see the further reading section at the end of this chapter.

Analysing data

The analysis of your data is a key part of the research process, because it is only at this stage that you can be certain that the results obtained are reliable. Decisions that you made at the outset now have implications for the type of data analysis that will be appropriate for you to use. However, whatever types you use, the onus will be on you to present your analysis in a way that can be understood, so that, for instance, patterns can be more easily identified.

It is not the purpose of this overview of the research process to cover all aspects of dealing with raw data in order to bring out and clarify what it means. For that you will need to go to texts such as Robson, Taber or Hopkins (see the further reading section at the end of this chapter). However, it is appropriate to briefly offer some guiding principles.

Quantitative (numerical) data may lend itself to complex statistical analysis. Tests can be used to assess whether your results have been obtained by chance or whether they are significant. Computer packages such as SPSS can be employed, but be careful. It is all too easy to generate piles of numbers that actually mean nothing! Unless the use of this type of analysis is a specific requirement of your project, and particularly for those without a good knowledge of these programmes and some statistical background, then often, simple numerical treatments will suffice. The priority is to make your findings clear through summary and display of the data. Here, percentages, means, standard deviations, tables and graphs can be your allies.

Some *qualitative* data can be formulated numerically. For instance, you could develop a number of categories for a set of verbal responses and then count the frequency of responses that fell into the categories. This sort of data can be summarized and displayed in similar ways to strictly numerical data. However, most qualitative data will be either verbal or visual, for instance, in the form of words, pictures, photographs or video. Reference to the texts at the end of the chapter will give information about ways of organizing and summarizing through using strategies such as editing, coding, displaying and conceptualizing. These are often iterative and time-consuming processes with insights gained from one strategy throwing light on other aspects and so on. This might involve nothing more technical than a paper and pencil to 'tease out' key ideas and themes, or if you have the skills (or time to develop them) the use of computer packages such as NUDIST or NVivo to help you do this. However, you need to be aware that these packages do not necessarily give you the 'instant' answer that some statistical software can when analysing numerical data.

It is also important to bear in mind that analysis of data can be a difficult enterprise and in small-scale classroom-based projects will probably not give you definitive or incontrovertible findings. What you are doing is perhaps adding another piece to the jigsaw, helping to make the overall picture of what is happening in a particular situation a little clearer.

Writing the report and publishing

Taber (2007) describes two ends of a continuum where, at one end, the purpose of your research is purely for professional development as a classroom practitioner and all you might wish to do is to evaluate existing ideas to find out if they work in your classroom or solve particular problems that you have highlighted. The knowledge gained from this endeavour might be personal to you and not shared, or you might only share it with a limited number of others, say colleagues in the same department. In addition, you might not want, or have the time, to spend on writing and publishing a formal report.

However, at the other end of the continuum, where you intend to put your work into the public domain, then a more formal report will be a necessity. This may be the case for you with any research assignment that you are obliged to do while in training, or as an NQT or as a more experienced practitioner undertaking a higher degree or professional qualification. Here, Robson (2007) notes that good reports share four common features, namely, that they are clearly structured, lucidly written, professionally presented and are your own work.

The structure of your report may well be determined for you via the regulations of your course or by the requirements of a particular journal if you intend to seek publication. Whatever the requirements, Taber (2007) offers some very helpful questions in his general model for writing up a piece of research to help you think about how to go about it. They are:

- Do I want to read this study? (your abstract)
- What is this study about? (your introduction)
- What do we already know about this? (the literature review)
- What is the issue/problem here? (the focus of your study)
- What am I trying to find out? (your research questions)

- How did I go about it (and why)? (your methodological decisions)
- What data did I collect? (an overview of the sample, methods and amount of data you collected)
- What did I find out (and how do I know)? (a discussion of the evidence to back your claims in order to make a persuasive case)
- So what? (your explanation of the significance of the findings, how they can be used and how generalizable you feel that they are)
- What are my sources? (your bibliography).

As an actual example of such a structure, a writing frame for a PGCE Science project can be found on the accompanying website.

In addition, the style in which you write your report will be determined by the audience for whom it is being written – a more formal or perhaps informal style as appropriate – but whatever the requirement, your writing should be lively and engaging for the reader. Make sure that you follow the conventions in relation to presentation of your report – for instance language style, word-processing formats and word limits. Looking at previous reports that got good marks and studying those in reputable journals can give you many pointers.

Overall, you should bear in mind that you are presenting an argument, with claims, reasons and evidence, to a particular audience. As Robson (2007) describes, you make a claim, because of (a reason), based on evidence and, if possible, supported by further evidence from the literature. For instance, you might write:

> Lack of communication (a claim), due to time (reason) was in fact identified by trainees in their questionnaire and interview responses in my research, as being part of ineffective mentoring (evidence). This is borne out elsewhere such as in the study by Jones (2000), where trainee teachers in England and Germany included lack of communication in their catalogue of unsatisfactory mentor behaviour (further evidence from the literature).

In this way, your claims should relate to the answers to your research questions; the data you have gathered and its analysis and interpretation will provide the evidence and your explanations, linked to the findings of others will help to persuade the reader about the reasons why (the 'because of').

Remember that it is essential that you acknowledge fully where information has come from, particularly in relation to other people's work. Direct quotes need to be referenced, as do ideas or findings taken from sources. You will then get credit for showing that you have read around the topic and have integrated this material into your argument.

Points for reflection

1. In preparation for your research project or dissertation:

   (a) Generate a possible list of topics that would be of interest to you.

   (b) Once you have done this, do a brief literature search starting with *School Science Review* to find two or three research articles that are connected to your two 'favourite' topics.

   (c) Use Taber's critical reading sheet (see further references for Taber, 2007) to analyse these.

2. If they are available, have look at some of the projects that have been done previously by people on your course. Use Taber's guidelines for writing up a piece of research (given on p 222–3) to decide whether these criteria have been fulfilled and thus whether you would consider the project(s) to be good pieces of research.

GAINING A TEACHING JOB

The sort of reflective activity and research work described earlier in this chapter should give you plenty of experience, ideas and material to allow you to put the 'icing on the cake' and be successful in gaining your first (and subsequent) teaching post(s). However, do not just expect a job to fall into your lap without taking some time to methodically prepare a good application and performing well at interview. So, how might you do this?

Formulating a good application

I would be a rich man if I had £1 for every trainee teacher that I have worked with who left their application letter until the end of their course, despite all the advice, support and warnings that this is too late. Applying for your first post should not be an afterthought. If you wait until you have got all your assignments out of the way and have finished all your school-based experiences before applying you will have missed the boat and all those ideal jobs will have been snapped up by others who have been much more on the ball.

What you must do is start reflecting on the type of school that you would ideally like to work in early on in your course. It would be a good idea to make a list of the criteria in order of importance. These might include:

- geographical area(s)
- type of institution (for example, 11–16, 11–18, sixth form college, further education college)
- ethos of the school, including any faith preferences
- state or independent
- size of school
- ability range
- opportunities that you are looking for (for example, teaching a second subject, being a form tutor, running school teams, taking part in extra-curricular activities)
- science syllabuses taught and schemes used
- NQT programme and support for professional development
- age profile of the staff.

Here, and perhaps obviously, your school-based experiences, both as a pupil and as a beginning teacher, will help to shape your reflections. Try to be flexible and include as wide a set of preferences as possible because this will give a wider selection of institutions to which you could apply.

Normally your first contact is via a job advert and you must do your 'homework' and study any job descriptions and accompanying school material carefully to match with your criteria. Look for the elements that the information *does not* mention as these can form your questions if you decide to apply for the post and are invited to interview.

You should also do some wider research. If you live near the school, you will already know something of its catchment and reputation. If not (or in addition), visit the school to see what it and the surrounding area looks like. Can you talk to people who went there or work there? What about asking in local shops, pubs and so on? Also, do not forget to look at the school's website and at the Ofsted website for any inspection reports as these can give you further vital information to use in your application and at interview.

It may be possible to make a preliminary visit. Sometimes this is available to anyone who is thinking of applying, or might be restricted to those who have applied or are going to be invited for interview. Whatever the circumstance, in my opinion a preliminary visit is a good idea as it not only gives you a chance to meet some of the staff (and maybe pupils!) and have a look around, it can also create a favourable impression of you as a conscientious professional with a bit of initiative. Beware the visit however – treat it as formally as you would any full interview. This includes formal attire, making sure you are on time and that you do not overstay your welcome, that you do your homework, have some questions to ask and that you keep your conversation professional at all times – you never know who is lurking behind that pillar in the staffroom!

I should mention here a couple of other potential scenarios. Even if you do not see a particular job advertised, it is not a wasted effort to send your CV (see the accompanying website for a possible format) and a letter of explanation to schools that interest you in the area(s) in which you want to teach. You might get an opportunity to visit the school and ask questions about working there, in which case the approach mentioned above for a preliminary visit applies. Creating a favourable impression might mean that should a post become available, the school will contact you to ask if you are still interested and invite you to apply.

You may also be in the position of having undertaken a successful school-based experience at a school and a post becomes available. You will have picked up the 'vibes' from colleagues as to whether you should apply. If you like the school, the staff and the pupils and have fitted in well, then this will not be a difficult decision. However, if this is not the case, do not be persuaded against your better judgement to apply for the sake of it (having done your homework as previously described and found few matching criteria from your list of desirable factors), but be prepared to give your considered reasons to colleagues as to why you are not applying!

If you do decide to apply, the next stage is the key to getting your foot in the door. Your letter of application needs to be crafted in order to convince the readers that you are worth inviting for interview. Key aspects of your letter are:

- professional presentation
- correct grammar and spelling
- including a concise story of what you have done and what you are good at.

Professional presentation means what it says on the tin. A well-printed (no variations in shade or density of ink colour – black is the convention!), word-processed letter/CV/application form on good quality paper (I advise my trainees to use a light pastel shade of a high quality, so that it stands out from the pile of letters written on cheap white paper). A guideline (unless this is given in the job advert or any material sent by the school) is two and a half A4 pages of 12-point font (such as Times New Roman or Arial), with single or 1.5 line spacing. Correct grammar and spelling are also vital – many a teacher has failed to get an interview because of errors. If you are worried about this aspect, get someone to check.

These are to some extent 'mechanistic' elements of your letter. The hardest part will be to tell your story in a concise way. A common and useful sequence for your letter is:

- Start with an opening paragraph saying why you have applied for the post. Here you need to say something specific about the school – its reputation, its ethos or type and its geographical location (particularly if you live in the area).
- Outline your academic profile in terms of any science or science teaching degree, PGCE or other teaching related qualification that you have done, or are currently undertaking. Emphasize your specialist subject(s) and specific areas of science interest.

- The next paragraphs are the key ones in your letter and should fill at least one page. You need to emphasize your teaching strengths as exhibited during your periods of school-based experience. The skill here is to 'blow your own trumpet' to say what you have done and are good at without going over the top and alienating the reader. My advice is to focus on the *areas of the teaching standards* and be specific about some of your good practice in relation to each:

  - your professionalism
  - how you have fitted into the departmental and school teams
  - your extra-curricular contributions
  - your planning
  - your teaching of a range of abilities/ages/topics
  - your classroom management skills
  - your relationships with pupils
  - your development of pupils' literacy, numeracy and ICT skills through science
  - your assessment strategies and successes
  - your evaluative and reflective skills.

- Then, give brief information about other skills and qualifications that you can bring to the school – musical, sporting, theatrical, and so on.
- For those with previous work experience, you should now mention this briefly. The strategy here is to relate your experience to any skills that you have that are transferable to a teaching context – such as managerial, organizational, team-working and time management.
- Next, you might include a paragraph about your philosophy of teaching to reflect any synergy with the school's ethos (this paragraph is particularly useful if the information that the school sends you is strong on a particular ethos).
- A short paragraph on your personal hobbies and interests comes next (to show that you are a 'well-rounded' human being and not, as pupils sometimes believe, someone who gets put into a cupboard at the end of the school day and is only brought out at the start of school the next morning). However, a word of warning here – do not include any activities that the readers of your letter might think are rather bizarre. I hesitate to suggest what these might be, so run these past another teacher or your tutor if you are not sure!
- A closing paragraph saying that you would look forward to discussing your application further at interview.

Do not forget to relate what you say to the job description/person specification as you compose the paragraphs suggested above. Make sure that you address the criteria given by indicating how you meet them and thus fit the description of the teacher that they are looking for. (An example format and illustrative letter can be found on the accompanying website.)

Finally, I think that you will find it useful to keep a record of your job hunting. Make a note of the details from any advert or materials that the school has sent you; whether you have applied and what you have sent; whether you have been invited for interview and perhaps some notes from the feedback that you will get if you are not appointed. (You will find an example format that you can use and adapt on the website accompanying this book.)

Teaching interviews

If you have written a good letter and you meet the criteria, you should be invited for an interview. This is where the real fun starts! Teaching interviews, in my experience, can be very varied, but may well consist of elements such as:

- meet and greet
- a chance to look round the school and meet the science department
- breaktime in the staffroom
- teaching an exemplar lesson
- being interviewed by a pupil panel
- lunch in the dining-room
- being interviewed by a senior management and governor panel.

All these elements need to be thought about before the interview, some more than others. Perhaps those that need most preparation are the exemplar lesson and the panel interviews. I will come to these shortly.

Your first challenge at the interview is the meet and greet. Try to remember any names and try to smile! Remember the old adage 'first impressions are lasting' and if you are dressed smartly, have arrived in good time and are well prepared, you should feel confident and ready to go. Try not to worry too much and remember some nerves and a little bit of adrenaline might not be a disadvantage as these will help you to be alert and on your toes.

The next obstacle to manoeuvre is the look around the school. This might be led by a member of the senior management team, the head of science or sometimes even a group of pupils and the secret here is to have some questions prepared in advance. For instance, you might ask about aspects of school organization, about science department resources or even do a bit of 'digging' if pupils are showing you round by asking them what their likes and dislikes are and especially whether they like science or not and why!

Also, turn up your powers of observation and try to comment favourably on what you see – perhaps an interesting corridor display or quiet atmosphere. Thus, you are making sure that you engage whoever is showing you round in conversation to show that you are observant and interested. However, beware of trying to dominate the conversation and not letting the other interviewees have their say. Remember, your guide is also interviewing you and will report their thoughts back to the interview panel. Breaktime in the staffroom and lunchtime in the dining-room can also be a good opportunity to chat to staff who are not part of the interview and pick up some useful pieces of advice, but avoid any 'off-hand' negative comments as these might find their way back and count against you.

Now we come to the parts of the interview that you must prepare most carefully for – the exemplar lesson and the panel interviews. One of the toughest situations that some of the trainees who I work with have encountered is where they have been given an hour (with textbook and PC resources) to prepare a lesson to a particular age and ability group on a particular topic and then they have had to teach it. In some ways, although this is putting you on the spot, it can be a blessing in disguise as you will not be able to spend hours or even days agonizing before the interview about what you are going to do – you will necessarily have to keep it simple and not rely on a mountain of pre-prepared resources.

However, this is tough, and more commonly you will be informed about who and what you are going to teach well in advance, thus giving you time to think and prepare fully. Nevertheless, the same principle applies as in the scenario above – *keep it simple* – this applies whatever the length of lesson you have to teach. My advice is to work to a three-part lesson format with an engaging start, main activity (or activities depending on the length of the lesson) and summative plenary. Make sure that you prepare a full lesson plan that has clear and specific learning objectives, relevant and engaging activities and appropriate assessment tasks. Have some spare copies to give to the people who will be observing your lesson.

You are trying to demonstrate to them that you have the ability to quickly form working relationships with pupils, that you are able to set and manage a good classroom learning environment and that you have got some creative teaching ideas. The way to do this is to get interacting with the pupils as soon as possible. Some of my trainees have facilitated this by asking pupils to wear sticky labels with their names on. Also you need to set a good pace so that pupils are busy and have activities that pupils will enjoy and be engaged in so that they are not bored and thinking about being disruptive.

In terms of an engaging start, an activity that is designed to help you find out what pupils already know about the topic (as opposed to what they should know from having perhaps studied it before!) is a good idea. I like activities such as *concept links* where pupils are asked to give two words related to the topic and then have to write a phrase which links the two words together in a meaningful way. You can increase the complexity by asking for further words and getting them to make further links (in fact, in the way that concept maps are formed). However, do not go 'over the top' with this – five minutes maximum will suffice.

The main body of the lesson will consist of activities (or just one activity perhaps if the lesson is only say 20 minutes long – do not try to pack too much in, which is a common mistake) that are designed to get pupils 'doing'. Obviously, a whole range of things would be appropriate here and this is where I would advise you to run your ideas past a more experienced teaching colleague (for instance, your mentor or your tutor). However, beware of trying to cram a multi-stage practical into too short a time frame.

The final part of your lesson is the plenary and this is a good opportunity to assess pupils' learning in your lesson. I am a fan of interactive game/quiz type activities (especially for interview lessons) as these avoid the 'classic' scenario where the teacher asks the questions, but only a couple of pupils answer. Again, there are many activities to choose from. My personal favourites are:

- 'Distillation' where you ask pupils for key words or phrases from the lesson and then ask them to vote on which they think is the most important
- 'Family Fortunes' where pupils have to pick the 'top five' answers
- 'Guess the Question' where, as the name suggests, you give the answer and the pupils have to offer the question
- 'Liar, Liar' where you say something and pupils have to shout 'liar, liar, your bum is on fire' if they think it is incorrect.

 Clearly some of these will work better with younger pupils! You will find some more examples of starters and plenaries on the accompanying website.

After the lesson, you need to be prepared to discuss it with any observers as part of any debrief. This might come in the panel interview or it might be a separate entity. You will remember from the information about lesson evaluation earlier in this chapter, that the 'feedback sandwich' is a typical debrief model. Thus, you should be able to discuss the successes of the lesson, any areas for further development and how you would go about this. Do this positively, by putting your own points of view forward clearly and listening carefully to your observers' feedback and advice. In this way, even if there was an aspect of the lesson that did not quite go to plan, your professional approach will help to mediate any such issues.

The final element(s) that you need to plan for carefully are the panel interviews. One thing that you can prepare beforehand to take with you is a small portfolio of material that you may be able to refer to. Include elements such as a well-prepared lesson plan, differentiated worksheet(s) or presentation slide(s); a highly complimentary lesson observation feedback sheet; photocopies of pupils' work to show marking with target setting and even photographs of pupils' work, for instance displays. Then, if the opportunity arises in the interview, you will be able to show the panel a concrete example to illustrate your answer.

Traditionally the 'adult' panel consists of four to six people including the head or a member of the senior team, the head of science or their deputy and one or more governors. In addition, you may encounter a pupil panel where specially chosen pupils have a set of questions that they will ask you and will report your answers back to the main interview team. This might be in addition to, or instead of pupils showing you round the school. Remember that this is also a formal part of the interview and so it is important to be professional and not criticize the school or any member of staff – you need to show that you are a teacher who treats them with respect and who has an interest in their learning and progress in science. As you will have done in your letter (and just like the way you will perform in front of the main panel), give specific teaching experience examples, including your exemplar lesson and materials in your interview portfolio, to illustrate your answers.

In the main panel interview try not to let your nerves and your tongue run away with you (something I can readily identify with). Listen carefully to the questions and ask for clarification if you are not sure what has been asked. Do not be afraid to have a 'thinking pause' before answering. A good interview is like a conversation with more of your contributions and fewer of theirs. Your answers need to stick to the point, but need to be balanced and analytical – saying why particular aspects of your teaching have gone well. Direct your answer to the person that asked the question, but do not forget to make eye contact with other members of the panel as you give your answer. You will find that any little nods and smiles from them can be very encouraging and supportive.

In my experience trainees have been asked a wide range of questions at interview, but there are some very common ones that you can think through beforehand. These include: 'Why have you applied for this post?' (a common opening question); 'Tell us about an aspect of your school-based experience that has gone particularly well'; 'How would you teach X topic to Y pupils?'; 'What are your strengths?'; 'What can you offer in terms of extra-curricular activities?' and 'Where do you see yourself in five years' time?'

In addition, beware of the 'negative' questions. By these, I mean the questions that ask you about your weaknesses or problems. The strategy here is to be honest without damning yourself. My strategy has always been to identify something that I have felt was an issue and then describe what I have done to try and improve – I have mentioned time management and prioritizing as areas that I have needed to work on. In the same vein, if you get the question asking you about any discipline problems describe these carefully but briefly and spend more time explaining the strategies that you used to overcome them or at least produce some improvement. In addition, and in response to a question about your weaknesses, Wright (2008) advises against the answer, 'I'm a perfectionist.' I would agree with him here in that any teacher who sets out to finish everything (that is, make things perfect) is heading for trouble!

(Some further examples of interview questions and some 'top tips' for interview can be found on the accompanying website.)

Throughout the whole proceedings, I believe the key thing that the interviewers are thinking is 'Will this person fit in here?' Thus, your thoughts should correlate with this – you should be thinking, 'Is this the right school for me?' You should in effect be interviewing the school against your criteria and making a decision about whether you want the post if it is offered to you. If you feel at any time that you do not want it and therefore to continue with the interview would be pointless, then let somebody know. It is much better to do this than 'go through the motions' or even get to the situation where they offer you the post and you decline it.

Points for reflection

Thinking about your application for a teaching post:

- Generate a list of criteria that will enable you to make your selection of which jobs to apply for (see p 225).
- Look at the example CV on the accompanying website and update/develop yours if necessary.
- Formulate your first draft letter of application and show it to your mentor(s) and tutor(s) for comment.
- Within the letter, prepare a paragraph which outlines your philosophy about science teaching which includes answers to the questions:
  - Why should science be on the secondary curriculum?
  - Why do you want to teach science?
  - How are you going to make it exciting and enjoyable for pupils so that they learn effectively?

PROFESSIONAL DEVELOPMENT

Professional development (PD) is a two-way process, with obligations on both you and the school. This is emphasized by the TDA who write that 'All teachers should have a professional responsibility to be engaged in effective, sustained and relevant professional development throughout their careers' (TDA, 2007a: 3). In addition, you are entitled to expect that your PD will be facilitated in the school where you work.

The same sorts of requirements apply to teachers throughout their careers, whether they are just starting out or whether they have many years of experience. At all points of assessment (for example, at the end of the induction year, for promotion to advanced skills teacher, head of department or year, or senior management) you need to demonstrate an ability to evaluate your own performance; a commitment to improve; a constructive attitude to innovation; a willingness to act on advice and an openness to coaching and mentoring (TDA, 2007a).

Your PD also relates to the way in which you develop characteristics that become deep-seated patterns of behaviour – how you do the job; your self-image, values and traits; how you approach situations and the motivation that drives your performance (HayMcBer, 2002). These involve a complex set of variables and encompass a wide range of knowledge, skills and attitudes that you need to acquire to become a successful science teacher.

As science teachers, Parkinson (1994) notes that 'we need to be constantly updating ourselves both in terms of knowledge of our subject and teaching methods'.

I would add knowledge of pupil learning, assessment and the use of new technologies to this. This can be achieved by proactive engagement with subject and pedagogical developments and reflection on and review of practice. To help you do this it is important to look for relevant PD. Bell (2006) describes PD as a 'complex amalgam' of a range of activities such as undertaking accredited and non-accredited courses; engaging in research; placements and sabbaticals; reading articles and books; attending conferences; using the Web to gather information, contribute to discussions and engage in online courses. A large number of sources provide such training, help, guidance and opportunity such as local authorities, higher education, independent providers, national strategies, public bodies and professional associations such as the ASE. The key is that the PD should be relevant and should develop knowledge, skills and expertise.

I would argue that the process of thinking about your PD as a science teacher begins the moment that you start your course of training. You will need to reflect on the knowledge, skills and qualities that you bring to teaching which have been acquired through previous work and life experiences and, as your training progresses and you learn more about the many facets of the profession, you will need to adapt and develop these in the context of your teaching role.

In order to be able to do this effectively, you need to have a method of collating and storing key material that will support your reflections and provide readily accessible and retrievable evidence of the activities that you have engaged in and also those that you have been successful in doing. Earlier in this chapter, I mentioned the common requirement for teachers in training to keep a professional portfolio. This seems to me to be the ideal vehicle to use to chart your professional development, not just during your training, but also throughout your teaching career. It will enable you to effectively formulate applications for teaching and other related education posts, enhanced status such as achieving the threshold and perhaps advanced skills status, and further accredited professional study such as undertaking a higher degree. An example portfolio of professional development can be found on the accompanying website.

The career entry and development profile

Towards the end of your training, you will be engaged in completing the first part of the national Career Entry and Development Profile (CEDP). This is an important checkpoint in your professional development where you will provide an overview of your training experience and identify specific strengths and areas for development. You will find that the completion of your CEDP will be very much easier if you have maintained a professional portfolio with a log of your progress against the teaching standards. Such a reflective activity, with the cataloguing of evidence of achievement against the standards will provide you with the detail that can be distilled into the specific elements required for the CEDP.

Your professional portfolio, of which the CEDP forms an important part, helps bridge the gap between your training and your first year in teaching, and you are required to use it to reflect on your professional development at key times during the beginning of your career. It also helps your first school co-ordinate your induction, PD and performance management, and provide you with a good start to teaching (TDA, 2007a; 2007b).

The completion of your CEDP is arranged around three 'transition points':

- at the end of your ITT programme, when the CEDP is first drafted under the supervision of your training provider
- at the beginning of your induction year, when it is reviewed by the induction tutor, and a programme of support for you is planned
- at the end of your induction year, when any targets that you have set for the year are reviewed and assessed.

Although your portfolio containing your CEDP is designed to be chiefly of benefit to you, another audience for it is the teacher in charge of newly qualified teachers at your first school, known as the *induction tutor*. This teacher will want to know something about your background and experience, and your portfolio and CEDP will provide this information. The areas that you have identified for further development will essentially form a written request for support in specific areas. My advice is to make a good job of this, as often one of the 'benefits' of induction is that you are more likely to receive a sympathetic ear and support for your developmental needs.

This part of your CEDP will guide your discussion with your induction tutor, which should involve a focus on how the school can support you in these areas. You will be able to make suggestions on how you think this might be done. The induction tutor may discuss whether this support can be provided in school or whether you may need to attend further training outside school.

You may find the following list of aspects helpful in formulating possible areas for further development:

- a wider range of work at KS4 or post-16
- experience in preparing pupils for external examinations
- working with particular groups of pupils (SEN, G&T, EAL, and so on)
- assessing against attainment levels
- assessing investigative and project work in science
- ICT knowledge and its use in the classroom (for example a particular programme to broaden your expertise)
- writing reports and communicating with parents
- how to predict GCSE grades, or how to set appropriate targets for individual pupils

- the role of the form tutor
- teaching PSHE
- citizenship education in the school
- getting involved in, developing expertise and gaining qualifications in extra-curricular activities.

The induction year and early years of teaching

The relief that you might feel at having successfully completed your teaching degree or training course and having secured your first post will probably be short-lived as you begin to think of your first year in teaching as a newly qualified science teacher. In the UK, even as an NQT, your training is still continuing and it is important for you to develop your knowledge, skills and experience while still retaining that flush of enthusiasm that you had when you started your journey to become a secondary science teacher. Thus, the induction year is a very important phase in your professional growth and development, because a successful experience can 'either catalyse or inhibit a lasting commitment to effective teaching' (Ginns et al., 2001).

One of the things that you will have assured yourself about when you were interviewed for your first teaching post was the existence of a well-planned induction programme in the school, which conforms to all the relevant government statutory frameworks and local authority (LA)guidelines and which meets your individual needs. Think of such a programme in terms of a number of aspects – 'How will your lesson observations be managed by your tutor?' 'Will your teaching timetable adhere to the requirement of no more than 90 per cent of a normal teaching load?' 'Will there be a school-based programme with input on various aspects of school, teaching and learning?' 'Will it offer you the opportunity to observe or shadow other teachers?' 'Can you team-teach?' 'Will you be able to visit other schools?' and 'Will you be allowed to participate in professional development courses such as those run by higher education or further education establishments, the Association for Science Education (ASE), the Science Learning Centres or the local authority?'

In my experience, the best programmes are those that are flexible and can be adapted and customized as you develop. Thus, as your induction year progresses, new aspects may be added to your targets while others are removed as a result of how successfully you become part of the science team, how effectively you teach and how well your pupils learn. This will be partly decided via a sequence of lesson observations, once in the first four weeks at the school, and then again at intervals of between six and eight weeks. The observations will be followed by discussions about your teaching. Then, you will have a more formal review of your progress at the end of each term and at the end of your induction year, you are assessed against the Induction Standards, which are similar to, but rather more demanding than the Standards for QTS.

A number of writers have described the professional growth of beginning teachers in terms of their absorption into the culture of the school and classroom. Fuller and Brown (1975) offer a useful three-stage model characterized by initial concerns for survival (coping with the busy pattern of work), followed by concerns about the teaching situation (for example, content, methods and materials) and thirdly, concerns about pupils (for example, their individual learning and emotional needs).

In your early years of teaching, you will benefit enormously from being in a department with a strong team ethic, where different teachers share ideas and share professional reflection. This support from colleagues is often particularly valued when it works on an informal level. This might involve sharing resources, strategies or activities, perhaps in relation to topics that you are struggling to teach.

Other support from within the school can be more formally organized through departmental meetings, performance review, and pre-arranged programmes of peer observation. The latter is commonplace, and tends to be highly valued by teachers as part of teaching and learning development. Before peer observation, you can pick on something specific, something that you realize that you should improve, and ask the observer to comment on that aspect of your work.

Performance review usually involves you having an annual professional development meeting with the head of science, where you will set yourself targets for the forthcoming year. They will then observe you teaching one or more times during the year and will ask you to update them on how the achievement of your targets is going and whether any of these need to be revised due to changes in circumstance. At the end of the year, you will have another meeting to see whether you have reached your targets, and what your new targets for the next year will be.

In addition, you may be observed teaching by an inspector as part of an Ofsted inspection of your school. These inspections are an established part of school life, and provide another, external, means of evaluating your teaching. Since 2005, all inspections are undertaken in partnership with the school, with the school's self-assessment providing the starting point for the work of the inspection team. The quality of teaching and learning across the school, however, remains one important focus for the inspection. This is only one of many judgements made by the team, but is probably the one that will affect you most directly as a newly qualified teacher or in your early years of teaching. Inspectors look at the quality of teaching and evaluate its impact on learning by looking at the way pupils respond in the classroom, whether they enjoy the work and whether they engage actively with the lesson. If you are observed, even for just part of a lesson, then you can expect some feedback from the inspector.

Support from local authorities, science learning centres and professional associations

Many schools also have access to support from the local authority advisory service. Among other things, staff in the advisory service co-ordinate training across schools, and provide additional support for major new initiatives. The authority also provides additional support for teachers and departments, including observing lessons and talks, offering ideas for development. Many local authorities have also set up facilities to make it easier for teachers to access web-based materials, particularly via the NGfL.

The Science Learning Centres are a national network for professional development, supporting science teachers and technicians in enhancing their professional skills by learning more about contemporary scientific ideas and in experimenting with effective teaching approaches and gaining experience of modern scientific techniques. There are nine regional centres in England and one national centre to serve the UK.

Courses began at the regional centres from October 2004 and the National Centre opened in autumn 2005. Each of the centres is equipped with new laboratories and ICT resources to provide advanced training. They also work with leading scientific organizations and businesses to ensure that the content delivered to teachers, technicians and further education lecturers is contemporary and relevant, with courses in the latest scientific research and industry, as well as education initiatives across all key stages and post-16. (You will find the web link to the Science Learning Centres home page in 'Useful websites' at the end of this chapter.)

There are also a number of well-established professional associations to which teachers of science can belong. The ASE is the professional body for those involved in science education at all levels from pre-school to higher education, including a growing number of technician members. The aims of the association are to promote high quality science education and foster the PD of its members. As a secondary member you will receive, among other benefits, the *School Science Review* four times a year and *Education in Science* five times a year. *School Science Review* is the journal for science teachers in 11–19 education and all those interested in this aspect of education. *Education in Science* is the in-house magazine for all members of the ASE. Its aim is to keep members up to date with association news and events, as well as topical issues in science education.

In addition, members of the ASE are invited to apply to become a Chartered Science Teacher (CSciTeach). This is a chartered designation in line with other awards, such as Chartered Scientist, Chartered Engineer, Chartered Accountant or Chartered Surveyor, which recognizes the professional standing of an individual working in that field. The introduction of the CSciTeach designation provides an opportunity for individuals to gain an award which accredits and values their all-round expertise in science education and their commitment to updating the knowledge, skills and understanding they require.

The Institute of Biology (IOB) is the professional body for UK biologists whose mission is to promote the biological sciences, to foster the public understanding of the life sciences generally, to enhance the status of the biology profession and to represent members and the biology profession as a whole to government and other bodies in the UK and abroad. The institute has several grades of membership, which include Fellows, Members and Graduates. Members and Fellows are awarded Chartered Biologist (CBiol) status, the professional qualification for bioscientists, recognized throughout Europe as a hallmark of excellence. It demonstrates a high level of attainment in biological experience, personal integrity, professional attributes and academic qualifications. All members receive free the peer-reviewed IOB journal *Biologist* four times a year. Members can also subscribe to the *Journal of Biological Education*.

The Institute of Physics (IOP) is an organization devoted to increasing the understanding and application of physics. It is a leading communicator of physics with all audiences, from specialists, through government, to the public. Its publishing company, IOP Publishing, publishes an internationally acclaimed range of magazines, journals and reference works. The Institute of Physics offers membership in several categories similar to the IOB and invites application for chartered status with three designations. As a member, you receive *Physics World,* a monthly magazine reporting latest news and developments, and *Interactions* which is the member newspaper.

The Royal Society of Chemistry (RSC) is the largest organization in Europe for advancing the chemical sciences. Supported by a worldwide network of members and an international publishing business, RSC activities span education, conferences, science policy and the promotion of chemistry to the public. Similarly to the IOB and IOP, the RSC has several grades of membership and awards chartered status. Members are sent *Chemistry World* and *RSC News* every month.

Thus, all these associations provide opportunities for you to keep up to date with new initiatives and recent developments as part of your professional development. This includes the publications sent to members as described, but also through other materials such as books, pamphlets, discussion papers and specialist teaching materials. Each organization holds conferences with keynote speakers, research reports, workshops and seminars. They also have local associations, whose members meet together on a regular basis. Active membership of one of the professional associations can also enhance your profile. Involvement in writing, in conferences or local associations demonstrates that you have an interest in science beyond the day-to-day demands of the classroom and indicates that you are open to new ideas and in listening to other teachers discussing innovation.

Weblinks to the various associations are given in 'Useful websites' at the end of this chapter.

Further professional developent

At the end of your training, your first priority will be settling in to your new job, and making it a success. However, even if you have not thought about them before, you should now give some thought to your long-term career aims and aspirations. As you progress, your growing experience in school will provide you with the opportunity to broaden your CV in a range of ways. One way that you can enhance your professional expertise, and at the same time increase your chances of promotion within teaching, is to undertake professional development courses. These can range from postgraduate certificates and diplomas to master's and doctoral degrees. Indeed, as this book goes to press, the government has announced its plans for all teachers to gain master's-level degrees.

If you have undertaken a PGCE then it may be that your training course already gives you the chance to gain credits that count towards a master's-level qualification. This would seem to me to provide an excellent opportunity to continue your PD as you already have a 'foot in the door' of higher-level study. These courses further develop you as a reflective practitioner by getting you to analyse the way that you do things in a particular way, make you question why and challenge you to think if there might be alternative, better ways. Criteria for success at master's-level include:

- comprehensive knowledge of the topic
- evidence of wide reading, together with the ability to synthesize a coherent argument, including consideration of opposing views
- an ability to support arguments with convincing evidence, accurately referenced
- critical reflection on your own classroom practice
- provision of evidence from your own research, comparing it with evidence from the literature
- independent thought.

I found that while doing my Master's, 'little lights' started to go on in my head as I made connections between aspects that I had studied as part of my training, my own classroom practice and the science education literature that I was now required to access. I would like to think it made me a better practitioner as a result, although you might have to interrogate some of the pupils that I taught in order to get a view that is minus the rose-coloured spectacles!

Such courses may also offer the chance to meet other people who are interested in research into science education. You may be able to make contact with someone engaged in a research project, perhaps one of the tutors of your course, and contribute to the project in some way. In fact, a lot of research consists of groups of teachers working together with academic staff from universities and they often report how much the project makes them reflect on and develop their own professional practice. In addition, if you have a particular area of interest, then you may be able to obtain guidance about how to set up a project yourself and this might lead to you studying for a doctoral degree, but that is another story!

Point for reflection

Reflect on your career progress to date (this might be at a suitable point in your training, induction year or perhaps beyond in your early years of teaching). You should do this by:

* listing your strengths and areas you feel need further development
* writing down your career goals and ambitions
* formulating an action plan to achieve these.

Your action plan might have the following components:

Area for development	Objective	Action required	Timescale

Further reading

Hopkins, D. (2002) *A Teacher's Guide to Classroom Research*. 3rd edn. Buckingham: Open University Press.

Robson, C. (2002) *Real World Research*. 2nd edn. Oxford: Blackwell.

Robson, C. (2007) *How to Do a Research Project. A Guide for Undergraduate Students*. Oxford: Blackwell.

Taber, K. (2007) *Classroom-based Research and Evidence-based Practice. A Guide for Teachers*. London: Sage.

All these four texts give lots of detailed practical guidance on conducting classroom-based social science research.

Useful websites

Live links to these websites can be found on the companion website www.sage pub.co. uk/secondary

www.ofsted.gov.uk/
The Ofsted website, containing links to school inspection reports, as well as information about the inspection process

www.blackwellpublishing.com/researchproject/
The website associated with Colin Robson's *How to Do a Research Project* book, with lots of related information and further weblinks

www.bera.ac.uk
British Educational Research Association, for a wide range of information on research, including research ethics

www.gtce.org.uk/tla/
The Teacher Learning Academy (TLA) of the General Teaching Council (GTC). The TLA seeks to offer public and professional recognition for teachers' learning, development and improvement work, particularly in relation to classroom-based research.

www.tda.gov.uk/teachers/induction/cedp.aspx.
The Career Entry and Development Profile document itself and guidance for completing it

www.tda.gov.uk/Recruit/becomingateacher/inductionyear.aspx
For further details about the induction year

www.sciencelearningcentres.org.uk/
The home page for the national network of Science Learning Centres

www.e-gfl.org/e-gfl/index.cfm?s=1&m=257&p=22,index&zs=n
This is an example of an LA Science homepage on the Essex National Grid for Learning.

Professional associations

www.ase.org.uk
Association for Science Education

www.iob.org
Institute of Biology

www.iop.org
Institute of Physics

www.rsc.org
Royal Society of Chemistry

BIBLIOGRAPHY

Adamczyk P., Willson, M. and Wiliams, D. (1994) 'Concept mapping: a multi-level and multi-purpose tool', *School Science Review*, 76(275): 116–24.

Adey, P. (1992) 'The CASE results: implications for science teaching', *International Journal of Science Education*, 14(20): 137–46.

Adey, P.S. and Shayer, M. (1994) *Really Raising Standards*. London: Routledge.

Adey, P., Shayer, M. and Yates, C. (1995) *Thinking Science: The Curriculum Materials of the CASE Project*. London: Nelson.

Adey, P., Shayer, M. and Yates, C. (2001) *Thinking Science – the Materials of the CASE Project: Third Edition*. London: Nelson Thornes.

Allum, N., Sturgis, P., Tabourazi, D. and Brunton-Smith, I. (2008) 'Science knowledge and attitudes across cultures: a meta-analysis', *Public Understanding of Science*, 17(1): 35–54.

Amos, S. and Boohan, R. (eds) (2002) *Aspects of Teaching Secondary Science*. London: RoutledgeFalmer.

Anderson, G. (1998) *Fundamentals of Educational Research*. 2nd edn. London: Falmer.

Arnot, M., David, M. and Weiner, G. (1999) *Closing the Gender Gap: Postwar Education and Social Change*. Cambridge: Polity Press.

Assessment Reform Group (ARG) (2006) *The Role of Teachers in the Assessment of learning*. London: Assessment Reform Group, Institute of Education.

Association for Science Education (ASE) (1979) *Alternatives for Science Education*. Hatfield: Association for Science Education.

Association for Science Education (ASE) (2001) *Topics in safety*. 3rd edn. Hatfield: Association for Science Education.

Battersby, J. and Gordon, J. (2006) *Preparing to Teach: Learning from Experience*. Abingdon: Routledge.

Bell, D. (2006) 'Continuing professional development: enhancing professional expertise', in V. Wood-Robinson (ed.), *ASE Guide to Secondary Science Education*. Hatfield: Association for Science Education.

Bennett, J. (2004) *Teaching and Learning Science: A Guide to Recent Research and its Applications*. London: Continuum.

Berg, B.L. (2001) *Qualitative Research Methods for the Social Sciences*. 4th edn. Boston, MA: Allyn and Bacon.

Black, P. and Harrison, C. (2001a) 'Feedback in questioning and marking: the science teacher's role in formative assessment', *School Science Review*, 82(310): 55–61.

BBC *Simple Minds: Education Special*. BBC World Wide Web.

Black, P. and Harrison, C. (2001b) 'Self & peer assessment and taking responsibility: the science student's role in formative assessment', *School Science Review*, 83(302): 41–8.

Black, P. and Wiliam, D. (1998a) 'Assessment and classroom learning', *Assessment in Education*, 5(1): 7–71.

Black, P. and Wiliam, D. (1998b) *Inside the Black Box: Raising Standards through Classroom Assessment*. Occasional paper. London: King's College.

Black, P., Harrison, C., Lee, C. and Marshall, B. (2003) *Assessment for Learning: Putting it into Practice*. Maidenhead: Open University Press.

Bloom, B.S. (1956) *Taxonomy of Educational Objectives, Handbook 1: The Cognitive Domain*. London: Longmans Green.

Boohan, R. (2002a) 'Learning from models, learning about models', in S. Amos and R. Boohan, (eds), *Aspects of teaching secondary science: perspectives on practice*. London: RoutledgeFalmer.

Boohan, R. (2002b) 'ICT and communication', in S. Amos and R. Boohan (eds), *Aspects of Teaching Secondary Science: Perspectives on Practice*. London: Routledge Falmer.

Borrows, P. (1984) 'The Pimlico chemistry trail', *School Science Review*, 66(235): 221–33.

Braund, M. and Reiss, M. (eds) (2004) *Learning Science Outside the Classroom*. London: RoutledgeFalmer.

Braund, M. and Reiss, M. (2006) 'Towards a more authentic science curriculum: the contribution of out-of-school learning', *International Journal of Science Education*, 28(12): 1373–88.

British Educational Research Association (BERA) (2004) *Revised Ethical Guidelines for Educational Research (2004)*. Nottingham: British Educational Research Association.

Brown, A. (2007) 'Transforming schools into communities of thinking and learning about serious matters'. in E.Scanlon, P.Murphy, J.Thomas and L.Whitelegg, *Reconsidering Science Learning*. London: Routledge Falmer.

Brown, J.S., Collins, A. and Duguid, P. (1989) 'Situated cognition and the culture of learning', *Educational Researcher*, 18(1): 32–42.

Brundrett, M. (2002) *Achieving competence, success and excellence in teaching*. London: Routledge Falmer.

Bruner, J. (1966) *Toward a Theory of Instruction*. Cambridge, MA: Harvard University Press.

Buldu, M. (2006) 'Young children's perceptions of scientists: a preliminary study', *Educational Research*, 48(1): 121–32.

Bullman, L. (1985) *Teaching Language and Study Skills in Secondary Science*. London: Heinemann.

Butler, R. (1988) 'Enhancing and undermining intrinsic motivation: the effects of task involving and ego involving evaluation on interest and performance', *British Journal of Educational Psychology*, 58, 1–14.

Capel, S., Leask, M. and Turner, T. (eds) (2005) *Learning to Teach in the Secondary School: A Companion to School Experience*. Abingdon: Routledge.

CapeUK (2005) *Creative Space: Collaborative Approaches to Science Learning in Schools*. Leeds: CapeUK.

Cerini, B., Murray, I. and Reiss, M.J. (2003) *Student Review of the Science curriculum: major findings*. London: Planet Science.

Chalmers, A.F. (1999) *What Is this Thing Called Science?* 3rd edn. Buckingham: Open University Press.

Cheminais, R. (2006) *Every Child Matters: A Practical Guide for Teachers*. London: David Fulton.

Cheyney, A., Flavell, H., Harrison, C., Hurst, G. and Yates, C. (2004) *Thinking Through Science*. London: John Murray.

Clark, L. (2008) Dimming down: How the brain power of today's 14- year-olds has slipped *'radically' in just one generation, Daily Mail* , 27 October, pp. 1 and 6.

Consortia of Local Education Authorities for the Provision of Science, (CLEAPS) (2005) *Banned Chemicals and Other myths,* Brunel University Bristol: CLEAPS. www.cleapss.org.uk/secfr.htm (accessed February 2008).

Cooper, H. and Hyband, R. (2002) *Children's Perceptions of Learning with Trainee Teachers*. London: Routledge.

Corry, A. (2005) 'Mentoring students towards independent scientific enquiry', in S. Alsop, L. Bencze and E. Pedretti (eds) *Analysing Exemplary Science Teaching*. Maidenhead: Open University Press. pp. 63–70.

Cowley, S. (2006) *Getting the Buggers to Behave*. 3rd edn. London: Continuum

Cox, M. (2000) 'Information and communications technologies: their role and value for science education,' in M. Monk and J. Osborne (eds), *Good Practice in Science Teaching: What Research Has to Say*. Buckingham: Open University Press.

Crace, J. (2006) 'Children are less able than they used to be', Crace, J. *Education Guardian*. p. 3.

Craft, A., Jeffrey, B. and Leibling, M. (eds) (2001), *Creativity in Education*. London: Continuum.

Dallas, D. (1980) *Teaching Biology Today*. London: Hutchinson.

Davies, F. and Green, T. (1984) *Reading for Learning in the Sciences*. London: Oliver and Boyd.

De Bono, E. (1970) *Lateral Thinking*. London: Penguin Books.

De Bono, E. (1992) *Teaching your Child to Think*. London: Penguin.

Deale, R.N. (1975) *Assessment and testing in the Secondary School*. London: Evans/Methuen.

Deale, R.N. (1975) Assessment and testing, *Secondary School Council Examinations Bulletin*, 32: 19–27.

Deng, Z. (2004) '*Knowing the subject matter of a school science subject*', paper presented at the Annual Meeting of the of the American Educational Research Association, San Diego, CA, 12–16 April.

Department of Education and Science (DES) (1990) 'The Outdoor Classroom', '*Building Bulletin* 71. London: DES.

Department for Education and Science (DES) (1989) Science in the National Curriculum. London: HMSO.

Department for Children, Schools and Families (DCSF) (2007) *Making Good Progress Consultation Document*   http://www.dcsf.gov.uk/consultations/downloadableDocs/How%20can%20we%20help%20every%20pupil%20to%20make%20good%20progress%20at%20school.pdf

Department for Education and Science (DES) (1987) *The Curriculum from 5 to 16. Curriculum Matters*. London: Her Majesty's Stationary Office.

Department for Education and Employment (DfEE) (1996) *Safety in Science Education*. London: HMSO.

Department for Education and Employment (DfEE) (1998) *Health and Safety of Pupils on Educational Visits*. London: Department for Education and Employment.

Department for Education and Employment (DfEE) (1999) *The National Curriculum for England, Science*. London: Department for Education and Employment.

Department for Education and Employment (DfEE) (2001) *Framework for Teaching Mathematics: Years 7, 8 and 9*. London: Department for Education and Employment.

Department for Education and Skills (DfES) (2002a) *Framework for Teaching Science: Years 7, 8 and 9*. London: Department for Education and Skills.

Department for Education and Skills (DfES) (2002b) *Assessment in Science: Resource Pack for Tutors*. Ref DfES 0369/2002. London: Department for Education and Skills.

Department for Education and Skills (DfES) (2003) *Every Child Matters Green Paper*. London: HMSO.

Department for Education and Skills (DfES) (2004a) *ICT across the Curriculum: ICT in Science*. London: Department for Education and Skills.

Department for Education and Skills (DfES) (2004b) *The Science National Curriculum for England*. London: Department for Education and Skills.

Department for Education and Skills (DfES) (2004c) *Removing Barriers to Achievement*. DfES publication 0117/2004. Nottingham: Department for Education and Skills.

Department for Education and Skills (DfES) (2004d) *Science Intervention Materials: Guidance Curriculum and Standards*. DfES publication 0077–2004. Nottingham: DfES

Department for Education and Skills (DfES) (2005a) *Every Child Matters: Common Core of Skills and Knowledge for the Children's Workforce*. London: Department for Education and Skills.

Department for Education and Skills (DfES) (2005b) *Leading in Learning: Developing Thinking Skills at Key Stage 3 School Training Manual*, London: Department for Education and Skills.

Department for Education and Skills (DfES) (2005c) *Higher Standards, Better Schools for All: More Choice for Parents and Pupils*. Norwich: HMSO.

Department for Education and Skills (DfES) (2006) *Learning Outside the Classroom Manifesto*. Nottingham: Department for Education and Skills.

Department for Education and Skills (DfES) (2007) *Assessment for Learning: 8 Schools Project Report*. Ref 00067–2007BKT. Nottingham: Department for Education and Skills.

Drake, P., Jacklin, A., Robinson, C. and Thorp, J. (2003) *Becoming a Teaching Assistant: A Guide for Teaching Assistants and Those Working with Them*. London: Sage.

Driver, R. (ed.) (1994) *Making Sense of Secondary Science: Research into Children's Ideas*. Abingdon: Routledge.

Driver, R., Leach, J., Millar, R. and Scott, P. (1996) *Young People's Images of Science*. Buckingham: Open University Press.

Driver, R., Squries, A., Rushworth, P. and Wood-Robinson, V. (2002) *Making Sense of Secondary Science: Research into Children's Ideas*. London: Routledge.

Dunn, R. Dunn, K. and Price, G.E. (1984) *Learning Style Inventory*. Lawrence, KS: Price Systems.

Edmonds, J. (2004) 'Creativity in science: leaping the void', in R. Fisher and M. Williams (eds), *Unlocking Creativity: Teaching across the Curriculum*. London: David Fulton.

Ellis, V. (ed.) (2007) *Learning & Teaching in Secondary Schools*. 3rd edn. Exeter: Learning Matters.

Erlauer, L. (2003) *Brain-compatible Classroom: Using What We Know about Learning to Improve Teaching*. Alexandria, VA: Association for Supervision & Curriculum.

Fautley, M. and Savage, J. (2007) *Creativity in Secondary Education*. Exeter: Learning Matters.

Feasey, R. (2005) *Creative Science – Achieving the WOW Factor with 5–11 Year Olds*. London: David Fulton.

Feasey, R. (2006) 'Creativity in teaching and learning science', in V. Wood-Robinson (ed.), *ASE Guide to Secondary Science Education*. Hatfield: Association for Science Education.

Fisher, R. (2005) *Teaching Children to Think*. 2nd edn. Cheltenham: Nelson Thornes.

Forster, S. (1989) 'Streetwise physics', *School Science Review*, 71(254): 15–17.

Frost, R. (1998a) 'The use of information and communication technology', in M. Ratcliffe, (ed.), *ASE Guide to Secondary Science Education*. Hatfield: Association for Science Education.

Frost, R. (1998b) *The IT in Secondary Science Book*. London: IT in Science.

Fuller, F. and Brown, O. (1975) 'Becoming a teacher', in K. Ryan (ed.), *Teacher Education*. Chicago, IL: University of Chicago Press.

Galton, M., Gray, J. and Ruddock, J. (2003) *Transfer and Transitions in the Middle Years of Schooling (7–14): Continuities and Discontinuities in Learning*. Report RR443. London: Department for Education and Skills.

Gardner, J. (ed.) (2006) *Assessment of Learning*. London: Sage.

Gilbert, J.K. (ed.) (1993) *Models and Modelling in Science Education*. Hatfield: Association for Science Education.

Gilbert, J.K. (2002) 'Science education and research', in S. Amos and R. Boohan (eds), *Teaching Science in Secondary Schools: A Reader*. London: Routledge Falmer.

Ginns, I., Heirdsfield, A., Atweh, B. and Watters, J.J. (2001) 'Beginning teachers becoming professionals through action research', *Educational Action Research*, 9(1): 111–33.

Glasersfeld, E. von (1995) *Radical Constructivism*. London: Falmer.

Glass, S. (2007) *Prove it! Scientific Enquiry in Action*. Oxford: Heinemann.

Greenfield, S. (2004) *Contemporary Issues in Science Learning*. SH806 Study Guide OU 1999 block 2. Milton Keynes. The Open University.

Gregory J. and Miller, S. (1998) *Science in Public Communication, Culture and Credibility*. London: Plenum.

Grevatt, A., Gilbert, J.K. and Newberry, M. (2007) 'Challenging able science learners through models and modelling', in K. Taber (ed.), *Science Education for Gifted Learners*. Abingdon: Routledge.

Griffin, J. (2004) 'Research on students and museums: looking more closely at the students in school groups', *Science Education*, 88(supplement 1).

Hammond, P. (2007) *Creative Activities for Scientific Enquiry Ages 7–11*. Leamingtion Spa: Scholastic.

Hann, K. (1995) Using Museums (*Heads of Science Bulletin No. 21*). Kingston upon Thames: Croner Publications.

Hargreaves, L. (2002) *Transfer from the Primary Classroom 20 Years on*. London: RoutledgeFalmer.

Harrison, B. (1998) 'Industrial links: purpose and practice', in M. Ratcliffe (ed.), *ASE Guide to Secondary Science Education*. Hatfield: Association for Science Education.

HayMcBer (2002) 'Teacher effectiveness', in B. Moon, A. Shelton Mayes and S. Hutchinson (eds), *Teaching, Learning and the Curriculum in Secondary Schools*. London: RoutledgeFalmer.

Hennessy, S. and Osborne, J. (2003) *Literature Review in Science Education and the Role of ICT: Promises, Problems and Future Directions*. Bristol: National Endowment for Science, Technology and the Arts.

Hill, M. (2007) 'Putting the fun back into education?', *Heads of Science Briefing No. 147*, Kingston upon Thames: Wolters Kluwer.

Hodson, D. (1998) *Teaching and Learning in Science*. Buckingham: Open University Press.

Hollins, M., Murphy, P., Ponchaud, B. and Whitelegg, E. (2006) *Girls in the Physics Classroom: A Teacher's Guide for Action*. London: Institute of Physics.

Honey, P. and Mumford, A. (1982) *Manual of Learning Styles*. London: P. Honey.

Hook, P. and Vass, A. (2000) *Creating Winning Classrooms*. London: David Fulton.

Hopkins, D. (2002) *A Teacher's Guide to Classroom Research*. 3rd edn. Buckingham: Open University Press.

Horton, P.B. (1992) 'An investigation of the effectiveness of concept mapping as an instructional tool', *Science Education*, 77(1): 95–111.

Inhelder, B. and Piaget, J. (1958) *The Growth of Logical Thinking from Childhood to Adolescence*. New York: Basic Books.

Ireson, G. and Twidle, J. (2006) *Reflective Reader: Secondary Science*. Exeter: Learning Matters.

Jardine, D.W., Clifford, P. and Friesen, S. (2008) *Back to the Basics of Teaching and Learning: Thinking the World Together*. Philadelphia. PA: Lawrence Erlbaum Associates.

Jones, A.T., Simon, S.A., Black, P.J., Fairbrother, R.W. and Watson, J.R. (1992) *Open Work in Science: Development of Investigations in Schools*. Hatfield: Association for Science Education.

Jones, M. (2000) 'Trainee teachers' perceptions of school-based training in England and Germany with regard to their preparation for teaching, mentor support and assessment', *Mentoring and Tutoring*, 8(1): 63–80.

Joubert, M.M. (2001) 'The art of creative teaching: NACCCE and beyond', in A. Craft, B. Jeffrey and M. Leibling (eds), *Creativity in Education*. London: Continuum.

Kelsey, M. (1995) *Developing the School Site as a Resource for Science Teaching*. Kingston upon Thames: Croner Publications.

Keogh, B. and Naylor, S. (2000) *Concept Cartoons in Science Education*. Sandbach: Millgate House.

Keogh, B. and Naylor, S. (2006) 'Access and engagement for all', in R. Hull (ed.), *ASE Guide to Secondary Science Education*. Hatfield: Association for Science Education.

Kozulin, A. (1986) *Thought and Language* (rev. ed.) Cambridge, MA: MIT Press.

Kuhn, T.S. (1970) *The Structure of Scientific Revolutions*. Chicago, IL: University of Chicago Press.

Kyriacou, C. (1998) *Essential Teaching Skills*. Cheltenham: Stanley Thornes.

The Learn Project (2000) *Guidance for Schools: An Assessment for Learning*: London: A DfES Publications.

Leibling, M. and Prior, R. (2004) *The A–Z of Learning: Tips and Techniques for Teachers*. London: RoutledgeFalmer.

Levinson, R. (2007) 'Teaching controversial socio-scientific issues to gifted and talented students', in K. Taber (ed.), *Science Education for Gifted Learners*. Abingdon: Routledge.

Lipman, M. (1991) *Thinking in Education*. Cambridge: Cambridge University Press.

Lucas, A.M. (1983) 'Scientific literacy and informal learning', *Studies of Science Education*, 10: 1–36.

Maag, J. (2004) *Behaviour Management from Theoretical Implications to Practical Applications*. 2nd edn. Belmont, CA: Thomson and Wadsworth.

Mannion, K., Brodie, M., Needham, R. and Bullough, A. (2003) *Transforming Teaching and Learning in Key Stage 3 Science*. Exeter: Learning Matters.

Marvin, C. (2003) *Access to Science: Curriculum Planning and Practical Activities for Pupils with Learning Difficulties*. London: David Fulton.

Massey, W. (1999) Science for all citizens: setting the stage for lifelong learning in E. Scanlon, R. Hill and K. Junker (1999), *Communicating Science*: *Professional Contexts*. London: Routledge.

McDuell, R. (ed.) (2000) *Teaching Secondary Chemistry*. London: John Murray.

McGregor, D. (2007) *Developing Thinking, Developing Learning: A Guide to Thinking Skills in Education*. Maidenhead: Open University Press.

McLean, A. (2004) *The Motivated School*. London: Paul Chapman Publishing.

McSharry, G. and Jones, S. (2000) 'Role-play in science teaching and learning', *School Science Review*, 82(298): 73–82.

McWilliam, E., Poronnik, P. and Taylor, P. (2008) 'Re-designing science pedagogy: reversing the flight from science', *Journal of Science Education and Technology*, 17: 226–35.

Mesure, S. (2005) 'Creativity in science: the heart and soul of science teaching', *Education in Science*, (214): 12–14.

Millar, R. (1989) 'What is Scientific Method and how can it be taught?', J. Wellington, (ed.) in *skills and Processes in Scientific Education: A critical analysis*. London: Routledge.

Millar, R. (2002) 'Towards evidence-based practice in science education', *School Science Review*, 84(307): 21–33.

Millar, R. and Osborne, J.F. (eds) (1998) *Beyond 2000: Science Education for the Future*. London: King's College London.

Monk, M. (2006) 'How science works: what do we do now?, *School Science Review*, 88(322): 119–21.

Moon, B. and Shelton Mayes, A. (1995) *Teaching and Learning in Secondary School Science*. Buckingham: Open University Press.

Morris, E. (2001) *Professionalism and Trust: The Future of Teachers and Teaching*. London: Department for Education and Skills.

Morris, P. and Wardle, J. (2006) 'Teaching science with ICT', in V. Wood-Robinson (ed.), *ASE Guide to Secondary Science Education*. Hatfield: Association for Science Education.

McCarthy, S. and Youens, B. (2005) 'Strategies used by science student teachers for subject knowledge development: a focus on peer support', *Research in Science and Technical Education*, 23(2): 149–62.

Murphy, P. and Whitelegg, E. (2006) *Girls in the Physics Classroom: A Review of the Research on the Participation of Girls in Physics*. London: Institute of Physics.

National Advisory Committee on Creative and Cultural Education (NACCCE) (1999) *All Our Futures: Creativity, Culture and Education*. London: Department for Education and Employment.

National Curriculum: Task Group on Assessment and Testing (1987) *A Report*. London: DES.

National Curriculum: Task Group on Assessment and Testing (1988) *Three Supplementary Reports*. London: DES.

Nichols, D. (1999) *Safety in Biological Fieldwork*. London: Institute of Biology.

O'Brien, P. (2003) *Using Science to Develop Thinking Skills at Key Stage 3. Materials for Gifted Children*. London: David Fulton.

O'Regan, F. (2006) *The Challenging Behaviours Pocket Book*. Alresford Teachers Pocketbooks.

Office for Standards in Education (Ofsted) (2000) *Handbook for Inspecting Secondary Schools, with Guidance on Self-evaluation*. London: HMSO.

Office for Standards in Education (Ofsted) (2004) *Outdoor Education: Aspects of Good Practice*. London: HMSO.

Office for Standards in Education (Ofsted) (2006) *The Annual Report of Her Majesty's Chief Inspector of Schools 2005/06*. London: Office for Standards in Education.

Office for Standards in Education (Ofsted) (2008) *Success in Science*. Report ref. 070195. London: HMSO.

Oliver, A. (2006), *Creative Teaching Science in the Early Years and Primary Classroom*. London: David Fulton.

Osborne, J. Duschle, R. and Fairbrother, R. (2002) *Breaking the Mould? Teaching Science for Public Understanding*. A report commissioned by the Nuffield Foundation. London: Nuffield.

Osborne, R. and Freyberg, P. (1985) *Learning in Science*. Auckland: Heinemann.

Overall, L. and Sangster, M. (2003) *Secondary Teacher's Handbook*. London: Continuum.

Oversby, J. (2002) 'Assessing conceptual understanding', in S. Amos and R. Boohan (eds), *Aspects of Teaching Secondary Science: Perspectives on Practice*. London: RoutledgeFalmer.

Parkinson, J. (1994) *The Effective Teaching of Secondary Science*. Harlow: Longman.

Parkinson, J. (2002) *Reflective Teaching of Science 11–18*. London: Continuum.

Parkinson, J. (2004) *Improving Secondary Science Teaching*. London: RoutledgeFalmer.

Peacock, A. and Dunne, M. (2006) 'Learning science outside the classroom', in V. Wood-Robinson (ed.), *ASE Guide to Secondary Science Education*. Hatfield: Association for Science Education.

Petty, G. (2006) *Evidence-Based Teaching: A Practical Approach*. Cheltenham: Nelson Thornes.

Piaget, J. (1972) *The Priciples of Genetic Epistoliology*. London: Routledge and Kegan Paul.

Popper, K. (1959) *The Logic of Scientific Discovery*. London: Routledge.

Price, G. (2007) 'Special educational needs', in V. Ellis (ed.), *Learning and Teaching in Secondary Schools*. Exeter: Learning Matters.

Qualifications and Curriculum Authority (QCA) (2004) *Creativity: Find It, Promote It*. London: Qualifications and Curriculum Authority.

Qualifications and Curriculum Authority (QCA) (2007a) *Science Programme of Study: Key Stage 3*. London: Qualifications and Curriculum Authority. http://curriculum.qca.org. uk/subjects/science/keystage3/ (accessed 22 Feburary 2008).

Qualifications and Curriculum Authority (QCA) (2007b) *Science Programme of Study: Key Stage 4*. London: Qualifications and Curriculum Authority. http://curriculum.qca.org. uk/key-stages-3-and-4/subjects/science/keystage4/index.aspx (accessed November 2008) http://curriculum.qca.org.uk/subjects/science/keystage4/ (accessed 22 Feburary 2008).

Qualifications and Curriculum Authority (QCA) (2008) *National Curriculum for Science*. London: Qualifications and Curriculum Authority. http://curriculum.qca.org.uk/ subjects/science/keystage3 (accessed March 2008).

Quita, I.N. (2003) 'What is a scientist? Perspectives of teachers of colour', *Multicultural Education*, 11(1): 29–31.

Ratcliffe, M., Batholomew, H., Hames, V., Hind, A., Leach, J., Millar, R. and Osborne, J. (2002) 'The nature of science education research', *School Science Review*, 84(307): 35–41.

Reeves, D.B. (2004) *Accountability for Learning: How Teachers and School Leaders Can Take Charge*. Alexandria, VA: Association for Supervision & Curriculum Development.

Reiss, M. (ed.) (2000) *Teaching Secondary Biology*. London: John Murray.

Rickinson, M., Dillon, J., Teamey, K., Morris, M., Choi, M., Sanders, D. and Benefield, P. (2004) *A Review of Research on Outdoor Learning*. Shrewsbury: Field Studies Council.

Robson, C. (2002) *Real World Research*. 2nd edn. Oxford: Blackwell.

Robson, C. (2007) *How to Do a Research Project: A Guide for Undergraduate Students*. Oxford: Blackwell.

Rogers, B. (2006) *Cracking the Hard Class: Strategies for Managing the Harder than Average Class*. London: Sage Publications.

Ross, K., Lakin, L. and Callaghan, P. (2000) *Teaching Secondary Science*: Constructing Meaning and Developing Understanding. London: David Fulton.

Ross, K., Lakin, L. and Callaghan, P. (2004) *Teaching Secondary Science*. 2nd edn. London: David Fulton.

Roth, W. (2002) *Being and Becoming in the Classroom*. Westport, CT: Ablex.

Roth, W. and Désautels, J. (2004) 'Educating for citizenship: reappraising the role of science education', *Journal of Science Mathematics and Technology*, 4: 149–68. www.educ.uvic.ca/ faculty/mroth/PREPRINTS/Citizenship.pdf (accessed July 2008).

Sang, D. (ed.) (2000) *Teaching Secondary Physics*. London: John Murray, for the ASE.

Sang, D. and Wood-Robinson, V. (eds) (2002) *Teaching Secondary Scientific Enquiry*. London: John Murray, for the ASE.

Scanlon, E., Hill, R. and Junker, K. (1999) *Communicating Science: Professional Contexts*. London: Routledge.

Scanlon, E., Murphy, P., Thomas, J. and Whitelegg, E. (2004) *Reconsidering Science Learning*. London: Routledge Falmer.

Schon, D. (1983) *The Reflective Practitioner*. New York: Basic Books.

Sharp, J. and Murray, B. (2006) 'The mystery of learning', in J. Sharp, S. Ward and L. Hankin (eds), *Education Studies: An Issues-based Approach*. Exeter: Learning Matters.

Sharp, J., Bowker, R. and Byrne, J. (2008) 'VAK or VAK-uous? Towards the trivialisation of learning and the death of scholarship', *Research Papers in Education*. DOI: 10.1080/02671520701755416.

Sharp, J., Ward, S. and Hankin, L. (eds) (2006) *Education Studies: An Issues-based Approach*. Exeter: Learning Matters.

Shayer, M. (1996) *The Long-term Effects of Cognitive Acceleration on Pupils' School Achievement*. London: King's College Department for Education and Professional Studies.

Shayer, M. (2000) *GCSE 1999: Added Value from Schools Adopting the CASE intervention*. London: King's College Department for Education and Professional Studies.

Shayer, M. and Adey, P.S. (1981) *Towards a Science of Science Teaching: Cognitive Development and Curriculum Demand*. London: Heinemann Educational.

Shayer, M. and Adey, P.S. (2002) *Learning Intelligence*. Buckingham: Open University Press.

Schulman, L.S. (1986) 'Those who understand: knowledge growth in teaching', *Education Researcher*, 15(2): 3–14.

Schulman, L.S. (1987) 'Knowledge and teaching: foundations of the new reform', *Harvard Educational Review*, 57(1): 1–22.

Simon, S. (2002) 'The CASE approach for pupils with learning difficulties', *School Science Review*, 83(305): 73–9.

Slingsby, D. (2006) 'The future of school science lies outdoors', *Journal of Biological Education*, 40(2): 51–2.

Solomon, J. (2002) 'Group discussions in the classroom', in S. Amos and R. Boohan (eds), *Aspects of Teaching Secondary Science: Perspectives on Practice*. London: Routledge Falmer.

Sotto, E. (2007) *When Learning Becomes Teaching: A Theory and Practice of Teaching*. London: Continuum.

Staples, R. and Heselden, R. (2001) 'Science teaching and literacy, part 1: writing', *School Science Review*, 83(303): 35–46.

Staples, R. and Heselden, R. (2002a) 'Science teaching and literacy, part 2: reading', *School Science Review*, 83(304): 51–62.

Staples, R. and Heselden, R. (2002b) 'Science teaching and literacy, part 3: speaking and listening, spelling and vocabulary', *School Science Review*, 84(306): 83–95.

Sutton, C. (1992) *Words, Science and Learning*. Milton Keynes: Open University Press.

Sutton, R. (2001) *Primary to Secondary – Overcoming the Muddle in the Middle*. Millom: Ruth Sutton Publications.

Taber, K. (2007) *Classroom-based Research and Evidence-based Practice: A Guide for Teachers*. London: Sage.

Thody, A., Gray, B. and Bowden, D. (2000) *The Teacher's Survival Guide*. London: Continuum.

Tilling, S. (2004) 'Fieldwork in UK secondary schools: influences and provision', *Journal of Biological Education*, 38(2): 54–8.

Timperley, H.S. and Robinson, V.M.J. (2000) 'Workload and the professional culture of teachers', *Educational Management and Administration*, 28(1): 47–62.

Training and Development Agency for Schools (TDA) (2007a) *Professional Standards for Teachers: Why Sit Still in your Career?* London: Training and Development Agency for Schools.

Training and Development Agency for Schools (TDA) (2007b) *Career Entry and Development Profile 2007/8*. London: Training and Development Agency for Schools.

Training and Development Agency for Schools (TDA) (2007c) *Professional Standards for Teachers: Qualified Teacher Status*. London: Training and Development Agency for Schools.

Vygotsky, L.S. (1978) *Mind in Society: The Development of Higher Psychological Processes*. London: Harvard University Press.

Watkinson, A. (2008) *The Essential Guide for Higher Level Teaching Assistants*. London: David Fulton.

Watson, R., Goldsworthy, A. and Wood-Robinson, V. (1999) 'What's not fair with investigations?', *School Science Review*, 80(292): 101–6.

Watson, R., Wood-Robinson, V. and Nikolaou, L. (2006) 'Better scientific enquiries', in V. Wood-Robinson (ed.), *ASE Guide to Secondary Science Education*. Hatfield: Association for Science Education.

Wellington, J.J. (1998) *Interactive Science Centres and Science Education*. Kingston upon Thames: Croner Publications.

Wellington, J.J. (2000) *Teaching and Learning Secondary Science: contemporary issues and practical approaches*. London: Routledge.

Wellington, J.J. and Ireson, G. (2008) *Science Learning, Science Teaching*. London: Routledge.

Wellington, J.J. and Osborne, J. (2001) *Language and Literacy in Science Education*. Buckingham: Open University Press.

West, A. (2007) 'Practical work for the gifted in science', in K. Taber (ed.), *Science Education for Gifted Learners*. Abingdon: Routledge.

White, R. (2002) 'Research, theories of learning, principles of teaching and classroom practice: examples and issues', in S. Amos and R. Boohan (eds), *Teaching Science in Secondary Schools: A Reader*. London: Routledge Falmer.

Wood-Robinson, V. (ed.) (2004) *ASE Guide to Secondary Science Education*. Hatfield: Association for Science Education.

Woolnough, B.E. (1994) *Effective Science Teaching*. Milton Keynes: Open University Press.

Wright, L. (2006) 'School self-evaluation of teaching and learning science', in V. Wood-Robinson (ed.), *ASE Guide to Secondary Science Education*. Hatfield: Association for Science Education.

Wright, T. (2008) *How to Be a Brilliant Trainee Teacher*. Oxford: Routledge.

INDEX

Added to a page number 'f' denotes a figure and 't' denotes a table.